LEADERSHI.

Why is it that leaders – in social, political, and (most importantly) organisational contexts – are seemingly unable to address meaningfully the wicked
problems and complex challenges that we currently face? There's enormous
busyness around reconfiguring departments and adopting 'transformational' operating models, but in general *plus ca change, plus la meme chose*.

Eyewatering amounts of treasure and time are spent in corporate life on
leadership development, with people working hard to try and demonstrate
that something useful has happened as a result. An entire pseudo-science
has emerged to try and prove its worth, in part to justify the economic
dividend that goes to those who make it to the upper levels of positional
power. The fetishisation of leadership, especially strong leadership, fills our
news outlets holding up carefully distorted images of great men (leadership is still deeply gendered) from across the worlds of politics, business,
and sports. This book explores the persistently disappeared and unacknowledged constraints that inhibit leaders in every context. It argues that
these constraints – defined in this volume in terms of five organisational
paradoxes and six management myths – are found at large in society and
are especially impactful in organisational life.

By calling attention to, and exploring in rigorous detail, these paradoxes
and myths, this book helps leaders, and the leadership systems they are part
of, to wriggle free of the tacit assumptions that lock them into a cul-de-
sac of simplistic prescription and heroic individualism. Once these mind-
forged manacles are removed, new forms of leadership practice become
possible, ones that are fit for purpose in engaging with a world facing
systemic crisis and existential risk.

This book is essential reading for leaders and managers at all levels looking for solutions to traditionally simplistic leadership practice and who want
to affect systemic change. It will be beneficial to all those in the world of
leadership development including business schools and HR departments.

Mark Cole is an OD practitioner with over 30 years' experience working on development in organisations in and around the NHS. Latterly, he has been critically thinking about work and the workplace and his book called *Radical Organisation Development* was published by Routledge in 2020.

John Higgins is an independent researcher, tutor, and coach specialising in how people use and abuse power throughout the workplace and society. He is widely published and has written extensively alongside the faculty and students of the Ashridge Doctorate and Masters in Organizational Change.

LEADERSHIP UNRAVELLED

The Faulty Thinking Behind Modern Management

Mark Cole and John Higgins

Routledge
Taylor & Francis Group

LONDON AND NEW YORK

First published 2022
by Routledge
2 Park Square, Milton Park, Abingdon, Oxon OX14 4RN

and by Routledge
605 Third Avenue, New York, NY 10158

Routledge is an imprint of the Taylor & Francis Group, an informa business

© 2022 Mark Cole and John Higgins

British Library Cataloguing-in-Publication Data
A catalogue record for this book is available from the British Library

Library of Congress Cataloging-in-Publication Data
Names: Cole, Mark, 1960- author. | Higgins, John, 1962 June 27- author.
Title: Leadership unravelled : the faulty thinking behind modern management / Mark Cole and John Higgins.
Description: Milton Park, Abingdon, Oxon ; New York, NY : Routledge, 2021. | Includes bibliographical references and index. |
Identifiers: LCCN 2021003154 (print) | LCCN 2021003155 (ebook) |
ISBN 9780367473471 (hardback) | ISBN 9781032033686 (paperback) |
ISBN 9781003035015 (ebook)
Subjects: LCSH: Leadership.
Classification: LCC HD57.7 .C6437 2021 (print) | LCC HD57.7 (ebook) |
DDC 658.4/092–dc23
LC record available at https://lccn.loc.gov/2021003154
LC ebook record available at https://lccn.loc.gov/2021003155

ISBN: 978-0-367-47347-1 (hbk)
ISBN: 978-1-032-03368-6 (pbk)
ISBN: 978-1-003-03501-5 (ebk)

DOI: 10.4324/9781003035015

Typeset in Joanna
by SPi Technologies India Pvt Ltd (Straive)

CONTENTS

ACKNOWLEDGEMENTS

Mark recognises the debt that he owes to John, in terms of the way in which their conversations and explorations have helped him to move his thinking forward and thence jointly to develop the analysis and ideas herein. It began with occasional discussions over coffee at the Caffe Tropea in Russell Square Gardens and developed into regular weekly calls as the pandemic took hold.

He also acknowledges the boundless support that he gets from his family. Aside from being constantly encouraging, Sarah also generously offered her services as a proof-reader for the work. And his son Thomas is a constant inspiration – not least because he is ceaselessly curious, as children tend to be, and looks at everything with completely fresh eyes. Regardless of our age, this is how we should seek to engage with the world.

John knows that anything good he has ever written has come about through his personal and professional relationships. In Mark he has found a co-conspirator who has a very different take on life – and also has to go on living in the world as it is (while John has temporarily withdrawn to the fringes as he tries to find a constructive way of engaging with life in the raw). He also wants to make a large nod, a bow even, to his long running 'other' research partner, Megan Reitz – who keeps dragging him back into the muck and bullets of organisational life.

At home he is kept in touch with both domestic priorities and the world of the portfolio non-executive through Rosie. Meanwhile Livia, at the start of her career, reminds him of why it's worth trying to shift the dial on what passes as good practice in the workplace – while Isobel keeps him in touch with debates around breast-feeding in the ancient world.

PREFACE

This book is an argument, one that takes to task the established beliefs about leadership, its role as a practice in organisational life and how the constellation of advisers, advocates, and apologists sustain an ideology which is forever denying its presence, while it ceaselessly shapes the workplace.

It is also an argument with itself, teasing out and picking at the contradictions within the world and with its own assertions and understanding. It stays with its own mess and the mess of the world, rather than rushing to tidy itself up and make itself look presentable according to established conventions.

It has been written to be expansive, to explore philosophical and ideological roots – and the tangle of meanings that exist around how the workplace gets organised (while of course having to grapple with what we mean by meaning). It has some distillations, some punctuation points, but its form is also its message. We need to relearn how to have sustained inquiry when it comes to matters of leadership in organisational contexts, stay with theoretical and inter-disciplinary complexity rather than allow ourselves off the hook by only privileging perspectives that are quick and easy to swallow.

In that regard, it represents a method in action. We have engaged critically with all that seems common sense and commonplace about how organisations are experienced at this time. We have looked to these taken-for-granted models, techniques, precepts, and approaches as if they were alien to us, things to which we have no real attachment. And we have pulled that method into our conversational and written exchanges, constantly asserting the need to take our thinking beyond the artifice of the presenting surface, to visit what lies behind or beneath.

Our method, then, has been dialogic, in conjunction with a commitment to reflexivity and critical thinking. As a metaphor it can be seen to resemble an old-fashioned vinyl record, which sees us circling around the subject and the stories that we feel are germane, returning to them time and again, knowing them through different lenses, refusing to accept that they can exist as definitive accounts of a singular experience. We quite deliberately have stepped away from the traditional linear narrative, which moves inexorably through a beginning, middle, and end – and all but inevitably results in a flattening of any depth of understanding as we rush towards some clearly identified endpoint, which in our established culture is readily conflated with the 'answer' or 'solution'.

We blend together high-theory with the quotidian, the ordinary experience of people who occupy all sorts of positions and perspectives throughout the organisational ecosystem. The much vaunted 'view from the top' is not only **not** privileged, as it is in so much consulting and business school verbiage, it is also explored with a critical eye and its political intention held up to scrutiny. Most of what we hold up to be evidence of a deeply suspect and self-serving discourse around leadership already exists, hiding in plain sight.

We spend time paying attention to the obvious, the overlooked, the taken for granted – a discipline which is actively undermined by most established organisational practices, which keep us too busy to ask the straightforward question, to be curious about what we discount, to inquire as to why the King is walking naked down the street while being acclaimed for the wonder of his (nearly always his) raiment.

We also address directly the slippery, pseudo-complexity, of the endless tsunami of leadership and management fads – and also name who benefits from all this noise and distraction. What don't we see when we're too busy chasing after the latest thing? What happens when everything is about the future, which is always rosy, and we ignore the deep shadows that live on however much we wish them away in our bubbles of optimism?

What happens when we consider our workplaces to be places of contention, argument, and difference – rather than totalitarian states with strict orthodoxies of all stripes, where everyone lives in harmony and all human vagaries are wished away by a single glorious vision or imposed statement of collective values?

There are loose threads to the argument we deliver in the book ahead, inconsistencies and points where we struggle to make obvious what is going on in the leadership discourse – much of this stemming from the seemingly deliberate smokescreen of linguistic confusion of those who sustain the status quo. There is also the endless incompatibility of what is claimed and what is lived – and our arguments can be frequently countered by the claim that what we speak of is in the past, while in the future all will be made good. This recurring pattern of escaping into an idealised future is one of the threads that runs through all we have to say and finds us curious about what purpose it serves.

Our intention is to avoid the laundry list of anodyne, superficial, thoughtless action beloved by the management literature – and which is to be found in the texts of what we call the 'Heathrow Academy', books designed to be read by busy executives, with no time to spare, looking for a soundbite or two to reinforce their existing self-knowledge. What we hope to do is stimulate curiosity and provide a way for the reader to engage with some of the weighty thinkers about the human condition, who have been disappeared by the existing leadership ideology. They have so much to teach us about what it means to be an axiomatically social animal, who needs to come together with their fellows while retaining a good sense of both personal agency and contingency.

Above all, this book should never be thought of as definitive: instead, it is intended to be declarative, in the hope that some of the investigations that we lay out spark a more oblique orientation to these topics, leading to a wider conversation about the 'deep structure' of organisational life. We aim to speak of things that may not normally be acknowledged – and in ways that challenge the 'normality' that we inhabit. Our hope is that we make a contribution to a different form of discussion, that discards traditional idiom and instead seeks out a new way of speaking about – and hence understanding (and changing, of course) – our workplace experiences.

1

AN INTRODUCTION... IN SEVEN UNEASY PIECES

The worlds of organisations and management are full of cliché and glibness. The mental disciplines that feed considered thinking and action have been rotted by bubble-gum habits of mind, trotted out as if they were the wisdom of the ages, something that looks good in a slide-deck. Meanwhile people's lives get turned upside down by a frenzy of pop-prescriptions that justify endless upheaval. given big-word titles such as 'transformation' and 'game changing' and 'world class' this or that. Nothing is allowed to be ordinary or human scaled. There is a lot of pain and little gain – except for the snake-oil salespeople and Quack Doctors who peddle the latest nostrums, dealers to corporate junkies too strung out to see who benefits from the exchange. There is a lot to despair at when looking at what has come to pass as good management and leadership, where its citadel of learning '[t]he business school.. has tended to become somewhere that produces knowledge for management rather that knowledge *about* management... It is knowledge... that relies on flattering those in power' (Parker, 2018, pp. 36–37).

DOI: 10.4324/9781003035015-1

In this book we draw on years of working in and studying organisations of all sorts to explore what got us into this state of affairs, so that it becomes possible for something different, something better to emerge in due time – free we hope of the false promises and soft-soap we've already staked out as part of our current organisational malaise.

We have written it for everybody who works for a living and has to be part of, or engage with, taken for granted institutional patterns, which leave them bemused as to how such strange behaviours have passed unquestioned, madness hiding in plain sight. For those of a literary bent we would say this is for anyone who has thought that 'there is something rotten in the state of Denmark', where Hamlet's Denmark stands for the common nonsense of accepted practices of organisational life.

In this introduction we'll sketch out how we came to this downbeat, but realistic, conclusion and outline how our analysis will unfold through the book and how we will cautiously outline what a better way might look like in terms of management and leadership. Its seven uneasy pieces are:

- Uneasy Piece 1 – The common sense we live by
- Uneasy Piece 2 – A superficial connection with reality
- Uneasy Piece 3 – What gets in the way of us stopping and wondering about our world
- Uneasy Piece 4 – The disappearance of collective sense and sense making
- Uneasy Piece 5 – The fragmentation of time, busyness, and the disconnected future
- Uneasy Piece 6 – Paying attention to the headwaters of our thinking
- Uneasy Piece 7 – What happens next

While wary of over-condensed conclusions, we will frame these introductory sections with our take on what might be seen as punctuating conclusions, while suggesting we all stay on our guard against potted knowledge that is easily swallowed and just as easily passed.

1.1 The common sense we live by

Here is a tale of the modern world – and insight perhaps into the way in which so many people experience it, which is crucial to the critique that we advance in this book. In May 2020, a story appeared in the virtual edition of the *Daily Mirror* newspaper in the UK, headlined 'Nursery teacher red-faced after discovering why newly purchased candle "disappeared"' (Cripps, 2020). A woman of 21 gave her 18-year-old sister a scented candle as a gift. When physics took its course and the candle burnt down, the recipient began a charged correspondence with her sister via text.

According to the story, she demanded to know 'where has the wax in my candle gone' and claimed it had 'disappeared'. It was explained that this is what happens with candles, which led the younger sister to complain in a disgruntled fashion that no one had told her that this might happen – and that, when she had seen her generous sibling replacing candles in the past, she had assumed that she had some sort of OCD about it or was some sort of candle expert.

Drawing attention to this story is not meant to denigrate in any sneering way the people in it. Instead, it seems to us to show the way in which so many of us experience our day-to-day lives, as something in which we are not fully invested but which we expect to endlessly meet our daily needs. In this instance, there are several noteworthy themes. Firstly, the report suggests that the first reaction was not to try to make sense of what had happened, but to argue that there was something wrong with the candle.

The lack of inquiry in the world is very apparent; it has been supplanted by emotional reaction. Things make us angry, sad, and happy these days… but very rarely do they make us feel curious. The clumsy and uncommunicative shorthand of social media leads us to push buttons, not sense make…and allows us to go from 0 to 60 in terms of emotional response, without any pause at thinking. When Scorsese's film *The King of Comedy* (IMDB, 1982) appeared in the UK in 1983, there's a scene where the entertainer Jerry Langford is approached on the street by an initially gushing and adoring fan, who then turns on a sixpence when Jerry makes his apologies about not speaking to her nephew Morris on the payphone that she's using. She bellows after him the vicious instruction that he contracts cancer, (YouTube, 2013) a curse that shocked at the time – but is now familiar behaviour on Facebook, Twitter, and the like.

Secondly, there is a failure of agency, with a sense that an infantilised perspective is at work here and across the wider social world. The response that no one said aloud that this might happen seems to allow an individual to abrogate their responsibility for making sense of the world – and instead sets up an insistent demand that the world should constantly be explained by others. We are nudging here towards a view of the world seen merely as a commodity that we are licensed to experience, rather than a place where we have an intrinsic and reflexive presence.

Lastly, there is a pathologisation of others based on one's own limitations, in terms of understanding a candle. Changing candles is explained away as part of some psychological condition. Interestingly, there is a flip side to this notion, which is to hide away behind ignorance and merely assert that those who have a reasonable grasp of key elements of the world can be dismissed as an 'expert' of some sort. In this case, it is to talk of the older sister as some sort of candle expert. One might reasonably suggest that this schema sees illness and expertise as pretty much part of the same 'weird' continuum, problems that need to be owned and fixed by another rather than an exposé of a lack of understanding on the part of the person who denigrates the other.

Let's leave those two sisters in their wax-and-wick based confusion. In the spirit of full disclosure, the following story is very similar and involves Mark. He left school on a Friday at 16 years old, racing around his school to get a chit signed by his form teacher so that he could finally leave the torture of compulsory education behind him. By the following Monday he was standing in a brand-new blue pinstripe polyester three-piece suit outside of a South London jewellery shop, at just after 8am, to start work as a shop assistant. Shy and gauche, he found the first day trying – and then, towards closing time, he was asked to vacuum throughout the store.

They had an upright vacuum cleaner, which was pointed out to Mark. He plugged it in and switched it on. However, he was perplexed by the fact that he could not work out how to release the upright part of the appliance. Instead, he gripped the handle with both hands and clumsily pushed the cleaner back and forth. It did the job, of course, but looked utterly ridiculous. The embarrassing fact about all of this was that his traditional working-class family – mum, dad, and younger brother – had a similar vacuum at home, which Mark had never once been expected to use nor had he ever volunteered to undertake any household chores. (The patriarchy was powerful in his background.)

Eventually, the kindly young woman who worked as the cashier in the shop walked over to Mark and showed him where the release pedal was. Mark was mortified, firstly that he did not know this himself and, secondly, that he had been seen by others to be so utterly inept. But it served as a reminder that, whilst his maternal home life had wrapped around him in so many ways with a strong cushioning effect, the world outside of that was harsh and demanded that he engage with it in order to better understand it and to be able to function meaningfully within it.

How do these tales give context to our project in this volume? Simply, it is our contention that our individual human existence in the world is increasingly passively experienced rather than actively lived. The commonsensical qualities of that world are increasingly unchallenged and our capacity for critique in the face of what passes for our engagement there is more and more limited. This haunts each and every experience in our lives, from our social exchanges through to our organisational presences. In essence, the very world that we inhabit can feel other-worldly, as if we are spectators rather than participants there.

1.2 A superficial connection with reality

Back in the late 1960s, the Situationists began to apply a critical approach to what they saw going on in the social, cultural, and economic cross-tides. They introduced the notion of the Society of the Spectacle, which sought to explain the passivity that existed in the face of a world that seemed to them to be in urgent need of change. This critique, deriving from (and building on) a Marxian understanding of capitalism in practice, asserts that,

> The fetishism of the commodity – the domination of society by "imperceptible as well as perceptible things" – attains its ultimate fulfilment in the spectacle, where the perceptible world is replaced by a selection of images which is projected above it, yet which at the same time succeeds in making itself regarded as the perceptible par excellence.
>
> (Debord, 2014/1967 p. 14)

From a philosophical perspective, then, the argument is that, 'The spectacle is *capital* accumulated to the point that it becomes images' (Debord, 2014/1967, p. 11).

The reason we consider this relevant to a book about leadership in the worlds of business and organisations of all sorts is that it speaks to a point of view that actively calls out the superficiality of our relationship with reality. It is a perspective that acknowledges the pre-eminence of the image – and our seemingly boundless fascination with representation rather than actuality – as a key development in the ways in which our society reproduces itself and limits the space available in which to think of a different way of shaping that society. The Situationists – and, in particular, Guy Debord – talked about the spectacle as an interactive and overbearing connection between advertising, commercial artwork, print media, and the broadcast networks.

However, this is not a straightforward argument of how those media reduce human beings to mere puppets of the ideas that they convey. They are not hypodermic needles, designed by a 'ruling class' as an ocular injection of acceptable ways of thinking that, at the same time, inoculate the subject against ways of thinking other than those that are held to be dominant. Hence, it is reasonable to observe that,

> Invasion by the means of mass communication is only seemingly a deployment of instruments that, even when badly used, remain essentially neutral; in reality the operation of the media perfectly expresses the entire society of which they are a part. The result is that direct experience and the determination of events by individuals themselves are replaced by a passive contemplation of images (which have, moreover, been chosen by other people).
>
> (Jappe, 1999, p. 6)

To ground this observation a little, the following offers some texture:

> As an example… Debord evokes celebrities, such as actors or politicians, whose function it is to represent a combination of human qualities and of joie de vivre – precisely what is missing from the actual lives of all other individuals, trapped as they are in vapid roles.
>
> (Jappe, 1999, pp. 6–7)

All of which nudges us to observe that the spectacle has – at a time of Big Brother, The Only Way is Essex, and formats like Britain's Got Talent, where a better title, considering how distant it is from the original talent showcases like New Faces, might be People Have Backstory – merely consolidated itself since the late '60s. And with the internet – and, in particular, the various social media platforms that it hosts – we are perhaps seeing the spectacle enriching itself with even more images and ways in which to view them (Vejby & Wittkower, 2010).

1.2.1 Parts 1 and 2 in summary

1. The common sense we live by
   - We have lost our capacity for inquiry and have learnt to privilege untrammelled emotion
   - There is a failure of personal agency for making sense of the world
   - Others are pathologised when they claim expertise and rare knowledge
   - Lives are lived passively rather than through enlivening engagement
2. A superficial connection with reality
   - There has been a triumph of the spectacle and the image
   - Social contexts create and sustain norms which give superficiality its weight (or currency)
   - The sense of personal aliveness has been outsourced

*   *   *   *   *   *   *   *   *   *   *   *   *

1.3 What gets in the way of us stopping and wondering about our world

Many of us will be familiar with the endless pursuit of the Road Runner by Wile E Coyote. Mark found himself sitting with his six-year-old son watching a portmanteau of Warner Brother cartoons, involving characters such as Daffy Duck and Elmer Fudd. It included a short from 1952 entitled *Operation: Rabbit*, which on this occasion sees the coyote character in pursuit of Bugs Bunny. The plot is pretty much as you'd expect: the coyote – ordinarily thwarted by his own absurd ambitions and reliance on a range of products and contraptions purchased from the ubiquitous Acme Company (surely a presentiment of the omniscience of Amazon) – is also constantly outsmarted by Bugs Bunny. One sequence resonated very strongly as Mark watched the show:

> The Coyote makes one last plan: filling a row of fake carrots with liquid nitro-glycerine inside an explosives shack within a construction site. Bugs, using a tractor and a rope lasso, pulls the shack to a nearby railroad line. The rope is released and the shack, with Wile E. inside, is sitting on the tracks. As Wile E. admires his new self-given title of

"Super Genius" while finishing his carrots, a train is seen approaching. Upon hearing the train whistle, the Coyote turns to the shack window to see the train bearing down on him, and futilely pulls down a window shade.

(Wikipedia, 2020)

Mark could not help but connect the actions of the coyote in this sequence with what he sees among leaders in organisations. First, there is the fetishised reliance on a plan – on this occasion, one last plan – as if the world is in some way amenable to being channelled and directed to some agreed outcome. It's a familiar trope in what passes for management thinking – a reliance on linear thinking and an expectation that effect follows cause – but its pre-eminence flies in the face of our day-to-day experiences of the world. The coyote's plan is ingenious, a delight in respect to its internal logic, and yet that exquisite quality only holds if one does not seek to operationalise that scheme because, at that point, the messiness of the world where one is seeking to actualise it interferes with its clockwork precision.

Second, whilst the coyote is utterly absorbed by the intricacies of his plan – and consumed with the hubristic excitement that this last plan might be the one to work (despite the fact that every other plan has failed to deliver the outcome that he was seeking) – the world is literally moving and changing around him. The coyote works on his plan – as Bugs hooks up the shack in which he is making his bombs and pulls it onto a railway track. The train appears – and initially, at least, the coyote disregards it. It is possible to call upon many examples in both our work careers where the corporate leaders are transfixed by the shiny elegance of their plans, which, in turn, leads them to neglect the practical nature of the reality all around them.

Lastly, the coyote's futile act of denial at the very last moment – pulling the blind and staring resignedly out at the viewer through the broken fourth wall – seemed to mirror the reactions of leaders when confronted with harsh reality, which ordinarily are either blithely to deny it or to acknowledge it and to double down on efforts to generate a greater sense of control. The coyote is defined as an agent in the world by his ceaseless efforts to chase and catch the Road Runner. Similarly, the 'leader' in our contemporary context is defined by their immediate efforts to grab the world and shape it to their will – notwithstanding that this remains an impossible dream and an abiding fiction to which we all end up subscribing. The responses of different organisations to the COVID inspired economic collapse of 2020 can be seen as instructive in this light. One, known to John, saw the senior executive respond to the collapse in its markets by doubling down on the sales targets of its staff, to deliver on what had been deemed possible at the end of 2019. They closed their eyes to the external reality and instead stayed inside the fantasy of their internal control.

Back to the cartoon. The coyote persists and never once considers the nature of what it is that he's doing. He commits resources to this pursuit, in terms of mental and physical effort, time, and material equipment, without ever seemingly stopping to think about whether what it is that he is doing makes sense. To an extent, he is caught in a script, an antagonist mindlessly chasing the protagonist without pause or reflection; he endlessly reproduces himself in terms of immersing himself unquestioningly in the thinking, attitude, and practices to which he has simply grown accustomed.

This, of course, leads us to an observation about the way in which organisations operate through scripting. Hence, it is argued that,

> Organizations present many predictable settings with reasonably predictable actions, events, and behaviours. As such, they would appear to represent a ripe setting for script processing to take place. The use of scripted behaviour generally requires typicality and some degree of repetitiveness. Organizations are attended by both, in the form of rituals, customs, procedures, symbols, and many other forms of institutionalized communication and interaction. Certain types of situation are likely to be handled with some degree of script processing.
>
> (Gioia & Poole, 1984, p. 454)

Scripts in this context are seen to be useful in two linked ways: 'Scripts provide dual benefits to people. They enable understanding of situations (and thus are schema-based sense-making structures…) and they provide a guide to behaviour appropriate to those situations' (Gioia & Poole, 1984, p. 450). But, from a more critical perspective, they can be seen to constrain the individual in terms of what they can imagine themselves saying and doing, and thence inhibiting and silencing human agency in organisational settings. And so those scripts that are being offered as guides to organisational practice merely offer shallow characterisations for people to inhabit in the performative terrain of the workplace, leading to an accusation of 'mindlessness' (Ashforth & Fried, 1988).

In contrast to this notion stands the idea of improvisation to understand better the day-to-day nature of presence in an organisational setting. Hence, we might consider how

> …orienting ourselves to organizational structure along the lines of the way jazz musicians orient to their structures in performing jazz could help us to generate a redescription of organizational structure that is compatible with the emerging vocabulary of organization studies.
>
> (Hatch, 1999, p. 77)

The jazz metaphor is popular – but it's not the only way to think about a freer organisational life with greater flexibility and agency attendant upon it particularly in light of the acknowledgement of the complexity and chaos that attends to organisational and business life (Cunha, et al., 1999). Indeed, efforts exist to stretch the notion beyond jazz and improvisational theatre to a more interdisciplinary approach (Hadida & Tarvainen, 2015).

Overall, though, whether we subscribe to notions of scripts or improvisation, these are – ultimately – mere managerial conceits, designs behind which our basic humanity can be hidden and the organisation promoted as the key unit of analysis, instead of focusing on the relational elements that bring animation and direction to organising endeavours. Hence, a foundational element of this book is – to borrow from the earlier example – to get the coyote to stop and wonder what it is that compels him to endlessly and fruitlessly chase the Road Runner. It is a challenge that we make to managers and leaders in organisations: in seeking to be seen to be performing the role of 'leader', what common sense notions, accepted ideas, and familiar practices trap them in – to borrow a key concept from Nietzsche – an 'eternal return' of endlessly repeating cycles (Westacott, 2020) of thought and action.

1.3.1 Part 3 in summary

3. *What gets in the way of us stopping and wondering about our world*
   - The fetishisation of the internal logic of cause and effect
   - The privileging of the wished for over actual reality
   - Living in the grip of a seemingly unchallengeable, eternal script (or 'truth')

* * * * * * * * * * * * *

1.4 The disappearance of collective sense and sense making

As we wrote this book, the coronavirus crisis hit the globe. It would seem, in fact, as though Patient Zero appeared at around the time that we signed the contract with the publisher. These circumstances formed a constant backdrop to our conversations and exchanges about the work – and the writing of the various chapters, not least the section that looks in detail at what we take to be the myths that impact adversely contemporary management and leadership practice.

The virus notwithstanding, the human reactions were the ones that gave both of us the greatest cause for concern. Mark visited a supermarket early in the crisis in the UK to see that the aisles of canned goods and even of eggs had been utterly cleared. During his mooch around a supermarket stripped of the sorts of staples upon which we all unthinkingly rely, he spoke with two elderly women, both of whom cast their minds back to recall their childhood times. One described coming to England from Ireland 65 years ago as part of a family of 11 (although she observed in passing that one had died in childbirth, so it was really a family of 12). She spoke dispassionately of a time in living memory when her family had shared the tiniest living space – and where there was no central heating or running hot water. It was, for her, a time that stood in sharp contrast to contemporary experience.

Underpinning her reminiscence was a strong sense of collectiveness. Strength to face the sort of adversity that she mentioned, in terms of overcrowding and the specific privations – not that, to be completely honest, it was seen as such at that time, as adversity is only really recognised in retrospect – came from the bond of a family that, to our modern minds, seems remarkably large. Some readers might be prompted to make the seemingly rational observation, 'If they couldn't afford a larger home, why did mum and dad have such a big family'? This patently disregards the social mores that would have prevailed at this time – and neglects the communality that will have derived from those ties and is in turn part of the taken-for-granted ahistoricism that hobbles so much of our current public discourse.

But that collective feeling was very much missing in the supermarket that day. A horde of rugged individuals had swarmed into the store with

limited concern for others. These individuals were those aggressively cel-
ebrated by neoliberal capitalism, promoted as the model of success in our
society. This was also the time when the individual of this type (a sort
of low rent superman or ubermensch) was being shown to be not quite
what we had all been told – all altruistic entrepreneur, self-made man, and
adventurer. As the Morning Star reported at the time,

> Airline Virgin Atlantic is asking 8,500 staff to take eight weeks of
> unpaid leave to reduce costs while it requests a taxpayer-funded bailout
> due to the coronavirus pandemic…Virgin founder Richard Branson has
> a net worth of £4bn. The cost of paying the 8,500 workers has been
> estimated at £34 million over eight weeks.
>
> (Lazenby, 2020)

For those who prefer their news with a less Stalinoid tinge, the story was
also carried by the Forbes business magazine. (Dawkins, 2020)

This picture of the atomised individual, forging their way through
sheer will and personal talent, has its provenance in Thatcher's oft-quoted
remarks that there is no such thing as society. Sympathisers often accuse
critics of misquoting her comments, so it's worth attending to what has
been officially transcribed as being said in the interview in question, which
was by Douglas Keay for Woman's Own:

> I think we have gone through a period when too many children and
> people have been given to understand "I have a problem, it is the
> Government's job to cope with it!" or "I have a problem, I will go and
> get a grant to cope with it!" "I am homeless, the Government must
> house me!" and so they are casting their problems on society and who
> is society? There is no such thing! There are individual men and women
> and there are families and no government can do anything except
> through people and people look to themselves first. It is our duty to
> look after ourselves and then also to help look after our neighbour and
> life is a reciprocal business and people have got the entitlements too
> much in mind without the obligations, because there is no such thing
> as an entitlement unless someone has first met an obligation…
>
> (Margaret Thatcher Foundation, 1987)

Certainly, the imputation seems to be that society should not be reified as some kind of abstract provider of support, because it is simply an aggregate of all of the individuals. It cannot exist as a notion without the individuals that foundationally constitute it. In this world view, then, the individual is the key unit of social analysis and the bordered, self-sufficiency of the individual assumed – and that focus served a distinct political purpose, which was to support the ambition to minimise the state's presence in people's lives. In this schema, society and state are being conflated for ideological effect.

As is so often the case with political discourse, a good deal is hidden behind the expression of a specific idea. Hence, to take a more historical perspective, it is argued that

> If we look at the word "individual" in historical dictionaries of the English or French languages, we will find that it first became current in the fifteenth century. The word "state", with its stipulation of a sovereign authority, became current at about the same time. And that is no accident, for the meaning of these two words depend upon each other. It was through the creation of states that the individual was invented as the primary or organizing social role.
>
> (Siedentop, 2015, p. 347)

Proceeding then from this bifurcation, it is possible to perceive of something that might be called individualism, defined as '…the retreat into a private sphere of family and friends at the expense of civic spirit and political participation' (Siedentop, 2015, p. 363). This can be strongly perceived in the Renaissance, where it is intimated that we saw the emergence of a '… cult of individuality, depicting the individual as the "victim" of social pressures and heroism as resistance to such pressures' (Siedentop, 2015, p. 337). Latterly, the argument is developed that modernity's '…fundamental feature…is an individuated model of society – a model in which the individual rather than the family, clan or caste is the basic social unit' (ibid).

This book makes a vital distinction in this regard. We are wary of the way in which the idea of 'individualism' enjoys a distorting pre-eminence. It derives from both classical liberalism and the sort of distinctive US libertarianism that finds its most pronounced expression in the fiction and thought of the writer Ayn Rand. This worldview resonates in our organisational settings, of course, particularly in practices such as performance appraisal (our work is almost exclusively a collective and collaborative endeavour – and yet our annual evaluation is invariably crystallised in a single rating of us as an individual performer) and resilience, wherein we are expected to absorb all of the pressure and stress of the modern workplace – and work on ourselves in order that we focus on our management of this, rather than working to change the oppressive context in which we find ourselves. There are parallels for us with the way that Albania used to, and North Korea still, run themselves – as self-sufficient and sovereign autarchies. In the ideology of individualism, the autarky of the individual is paramount and so notions of inter-dependency and mutuality are lost. It is all for themselves and let the devil take the hindmost.

Whilst we reject individualism – as a political project with powerful implications in our lives – we embrace the idea of the individual. Therein lies the critical faculties and capacity for connection that amplifies impact in terms of making sense of the world and seeking to build a better one. Whilst individualism fetishises the individual, and allows only for a very particular type of self-sufficient individuality, we seek to celebrate the power that exists within the individual. The distinctive power for us is that of being able to take an oblique view of commonsensical ideas that constrain us with their widespread currency, normality, and apparent sensibility. Where individualism places the individual on a very specific de-socialised pedestal, we locate the individual as a social being amidst other individuals, reaching out to others in dialogue and in concerted effort to rethink the present that we all of us have to occupy and live through.

This tension between a prevalent individualism and the urgent need to rediscover the individual is something we want to call attention to, as one of the key precepts that we earnestly hope the reader can see in our work as a systematic critique of every aspect of life – particularly in an organisational context (which is, of course, both a reflection and a reinforcement of the wider socio-economic setting in which we find ourselves). We have opted here in the opening chapter to highlight what we take to be one of the foundational messages that flow from this exploration of all that is currently held dear in the world of business leadership and beyond.

1.4.1 *Part 4 in summary*

4. *The disappearance of collective sense and sense making*
    •   The emergence of the de-socialised society

- The triumph of rugged, autarkic individualism
- The hi-jacking and strait-jacketing of individuals by individualism

* * * * * * * * * * * * *

1.5 The fragmentation of time, busyness, and the disconnected future

Alongside hopefully unshackling the resourceful and connected individual from the wearisome politics of individualism, we also look to the way in which we think about time in organisational settings. Patently, there is much made about ensuring that the tasks that need to be completed spill over from the bounding of the working day, so that all of us can subscribe to the idea that 'busyness' is a critical feature of the valuable worker. To an extent, this may well flow from the fact that many of us – including both authors here – are absorbed by what has been described as 'bullshit jobs', a broad category that encompasses financial services, telemarketing, or expanded sectors such as corporate law, academic and health administration, human resources, and public relations, alongside all the support roles that sit around these pursuits – up to and including people employed to do things because those in 'bullshit jobs' do not have time to do them (Graeber, 2013).

To appreciate what this means overall, the following encapsulates the socio-economic theorising that sits behind this somewhat crude shorthand:

> Real, productive workers are relentlessly squeezed and exploited. The remainder are divided between a terrorised stratum of the, universally reviled, unemployed and a larger stratum who are basically paid to do nothing, in positions designed to make them identify with the perspectives and sensibilities of the ruling class (managers, administrators, etc.) – and particularly its financial avatars – but, at the same time, foster a simmering resentment against anyone whose work has clear and undeniable social value. Clearly, the system was never consciously designed. It emerged from almost a century of trial and error. But it is the only explanation for why, despite our technological capacities, we are not all working 3–4 hour days.
>
> (Graeber, 2013)

That time implies succession I do not deny. But that succession is first presented to our consciousness, like the distinctions of a "before" and "after" set side by side, is what I cannot admit. When we listen to a melody we have the purest impression of succession we could possibly have – an impression as far removed as possible of that of simultaneity – and yet it is the very continuity of the melody and the impossibility of breaking it up which makes that impression on us. If we cut it into distinct notes, into so many "befores" and "afters", we are bringing spatial images into it and impregnating the succession with simultaneity: in space, and only in space, is there a clear-cut distinction of parts external to one another. I recognise moreover that it is spatialized time that we ordinarily place ourselves. We have no interest in listening to the uninterrupted humming of life's depths.

(Henri Bergson, 1946, p. 176)

How we perceive of time is a key element of human existence. We are – as a species – blessed (or perhaps it might be more accurate to say blighted) by an acute awareness of it and its passing; existentially, we are alert to its finitude for us as organisms, leading to a constant admonition that it should not be wasted. We are conscious of the sentiment expressed in the Ben Folds Five song, *Jackson Cannery* – of moments passing slowly, while the years pass in the blink of an eye (Ben Folds Five, 1995). Of all the epigrams that Albert Einstein never actually said – other than out on the muddied waters of the internet, where all manner of statements are fallaciously attributed to him – the one that contrasts the joy of spending two hours in delightful company, which seemingly passes in a mere moment, with placing one's hand on a hot stove for a minute, which will feel like an extraordinary long time, is the most effective one in encapsulating how human beings actually experience its passage on a day-to-day (or moment by moment) basis.

Our organisational lives are shaped and directed by the whole notion of time, of course. It might be argued that the most important machine of the Industrial Revolution was the clock, a crucial element of the development of means of mass manufacture (Davies, 2019). Factory life cannot exist without the timepiece, which allows for the segmentation and regularisation of process in space and time. It also dictates the discipline of the industrialised workplace – or at least did do, until such time as a further technological development (in terms of smart phones and the like) engendered a 24/7 expectation of work availability (Crary, 2013). The COVID-19 pandemic doubled-down on this by encouraging more remote and home working, which – alongside its benefits – carries a shadow of work intensification and digital presenteeism (Stringer, et al., 2020).

But the question of time is embedded at a far deeper level of management and leadership thinking – and goes beyond the mere calibration of what gets done and when, by whom and how. We are all acutely aware of the 'working week' – familiar with tropes such as referring to Wednesdays as 'hump day', meaning that it is then downhill all the way into the weekend, or (more sharply) describing Thursday as 'Day Four of the hostage situation' – and of the intense nature of the 'working day', with its demands around visibility (at your desk, on the phone, in the meeting – always seen to be doing something, without much consideration as to whether that something has any genuine value to the individual or the endeavour to which they sell their labour) and expectations of 'busyness', expressed in the artefact of the Outlook calendar (pointedly accessible to all) that is chockful of back-to-back activity of one sort of another, leading one to wonder when it is that the work gets done.

Time, then, is a vital currency in organisational life: some senior leaders make a great deal of fuss about not having enough of it, a self-justifying conceit that seems to aim to reinforce their 'busyness' and declares that they are making an invaluable contribution. After all, how could someone so completely absorbed by 'work' not be essential to their business? Within the organisational context, there is the linguistic sleight of hand that replaces the term 'time' with that of 'capacity'. Invariably, this is how managers discuss whether they might be able to offload yet another piece of work on an unsuspecting member of staff. And that person almost certainly ends up collapsing exhausted at home after the travails of the day and wishing that there were more hours in the day.

Underpinning all of this, to our mind, is a more pervasive and impactful structuration around chronology. Specifically, another fundamental element of our argument is the simple notion that, whilst we all live in the present wherein we act – individually and in concert in order to exercise agency in the world – organisational life instead ceaselessly privileges the future. Our past is merely a terrain littered with the not quite good enough (regardless of how effective or acceptable it might actually have been), whilst our present is not a place where we might reflect and think but merely a stepping off point into the future. And it is a future that is heavily freighted with notions of progress and betterment. Hence, chronology in the world of business and work writes off the past as a failure, sees the present merely as a staging point, and fetishises the future as something that we must constantly 'envision', plan, and actively create.

That constant feeling of being thrown forward leaves everyone dizzy and unable to focus on the here and now – or, indeed, to recognise the past as a rich resource of attainment and achievement. To an extent, it is about the pursuit of a commoditised notion of novelty, as suggested by the whole idea of 'disruptive innovation' (Christensen, 2016) – and the sense to which,

> We are not good at thinking movement. Our instinctive skills favour the fixed and the static, the separate and self-contained. The dynamic and precariously balanced nature of our social world frequently escapes our attention because of deeply ingrained habits of thought which surreptitiously work to elevate notions of stability, continuity, and permanence over transience, flux and transformation. Taxonomies, hierarchies, systems, structures and end-states represent the instinctive vocabulary of institutionalized thought in its determined subordination of the language of movement, change, emergence and becoming.
>
> (Chia & King, 1998, p. 462)

Hence, whilst flow and movement are crucial aspects of developing a human understanding of our presence in the world, there is a tendency for businesses to seek to fix these things through the generation of a range of artefacts. We seek to seize the world by our indulgence of a range of practices that are familiar to us all from organisational life, such as policies, standard operating procedures, project plans, and – perhaps most hubristically – strategies. In respect to the latter, this is where we sense the constant impulse to move into the future; leadership practice privileges notions such as creating and communicating a vision, sketching out the directions of travel, and developing an awareness of the challenges to one's company that might be on the horizon. And it is not just the senior leaders that are encouraged to occupy this future space, because they – in turn – ceaselessly encourage their workforces to be scrapping the past and using the present as a stepping stone into an always better future.

We want to advance the view very forcibly that this is the wrong place in which to position people. The past is not a scrapyard full of failed attempts to control the world. It is, instead, the very richest resource of practical experience, offering insight for us into the things that worked and the context that supported them so to do – and also the experiments that did not deliver what we expected of them, oftentimes precisely because of the unknowability of the circumstances in which we were trying to work at that time. Similarly, the present is where we are and where we do the work that is intrinsic to our efforts around organising; it is not merely a platform from which we endlessly leap into a future that – through our indulgence of the fictions of managerial practices – we feel as though we have defined as a destination to which we must constantly be heading.

To that extent, we believe that leadership needs to liberate itself – and those with whom it finds itself alongside – to think very differently about chronology. First, the fetishisation of 'busyness' needs to be set aside once and for all. Quite simply, your status does not derive from the volume of demands that exist on your time. That is an altogether artificial aspect of your leadership status, where your position leads people unthinkingly to make those demands. Your calendar is busy, not because that preoccupation brings value and thereby determines the impact that you are having on the organisation as a leader, but because you are seen to be a leader and hence people have been entrained to draw down on your time.

Second, having put aside 'busyness', it is essential that leaders steer their workforces to a new and more enlightened understanding of speed in business. We are all used to the familiar business meeting mantra wherein someone in a senior position intervenes to make some remark along the lines of, 'We have done enough talking, we need to do something'. The understanding of time in business settings means that action is endlessly privileged over reflection and consideration. Patently, the two are in a subtle balance – or, at the very least, they most certainly should be: as the old business saw reminds us, 'reflection without action is mere daydreaming, whilst action without thought is a nightmare'. So, the leader needs to encourage those around them not to be transfixed by the speedy sweep of the second hand, nor indeed transfixed by the observable whirl of the minute hand. Instead, they need to help people to refocus on the slow progress of the hour hand – and use that motion as a means of structuring their exploration of lines of inquiry and development of ideas as to how things might be approached.

Lastly, having nudged people back into a slower pace wherein thinking and practice might be carefully undertaken, the leader needs to encourage a turn away from the endless focus on the future in favour of a commitment to learning from the past alongside sensemaking in the present. Hence, a liberated leadership would abandon the traditional, common sense ideas that haunt managerial practice in favour of an approach founded upon an embrace of thoughtfulness and a reasoned, critical orientation that seeks to call into question everything.

1.5.1 *Part 5 in summary*

5.   *The fragmentation of time, busyness, and the disconnected future*
  - The squeezing of the productive few and terror of the bullshit many
  - The fragmentation of worktime and disappearance of the flow of the whole
  - The focus on an unrooted, disconnected future
  - The need to liberate leadership from busyness, the sugar-rush of action, and embrace the speed of the hour hand

* * * * * * * * * * * * *

1.6 Paying attention to the headwaters of our thinking

When we discussed this book, we were very clear about its foundational premise: we wanted to lift ourselves out of the whirling maelstrom of unthinking leadership practice and make our way to the headwaters of management thinking. And, in doing so, we wanted to encourage others to do the same (although, in all honesty, we are not hugely hopeful that people will be so content to surrender the benefits that attend to doing things in the way that they've always been – and to push their way into a space of uncertainty where they will be expected to find a way through the day-to-day challenges). It is an act akin to going beyond the turkey voting for Christmas to a situation where the fowl also willingly plucks itself, leaving it naked and susceptible to being shoved without ceremony into the pre-heated oven.

Nevertheless, our intention is to demonstrate how management practice and leadership thinking is unthinkingly absorbed and endures no meaningful challenge; it is constantly reproduced by the fact that we choose not to think our way out of it…and to tackle its source. This is what we mean when we speak of wanting to tackle the headwaters of the tradition of how management and leadership gets done, rather than wanting to paddle around downstream where one is simply buffeted by the current and the detritus accumulating around us as the consequence of some unacknowledged source.

This sense of purpose arose out of a series of reflexive conversations that we enjoyed over the course of 2019. They proceeded from a starting point of Mark pondering why it was that it seemed so difficult to encourage leaders to engage with the ideas surrounding what was described as 'systems working' in health and social care. Naturally, a starting point was whether Mark was a sensible advocate for this approach or whether his communication of the key ideas was as clear and persuasive as it might be. At some point, a conversation with someone through LinkedIn led Mark to wonder whether simply broaching the topic of this approach was actually merely flooding his audience with terrible anxiety. Latterly, the conversation landed at a point where it was possible to see the very notion of 'systems leadership' as yet another off-the-peg management response to the challenge of giving direction to human organising.

Hence began a period of critique in respect to precisely that: what is it about management and leadership that prompts slackness of thinking and creativity in respect to practice. This encouraged an inquiry into precisely those headwaters of which we have spoken – and the various agents who sustain the traditions of thinking and doing in that realm, such as the business schools and the professional services companies. In practical terms, we found ourselves engaged in two pieces of work: first, in respect to a presentation to a CIPD Student's Conference, there was an examination of a selection of what were described at face value as paradoxes of modern organisational life. The arguments about those paradoxes are developed herein – and the analysis of them is extended to concede that these may not strictly speaking be paradoxes.

Instead, they each represent a harsh corporate reality that is delicately wrapped in a soft ideological coating – either knowingly or unwittingly – by those who work as leaders or managers in corporate life. This resonates with a stipulation that there would be great benefit to the application of critical theory to notions of organisational paradox:

A concern with power is at the heart of [Critical Management Studies] and runs through the various paradoxes that it addresses. To understand these kinds of organizational processes, paradox scholars need to start by looking at these underlying tensions which have been explored by researchers working in a critical tradition. Doing so could uncover instances of ideology and control in what at first sight appear to be benign paradoxes.'

(Van Bommel & Spicer, 2019, p. 157)

This speaks to us strongly in respect to what we have discovered in respect to paradoxes in organisations.

Second, we began to tackle what we took to be a number of management myths that complimented the raft of so-called paradoxes that we had identified, in respect to the preparation of a paper for the International Critical Management Studies conference held at the Open University in 2019. In this regard, we were careful to make the case that these were mythical beliefs. Partly, this reflects the way in which they contribute to a wider and significantly dominant discourse of management and leadership – and the specific way in which they achieve their effect.

So, our starting point derives from Claude Levi-Strauss, the structural anthropologist, who argues that '...the purpose of myth is to provide a logical model capable of overcoming a contradiction (an impossible achievement if, as it happens, the contradiction is real)' (Levi-Strauss, 1963, p. 229). To our mind, the world of leadership and management – particularly when considered in the context of a capitalist socio-economic system – is riven with contradictions. To confront them would be to unravel the very fabric of those arrangements, a possibility that is unacceptable and so constantly ideologically overlaid until it seems to have disappeared.

Within this schema, there is the relationship between myth and ritual, which leads to the observation that 'Regardless of whether the myth or the ritual is the original, they replicate each other; the myth exists on the conceptual level and the ritual on the level of action' (Levi-Strauss, 1963, p. 232). Here is the crucial element in terms of impact: the potential for myth to generate ritual, for the two to be closely associated. In this regard, we seek to make the case that the repertoire of management myths that we perceive in and through our practice in organisations directly shape the limits of thinking in the field – and define ritualised responses in that context amongst those who cast themselves as leaders or managers in firms and all types of organisations.

Work that orients via both Bergson and Levi-Strauss states quite expressly how myth might play out in organisational life. Building on the latter's position, it is more widely asserted that Levi-Strauss took the view that

> ...myths are machines for the suppression of time. In other words, they attempt to turn difference into repetition. Unfortunately, much of the work on myth and symbol in studies of organizational culture never fully understcod this remark and thus never really moved past it. Cultural formulations such as myth attempt to capture anthropological problems and responses and symbolically project both problem formulation and response as though they are not specific to a time or culture but are perennial, to reassure by suppressing difference and contingency.
>
> (Linstead & Mullarkey, 2003, p. 4)

Equally, the work of Roland Barthes offers a crucial understanding of myth as a linguistic element and the function that it might play in generating the common-sense normalcy of a particular social formation. Most importantly, Barthes reminds us that, ...myth cannot possibly be an object, a concept, or an idea; it is a mode of signification, a form' (Barthes, 1972, p. 107). He goes on to suggest:

> Semiology has taught us that myth has the task of giving an historical intention a natural justification, and making contingency seem eternal [...] myth is constituted by the loss of the historical quality of things: in it, things lose the memory that they once were made.
>
> (Barthes, 1972, p. 142)

The myths we highlight here – and there are likely many more, with which the reader will be acquainted and on which they may then wish to take a critical view – serve to create the sense of ahistoricism in respect to managerialism. Myths make it seem a timeless endeavour, without beginning or end...and it creates the illusion, through that, of a universal truth that feels like it might lie behind them. But just like myths themselves, this is of course merely a convenient fiction – and one which must now be located more firmly in its wider cultural and chronological context. As an analysis of the relationship between myth and psychoanalysis helpfully explains, 'Lacan's focus on myth shows how a fiction should not be understood simply as something "false" but as something that can be used to organize disparate and traumatic material' (Leader, 2003, p. 42).

In essence, then, it can be argued that myth offers a way to consider and manage concepts in life that seem contradictory and irreconcilable. As Barthes helpfully observes in this respect,

> Myth does not deny things, on the contrary, its function is to talk about them: simply, it purifies them, it makes them innocent, it gives them a natural and eternal justification, it gives them a clarity which is not that of an explanation but that of a statement of fact.
>
> (Barthes, 1972, p. 143)

The myths that we detect in respect to management do precisely this: they acknowledge and yet obscure the wicked problems and the challenges of working in complexity – all of the positions that seem to sit in opposition to one another – in order to generate a certainty that can be repeatedly asserted and actively pursued, even when it is seen to fail to deliver. With these orientations in mind we assert the following myths as having a significant impact on the capacity for action amongst leaders (and, indeed, the wider workforce) to affect positive change in managing their organisations. As will be seen, however, the myths are not merely managerial and actually reside across society.

1.6.1 Part 6 in summary

6. Paying attention to the headwaters of our thinking
   - The lack of thoughtful challenge to what is taken for granted in leadership and management
   - Not being an 'off-the-peg' replacement to the current 'off-the-peg' ideology of management
   - How we came to the paradoxes and myths we see underpinning and sustaining current practice
   - The role of myth in normalising and eternalising management and leadership practices

* * * * * * * * * * * * *

1.7 What happens next...

The remainder of the book intertwines a more sustained exploration of the thinking underpinning current practice with some suggestion as to what a better, or at least more thoughtful, approach to leadership and management could look like. This is built around an examination of five paradoxes and six myths.

1.7.1 The five paradoxes

Wellbeing contra overbearing busyness – a fashionable focus on workforce wellbeing initiatives alongside the overbearing corporate culture of busyness.

Inclusive compassion contra heroic control – a public declaration (particularly in the NHS) in favour of compassionate and inclusive leadership in contrast to a practical adherence to heroic leadership and command-and-control.

Diversity of voice contra enforced homogeneity – an emphasis on diversity – particularly of voice – in organisations alongside the cultural totalitarianism of values alignment, with its orientation towards enforced homogeneity (Willmott, 1993).

Authenticity contra part of the superstructure – an invocation that leaders should be their authentic self in the workplace juxtaposed with a constant organisational drive for performance, which – for middle managers – merely renders them an element of the superstructure that manages the delivery of output and outcome.

All to be heard contra the privileging of extraversion – the invitation in a corporate setting for all voices to be heard yet the continued (and encouraged) dominance of an extraverted culture in this context, where thoughtfulness, reflection, and quietness is ascribed an otherness in contrast to the dominance of decisiveness, action, and noise that is privileged in nearly every organisational setting (Cain, 2013).

1.7.2 The six myths

All is fixable – we live in a consequence free world, where solutions to all situations exist, where pills and modern medicine, technology, the market, new so-called 'thought leadership', and a battery of management techniques, will be a *deus ex machina* (or *deus ex McKinsey*) stepping in to make everything better. This fictional certainty encourages leaders to ignore the messy complexity of the here and now and instead focus on the dream of a visionary tomorrow. Advocacy dominates inquiry. Action, especially fast action, trumps understanding.

Perfection is the only state worth pursuing – idealism and the pursuit of 'world class' operating models dominate the leadership discourse. 'Good enough' and contextual realities have been abandoned in the face of an ideal which is being permanently recast. Perpetual revolution and reinvention have become the new normal. We are consumed by the 'innovator's dilemma', yearning for that breakthrough in terms of newness that will disrupt our markets and catapult us into the lead (Christensen, 2016). Perfection co-exists, of course, as a part of fixability: it can only truly be fixed if it's seen to be perfect.

There is just one true way of doing things – bleeding through from the (Newtonian/Material) scientific method is an unfortunate belief that social systems can be reduced to a mechanistic model of cause and effect, where a single approach to knowing the world can be identified as an 'objective' truth. This is further fuelled by a belief that all approaches need to and can be scalable and replicable – resulting in local realities being trashed and everything being recast in terms of the lowest common denominator of what can be seen as the same. This bleeds into the game of piloting, where the pilot is an experiment that tests a hypothesis and if, in the precise moment of piloting there is a positive outcome, then the hypothesis is proven and the steps of the 'experiment' become a process or a method for delivering that outcome. Most of which is unsupported by our day-to-day experience of the lived world. Commensurability is all and that which is non-commensurable irrelevant.

Metrics reflect an objective reality – modern management is in the grip of the 'tyranny of the tangible' (Reynolds, et al., 2020) and now lives with the consequences of reporting systems which have little connection to the lived experience of customers, patients, and employees. Measurement has become a lousy master rather than a useful tool. Metrics prevail because they allow management practice to ape the so-called 'scientific method'. They also create a simulation of reality wherein those measurements can be bent and stretched into shapes that seem, to those who buy into this fiction, to show the fixability, perfection, and speed of change that corporate life craves. Changing the numbers is always much easier than engaging with the complexity of meaningful workplace reconfiguration.

Values bind the organisation – they don't. They may bind the executive team and keep their competitive instincts in check. For people involved in the primary task of an organisation abstract values have little meaning in comparison to the lived experience of what actually gets valued in the here and now. However, the corporate values encroach upon them as hoops through which they are expected to jump: job applicants are asked to demonstrate their understanding of an organisation's values and their individual and entirely hypothetical capacity to apply them in practice as part of the selection process. That process offers no space or opportunity for a candidate to outline the values – individual or social – that motivate them as a human being; it is solely about whether they can absorb the Orwellian Newspeak of the company's carefully crafted values.

'We're all in this together' – workplaces are political systems where individuals and groups have distinctive priorities and interests. The excessive advocacy and policing of compliance to a single narrative fuels an underground culture, where difference is fought out in the shadows and cannot be acknowledged, sustaining the chasm between espoused and actual experiences of leadership. This myth allows people to indulge the illusion that resistance has evaporated from the workplace, when more diligent and thoughtful writers seek to remind us that it persists, even amidst the idea that organisations are more akin to 'happy families' than spaces in which we constantly contest our positions (Fleming, 2014).

1.7.3 An end to the introduction

We do not have answers. We have real doubts about the values of the hidden-hand currently directing how the world of management and leadership is known and talked about. We wish we could assuage ourselves with some new model, some easy to digest piece of consensual pseudo-objectivity (presented to senior leaders on one page of A4...). We wish we could lie to you, as so many have in recent times, by recommending that management and leadership 'follow the science'.

But that is not how social reality gets created, sustained, challenged, and changed. What counts as socially normal is always an expression of subjective values and philosophy, which privileges particular ways of knowing and particular groups – it is this intertwining of values, privilege, and knowing that is at the heart of what we see as Michel Foucault's insistence on talking of truth-power, rather than independent categories of 'truth' and 'power'. In human society and in its work-places what counts as true is an expression of, and shaped by, what is experienced as power by and through people.

What this book intends to do is expose a dominant truth-power ideology and practice, which we contend does not serve the majority of people at all well. It also suggests ways in which that ideology, its practices, and the groups who serve it and are served by it may be challenged and with luck over-turned. It is time to take on William Blake's mind-forg'd manacles (Blake, 2020) that make slaves of so many of us and strips life of its liveliness. Who knows, it may even be 'transformational'.

References

Ashforth, B. E. & Fried, Y., 1988. The mindlessness of organizational behaviors. *Human Relations*, 41(4), pp. 305–329.

Barthes, R., 1972. *Mythologies*. New York: The Noonday Press.

Ben Folds Five, 1995. *Ben Folds Five*. [Sound Recording] (Passenger Records).

Henri Bergson, 1946. *The Creative Mind*. New York: Philosophical Library.

Cain, S., 2013. *Quiet: The power of introverts in world that can't stop talking*. London: Penguin.

Chia, R. & King, I. W., 1998. The organizational structuring of novelty. *Organization*, 5(4), pp. 461–478.

Christensen, C. M., 2016. *The innovator's dilemma: When new technologies cause great firms to fail*. Boston, Mass.: Harvard Business Review Press.

Crary, J., 2013. *24/7: Late capitalism and the ends of sleep*. London: Verso.

Cripps, J., 2020. *Nursery teacher red-faced after discovering why newly purchased candle 'disappeared'*. [Online] Available at: www.mirror.co.uk/news/uk-news/nursery-teacher-red-faced-after-22110705 [Accessed 29 May 2020].

Cunha, M. P., Cunha, J. V. & Kamoche, K., 1999. Organizational improvisation: What, when, how and why. *International Journal of Management Reviews*, 1(3), pp. 299–341.

Davies, A. C., 2019. *The industrial revolution and time*. [Online] Available at: www.open.edu/openlearn/history-the-arts/history/history-science-technology-and-medicine/history-technology/the-industrial-revolution-and-time [Accessed 8 July 2020].

Dawkins, D., 2020. *Bad times for billionaire Branson – staff at Virgin Atlantic asked to take unpaid leave as coronavirus cripples air travel*. [Online] Available at: www.forbes.com/sites/daviddawkins/2020/03/16/bad-times-for-billionaire-bransonstaff-at-virgin-atlantic-asked-to-take-unpaid-leave-as-coronavirus-cripples-air-travel/#9e44ab358ef5 [Accessed 18 March 2020].

Debord, G., 2014/1967. *The society of the spectacle*. Berkeley, CA: Bureau of Public Secrets.

Fleming, P., 2014. *Resisting work: The corporatization of life and its discontents*. Philadelphia: Temple University Press.

Gioia, D. A. & Poole, P. P., 1984. Scripts in organizational behavior. *The Academy of Management Review*, 9(3), pp. 449–459.

Graeber, D., 2013. *On the phenomenon of bullshit jobs: A work rant*. [Online] Available at: www.strike.coop/bullshit-jobs [Accessed 7 July 2020].

Hadida, A. L. & Tarvainen, W., 2015. Organizational improvisation: A consolidating review and framework. *International Journal of Management Reviews*, 17(4), pp. 437–459.

Hatch, M. J., 1999. Exploring the empty spaces of organizing: How improvisational jazz helps redescribe organizational structure. *Organization Studies*, 20(1), pp. 75–100.

IMDB, 1982. *The king of comedy*. [Online] Available at: www.imdb.com/title/tt0085794/?ref_=tttr_tr_tt [Accessed 2 June 2020].

Jappe, A., 1999. *Guy Debord*. Berkeley, CA: University of California Press.

Lazenby, P., 2020. *Virgin ask staff to take eight weeks' unpaid leave*. [Online] Available at: www.morningstaronline.co.uk/article/virgin-staff-unpaid-leave [Accessed 18 March 2020].

Leader, D., 2003. Lacan's myths. In: J. Rabate, ed. *The Cambridge companion to Lacan*. Cambridge: Cambridge University Press, pp. 35–49.

Levi-Strauss, C., 1963. *Structural anthropology*. New York: Basic Books Inc.

Linstead, S. & Mullarkey, J., 2003. Time, creativity and culture: Introducing Bergson. *Culture and Organization*, 9(1), pp. 3–13.

Margaret Thatcher Foundation, 1987. *Interview for woman's own ("No such thing as society")*. [Online] Available at: www.margaretthatcher.org/document/106689 [Accessed 18 March 2020].

Parker, M., 2018. *Shut down the business school: What's wrong with management education?* London: Pluto Press.

Reynolds, A., Houlder, D., Goddard, J. & Lewis, D., 2020. *What philosophy can teach you about being a better leader*. London: Kogan Page.

Siedentop, L., 2015. *Inventing the individual: The origins of Western liberalism*. London: Penguin.

Stringer, L., Mustchin, S. & Dundon, T., 2020. *The downsides of homeworking*. [Online] Available at: www.alliancembs.manchester.ac.uk/news/the-downsides-of-homeworking/ [Accessed 8 July 2020].

Van Bommel, K. & Spicer, A., 2019. Critical Management Studies and paradox. In: W. K. Smith, M. W. Lewis, Jarzabkowski & A. Langley, eds. *The Oxford handbook of organizational paradox*. Oxford: Oxford University Press, pp. 143–161.

Vejby, R. & Wittkower, W. E., 2010. Spectacle 2.0? In: W. E. Wittkower, ed. *Facebook and philosophy: What's on your mind?* Chicago: Open Court Publishing Company, pp. 97–108.

Westacott, E., 2020. *Nietzsche's idea of eternal recurrence*. [Online] Available at: www.thoughtco.com/nietzsches-idea-of-the-eternal-recurrence-2670659 [Accessed 7 July 2020].

Wikipedia, 2020. *Operation: Rabbit*. [Online] Available at: en.m.wikipedia.org/wiki/Operation:_Rabbit [Accessed 6 July 2020].

Willmott, H., 1993. Strength is ignorance; slavery is freedom: Managing culture in modern organizations. *Journal of Management Studies*, 30(4), pp. 515–552.

YouTube, 2013. *I hope you get cancer*. [Online] Available at: www.youtube.com/watch?v=wjaKdtYbTto [Accessed 2 June 2020].

2

THE USE AND ABUSE
OF PARADOXES IN
ORGANISATIONAL LIFE

2.1 Setting the scene

This chapter gets under the skin of a word that we should find deeply troubling, one that should create an emotional jolt as it brings into exquisite attention the incoherence that shapes much of our working lives. Instead 'paradox' has been shape shifted into another bland piece of management think, where conflicting priorities, interests, and ways of knowing the world are disappeared into a continuum of choices which we unproblematically toggle between – one moment strategic and the next operational, as we breathe in we are concerned with the global perspective and as we breathe out so we shift to what is local.

In this chapter we explore the consequences, intended and unintended, of treating what should be sources of profound conflict and tension as if they were polarities in search of a world of equilibrium, where the golden mean holds sway. We explore whose interests are served by presenting the world through the lens of resolvable paradox and why this might well be

DOI: 10.4324/9781003035015-2

one of the ways in which the naked reality of power, coercion, and control play out in our faux-nice workplaces of teams, collegiality, and wellness initiatives.

We will do this by:

- Exploring how paradox has become another piece of managerial instrumentalism
- Introducing you to five of the commonplace so-called paradoxes and the diverse qualities that are presented as polarities
- Reviewing the implications for management practice of working with what lies behind the veil of paradoxical managerialism

And our argument that reflects this unfolds under the following headings:

- Starting with the personal in the context of the systemic – the non-inevitability of equilibrium
- On the notion of paradox – the game where two irreconcilable propositions co-exist
- Paradoxes in organisational life – how words create worlds and legitimise one-dimensional management
- Dismantling five impactful paradoxes – an overview

2.2 Starting with the personal in the context of the systemic: the non-inevitability of equilibrium

The work day commute is a familiar feature of many people's lives. At its best, it offers a brief period of down time before the start and at the end of the doubtless hectic working day, to admit to being anything but hectic at work being of course a modern-day heresy. Mark is old enough to enjoy buying a paper copy of a daily newspaper and reading it on his 20-minute jaunt, when things run smoothly, into the capital. And he ploddingly reads a chapter or two of a novel on his way home – this despite the fact that his bag is invariably stuffed with work material and articles that he feels he should be reading, but which never comes out of the rucksack during those travels.

But equally it can be a time of stress and frustration, as travellers can oftentimes acutely feel the powerlessness that derives from being wholly reliant on a large faceless system of competing corporations and statutory priorities to deliver a service upon which they the passengers depend, but seem to be all but disappeared when it comes to having a meaningful voice. A cursory glance at the Twitter feed of any railway company and providing body during a period of disruption demonstrates how those sorts of experience can bring out the worst in people, particularly where social media is involved. Ultimately, of course, those invariably barbed – and sometimes just brutal and vile – comments don't speak about the experience of not catching a train, or sitting abandoned in a siding for hours, but about how so many of us feel in the face of a society where we are told that we are free citizens but where the reality is that we are embedded in webs of power that deny us any felt sense of agency.

One might reasonably assume that we are all involved in making some sort of trade-off between commuting and compensation: the latter needing to be significant enough to the individual to justify the time and psychological effort required to put up with travel to work. There is some form of explicable and mutually beneficial cost/benefit analysis in play, with the market (however imperfect) working its invisible magic. Yet it is suggested that this is not the case, which offers up a noteworthy paradox wherein research reports that '...people with long journeys to and from work are systematically worse off and report significantly lower subjective well-being. For economists, this result on commuting is paradoxical' (Stutzer & Frey, 2004, p. 3), with people 'choosing' to be worse off than they need to be – the invisible hand being more of a clunking fist or blind watchmaker, rather than a sensitive reconciler of social and economic differences.

Interestingly, from this perspective, paradox is seen to arise where an expected equilibrium fails to materialise. This presupposes that equilibrium is a natural – and indeed desirable – state, towards which we should all be actively working. Contrariwise, it may actually be the case that the messiness of life means that contradiction and tension – which we might usefully describe as paradox, as is the case in the commuting example offered earlier – is as much a feature of life (especially life in an organisational setting) as equilibrium. An exploration of what is meant by paradox in this context offers a useful starting point.

2.3 On the notion of paradox: the game where two irreconcilable propositions co-exist

For many of us, our first exposure to the idea of paradox comes from classical literature. We have a nodding acquaintance with it as a notion in respect to the idea of stepping into a river, which is drawn from the writings of Heraclitus. Here it is argued that, because of the flow of the waters, it is impossible to step into the same river twice. The waters of the river flow by second by second – so it is entirely different each time you step into it.

The paradox exists between the water that constitutes a river and the very idea of a river that we carry in our heads. The Thames has flowed from its fountainhead for countless years; we ascribe to it a sense of permanence, yet we know that it is constantly changing. The fact that it is a river and a flow of water at the same time is the paradox in terms of our thinking. In an effort to reconcile this, there are a number of possible resolutions, one of which is to assert that '…the river is not identical with its waters: rather it is composed of waters and composed of different waters over time. Were it not composed of different waters, it would be a long, thin lake, not a river' (Cave, 2009, p. 74). The conversation becomes part of a language game, where who owns the definition becomes part of the truth/power game within which language plays its part – and social standing and status dictates which truth traditions hold sway.

A contentious yet highly illustrative example of the concept is offered in the work of the philosopher Kierkegaard, in respect to the very idea of having belief in God. In a commentary on his work, it is argued that:

> For Kierkegaard the object of faith must by definition be something uncertain – that is, objectively uncertain. This contrasting certitude (inner certainty) and uncertainty (objective lack of certainty) of faith he called the paradox of faith.
>
> (Heywood Thomas, 1957, p. 103)

In this picture, the certainty and uncertainty simply have to be acknowledged: they cannot be reconciled, so faith is the idea that bridges these two ideas that sit in endless tension. Douglas Adams, of *Hitchhiker's Guide to the Universe* fame, presented a similar argument about the Babel Fish and its legendary capacity to act as a universal translator. The argument was that the

Babel Fish was a dead giveaway for the existence for God, resulting in God disappearing in a puff of human logic, followed on shortly by mankind getting killed on the next zebra crossing (having used the power of logic to prove that black was white).

The notion of paradox requires us to pay close attention to our ways of knowing the world, how we deploy our conceptual framing, and how much of that deployment is an expression of social convention and the power-relations of social life. This can feel unsettling, as if we're falling down a rabbit hole, where nothing is fixed and all is filled with contradiction and we are left with no idea of which way is up or down. In a world that so admires clarity and certainty, where we don't have the time to stay with these conceptual prattlings, it is not surprising therefore that so much of our life is built on sand – because we have not learnt, or have lost, the necessary discipline to explore and stay with the irreconcilability, the non-commensurability that is at the heart of the notion of paradox. This is especially the case when we have divided up the world of theory and practice so they are seen as separate, that understanding and action are independent frames rather than conjoined twins; inevitably we therefore eschew praxis which might be the only way out of the mindlessness of doing without thinking and the irrelevance of thinking without doing.

2.4 Paradox in organisational life: how words create worlds and legitimise one-dimensional management

All of these, of course, are logical paradoxes, which can be seen as amusing philosophical puzzles for us to try to solve – although we think they also point to a deeper problem, a lack of philosophical rigour in our habits of mind which encourage us all to stay at a superficial, or first order, understanding of the world. So the BBC news recently pumped out from 6am to 10pm the great glad news that an AI programme in the US had been able to identify a new form of anti-biotic in a fraction of the time usually taken – at no point did the news raise questions around what it was in our current approach to antibiotics that was rendering them useless at an alarming rate, a concern the previous Chief Medical Officer, Dame Sally Davies, had repeatedly tried to raise but which had gained little traction, even as she equated it as presenting a threat as profound as accelerating climate change (Harvey, 2019).

But we also face what appear to be paradoxes in life, which have a greater impact on us than simply engendering bemusement and frustration – and which is why we introduced the term praxis earlier, where logical rigour comes face to face with that which we experience in the ways we go about our day-to-day lives. It is organisational paradox that fascinates us, simply because many firms clutch these contradictions dumbly to their hearts, so as to remove them from the public view of everyone working in such a world.

We contend that hiding them in the shadows denies people the opportunity to engage with them – and to recognise the covert ways in which they influence culture and practice in the workplace. What does and doesn't get talked about doesn't happen by accident – it is an expression of power, and in our modern workplaces power is largely disappeared into a technocratic debate around leadership (presented as a thing, rather than as an expression of social organising) and its associated fads and fashions. In John's recent authorial work he has been struck by how much he had to tussle with one of the then editors of the *Harvard Business Review*, who was insistent on his taking out his references to organisational hierarchy – the ideology of the editor and the magazine being that the world is getting flatter, despite all the evidence of the last 30 years pointing in the opposite direction in terms of wages, income inequality, and the scope of senior executive authority.

We are, of course, not the first to call attention to the issue of paradox in an organisational context. There is a noteworthy psychodynamic tradition in this regard. Here, we find the declaration that:

> The simultaneous presence of opposite and contradictory forces and the repetitious 'stuckness' that often accompanied these forces led us to consider that what we were observing was the expression of the paradoxical nature of group life.
>
> (Smith & Berg, 1987, p. 62)

This perspective contrasts with our own: it intimates that these tensions live on the surface and inhibit effectiveness, whereas we take the view that these paradoxes sit at the heart of organisation and serve a distinct ideological purpose through denying people the chance to explore these issues; in other words, paradox is purposeful, not accidental or an enduring, natural psycho-social phenomenon.

Writing this on March 18th 2020 it is striking how the debates about the NHS being overwhelmed by those potentially hospitalised by the coronavirus crisis is largely spoken about as if it was purely a natural phenomenon, the drama of the crisis dominates the public discourse. The hollowing out of the number of available critical care beds in the US and UK, in comparison to countries such as Germany and Japan, is relegated to a side issue (Stacey & Romei, 2020).

Elsewhere, in what the author Kets de Vries described as a clinical approach to management, a number of workplace paradoxes were interrogated through a psychoanalytical lens. One of these looked at the tensions that exist in the role of entrepreneur, where the psychological profile of that abrades against the expectations of stability in an organisational context (Kets de Vries, 1995). In the same volume, there is a fascinating exposition – prefiguring some of our contemporary perspectives on organisational form – on how 'organic' and so-called post-bureaucratic structures seem to offer a greater sense of liberty and apparent licence to act for the person and yet, at the same time, encompass uncertainty and ambiguity, which can be seen to be engendering stress amongst the workforce (Kets de Vries, 1995, pp. 46–47).

The world of management fills up with elusive phrases, from holocracy to sociocracy, which require an extraordinary amount of effort to understand (if they are comprehensible at all) and are largely predicated on assumptions of shared and amenable purpose and hide in plain sight the widespread casualisation of the workforce and the removal of security of employment. The popularised term 'Me Plc' for instance can be an appealing phrase to some, playing into notions of rugged, self-actualising individualism and entrepreneurialism, while disguising the sleight of hand that is transferring the risks of employment from the employer to the employee, from the well-resourced to the less-resourced. This reality is now exploding in people's faces as rugged individuals discover for themselves John Donne's insight that nobody can live in glorious isolation, experiencing how cold it is when you don't have enough collective resources to fall back on or into.

The discussions around paradox in organisations are not in the least bit new. Nearly 20 years ago, it was observed that, 'Managers [...] are asked to increase efficiency and foster creativity, build individualistic teams, and think globally while acting locally. "It's a paradox," however, is rapidly

becoming the management cliché of our time – overused and unspecified'
(Lewis, 2000, p. 760). More recently, Chris Mowles offered an examination of paradox in organisational life through the lens of complexity. He
specifies therein that the literature in this area takes two forms: the minority position accepts paradox as unresolvable and hence a useful way of
acknowledging contradiction in organisations; and a more prevalent and
accepted perspective, which is '...generally managerialist in character and
assumes an instrumentalizing approach to paradox' (Mowles, 2015, p. 40)
and which leads people into the world of polarities to be managed, slid-
ing scales to be modulated, rather than conflicts and contradictions to be
fought and debated over.

Through the prism that Mowles uses, a number of fascinating paradoxes
are explored. He attends to the tension for managers that exists between the
operational and strategic, ensuring the business functions whilst trying to
explore new ways for it to develop (with no consideration of what 'develop'
means or who a particular definition serves best). Similarly, he reviews culture through the delicate equipoise between the local and the global. And
he investigates the contested notion of 'innovation', both in terms of how
the traditional balance between stability and change is presented – and the
notion of whence innovation springs, namely from senior leaders setting in
train grand ideas or out of the day-to-day practice of those actively involved
in working towards the purpose of that organisation (Mowles, 2015). Both
perspectives are valid and co-exist, like the Gestalt pictures which can be
seen both as one thing and another; there is no tension – they are simply
both there depending on the framing of the viewer, the question as to how
relative power and authority play out in privileging one view over another
are not part of the consideration. As another writer notes, there is a paradox
at the heart of the need to accommodate complexity through collective
engagement, which is argued to be more difficult to attain in the culture of
the contemporary workplace (Day, 2020, p. 30).

Once something is framed as a managerial challenge, of course, there
is likely to be a technical response, notionally allowing leaders to 'work
through' that challenge in a decisive and directive manner. The response
to paradox conceptually allows the leader to toggle between the two contradictory states by recasting them as 'polarities' and offering us up the
option of managing them (Johnson, 1996). This is an exercise that seems
to have a satisfying internal consistency – but which can be seen to leave

reality largely untouched. Its function is to make leaders feel that they have addressed and resolved an issue, a crucial factor to which we return in far greater detail in the chapter on management myths.

This method is made attractive by the idea that it renders issues which do not lend themselves to solution **manageable**, or rather the simulacrum of manageability – which may itself have value in containing overwhelming anxiety on occasions. Beyond this, some have asserted that paradox itself might be seen as a lens through which to explore work in respect to organisational change: their formulaic response runs through four linear stages, namely: formulating the mess (an initial problem definition phase); exposing the dilemma that derives from either/or thinking; using paradox to discover the link; and heading towards a more workable certainty (Luscher & Lewis, 2008, p. 231). Conflict and difference are disappeared, the warm bath of the melting pot (to mix up all sorts of metaphors) comes to our psychic aid, the prophylactic of closure is put on. In the world of workshops and leadership development, people are never left too disturbed (stimulated never provoked). Instead, they stride out of the sealed world of the business school, having been offered the 'edutainment' giving the experience good ratings, because they have once again been saved from the emotional anxieties of having to choose between competing world views, or of simply not knowing, or having to look at the naked truth of the reality of someone outside their world.

To our mind, this is all an illusion – and a dangerous one at that, for a number of reasons. First, it carries within it the faulty idea that everything can be resolved, smoothed off to make it supposedly comfortable for the human mind. In this sense, it is a discursive practice, something that contributes to the commonplace and generalised notion that equilibrium is the desirable state and that tension is a negative facet of human connection and organising. In John's work with people who work in the world of Diversity & Inclusion he experiences their frustration at this avoidance of felt discomfort, how being a woman from a BAME background is a discordant experience in a world where, to quote from private papers held by John, 'white is still seen as right' and the fragile white insists on its right not to be too discombobulated. A belief in equilibrium and emotional comfort silences and disappears those who don't see equilibrium and comfort as neutral states, but as part of the power game which keeps their discordant reality at arms-length.

Elsewhere, though, people are minded to put irresolvable matters in organisational life at centre stage, worthy of acknowledgement and exploration in themselves – and not merely 'problems' that need to be solved. Hence, business paradoxes are expressly referenced and these include such things as individuality in contradistinction to collective effort, something that appears in pronounced form in the course of job interviews or the annual appraisal, both focused on a single human subject but which publicly values the idea of 'teamworking' as the best possible way to get things done in a corporate context. Anyone who has attended an interview panel or submitted an application for a job knows this game, the need to foreground the collective effort while making sure that as an individual you were the controlling mind.

Then there is the so-called balance between control and autonomy, which can be seen to engender all manners of noisy conversation about so-called post-bureaucratic organisational formations and which cunningly avoid talking about power and hierarchy (except as qualities to be disappeared as old-fashioned, rather than persistent and sustained through established forces of social reality). In a recent conversation with a senior Director of a Technology company this control/autonomy tension was raised with John. The founder CEO's ongoing 92% ownership of the company, and the therefore explicit controlling power she retained, was touched on as no more than a background consideration, assumed away as unimportant when trying to understand why people's felt reality of being controlled didn't fit with the espoused collective value of personal, distributed autonomy. Meanwhile in the world of the global enterprise, there is also the need to encompass both local and global mindsets, a particular challenge for leaders of organisations with supply chains that spread from Wuhan to Watford (Waldman, et al., 2019).

From our perspective, these paradoxes are not things to be overcome through managerial and leadership practice. Indeed, we're not convinced that they are even amenable to this, notwithstanding the wider philosophical notion that we can discern 'dead paradoxes', wherein the contradictions have resolved themselves in practice; this leads to the interesting observation that,

> Whether or not something counts as a paradox is relative to a time or a culture. In considering how many paradoxes lie ahead, we should

include even those doomed to die, for, with paradoxes, death is progress: the satisfying resolution of apparently conflicting appearances.

(Sorensen & Sainsbury, 2020)

However, that perspective notwithstanding, we are of the opinion that paradox in organisational setting – and, in particular, the five that we intend to explore critically in the rest of this chapter – does inhibit fresh thinking, where fresh is both rigorous and seeks to pay attention to the informing assumptions that keep organisational life on a treadmill of compelling busyness and one-dimensional management. Perhaps more than this, we are uncertain as to whether they are truly paradoxes. In fact, as we investigate these, we wish to promulgate the view that these are not seemingly contradictory and irreconcilable linked positions but represent crucial conjoined elements that serve to form our everyday and shared understanding of organisational life, creating and legitimising particular regimes of power and control.

In broad terms, each of these so-called paradoxes have the appearance of contradiction. In fact, they represent an encapsulation of the reality of our day-to-day experience – and an ideological veil that is drawn across this, through our willingness to subscribe actively to these secondary aspects and avoid looking directly into the sun of power and the truth it shapes, rewards, and punishes. Let's look at the five faux paradoxes that we take to be particularly impactful in the workplace context.

2.5 Dismantling five impactful paradoxes: an overview

In overview these five impactful paradoxes are:

* **Well-being contra overbearing busyness** – a fashionable focus on workforce well-being initiatives alongside the overbearing corporate culture of busyness.
* **Inclusive compassion contra heroic control** – a public declaration (particularly in the NHS) in favour of compassionate and inclusive leadership in contrast to a practical adherence to heroic leadership and command-and-control.
* **Diversity of voice contra enforced homogeneity** – an emphasis on diversity – particularly of voice – in organisations alongside the cultural

totalitarianism of values alignment, with its orientation towards enforced homogeneity (Willmott, 1993).

- **Authenticity contra part of the superstructure** – an invocation that leaders should be their authentic self in the workplace juxtaposed with a constant organisational drive for performance, which – for middle managers – merely renders them an element of the superstructure that manages the delivery of output and outcome.
- **All to be heard contra the privileging of extraversion** – the invitation in a corporate setting for all voices to be heard yet the continued (and encouraged) dominance of an extraverted culture in this context, where thoughtfulness, reflection, and quietness is ascribed an otherness in contrast to the dominance of decisiveness, action, and noise that is privileged in nearly every organisational setting (Cain, 2013).

These seeming paradoxes, which are part of the discourse in most organisational settings, create a context of incoherence where people have to fight against a wall of verbiage and seeming nonsensicality. The world gets dangerously close to Orwell's novelistic assertion from 1984 that two plus two equals whatever those in power mean it to mean, and over time we become skilled at giving the answer that is expected of us – even genuinely believing that two plus two equals five, if that is what is required of us.

In critiquing these paradoxes we can find ourselves at times trying to grapple with mist, where terminological obfuscation is part of the game and writers (including ourselves) can go the way of Humpty Dumpty in Lewis Carroll's *Through the Looking-Glass* (1871): 'When I use a word', Humpty Dumpty said in a rather scornful tone, 'It means just what I chose it to mean – neither more nor less'. When the words we use are cut off from an understanding of their relational context, from the lived experience of how truth shapes power and power shapes truth, then we are left with what we have – a world of seeming paradox which we try to manage without any understanding of why our inability to manage or make sense is in turn wrapped up in the invisible (or undiscussable) world of power relations.

2.5.1 Paradox one: well-being contra overbearing busyness

A fashionable focus on workforce well-being initiatives alongside the overbearing corporate culture of busyness.

2.5.1.1 *In brief...*

The themes we explore in association with this paradox are:

- Anxiety around employee engagement with work and how focusing on wellness disappears the need to pay attention to the actuality of the work
- The blurring boundaries between working, not working, and being available to work and how the worldview of workplace organisation has permeated our every waking hour
- The seduction of belonging to a group by thinking in the way approved of by those seen to have power and authority
- The imprecision and fuzziness of what counts as well-being in the workplace — what is meant by it is not obvious, is inherently subjective and is an ethical not technocratic consideration

2.5.1.2 *The paradox in full...*

We explore the paradox under the following six headings:

- The framing of well-being as being in the service of productivity
- The organisational response to workforce disengagement which threatens productivity
- Busyness and the penetration of work-think into the home
- The intended and unintended consequences of ICT
- The imprecision of what is meant by health and well-being
- The addiction to persistent, executively framed, programmatic upheaval (aka 'change')

And we begin our argument with the first one of these six headings.

2.5.1.2.1 THE FRAMING OF WELL-BEING AS BEING IN THE SERVICE OF PRODUCTIVITY

The International Labour Organisation (ILO) is an agency of the United Nations. In one corner of its extensive web presence, it declares as follows: 'Workers well-being is a key factor in determining an organisation's long-term effectiveness. Many studies show a direct link between productivity levels and the general health and well-being of the workforce' (International Labour Organization, n.d.). For those who imagine that the current fascination amongst many employers in respect to the health and well-being of their workforce is attributable to some unexpected altruistic impulse, the ILO helpfully lays bare the underlying (even true...) motivation in this regard.

At its most extreme, the focus on well-being reflects an anxiety about a lack of engagement with work at a time when work has become more and more routinised through the enforcement of standardised operating models, embedded and policed through computerisation of the workplace. Hence, it is noted that, '...25 per cent of us enjoy our work but the rest of us do not. Productivity suffers as a consequence, due to the workplace being more a place of conflict and dissatisfaction' (Clements-Croome, 2013, p. 45), conflict arising in part from a need for people to have some personal discretion over an increasingly micro-controlled world.

In a visit the two of us made to an Amazon warehouse in January 2020, the tour guide described Amazon as being first and foremost a software company with some clever algorithms randomly managing warehouse space – and co-incidentally creating working patterns where people were similarly randomly distributed and followed completely scripted tasks, down to what food employees were allowed to bring in i.e. unwrapped, individual boiled sweets. This last piece of data found by John as he lagged behind the main group and read the small print of the health and safety notices, while Mark and everyone else were swept along to enjoy the pictures of the 2019 Christmas party, held in January 2020 once the Christmas rush was over and wouldn't get in the way of service productivity.

Lack of productivity shows up in many ways, such as 'absenteeism, arriving late and leaving early, over-long lunch breaks, careless mistakes, overwork, boredom, frustration with the management and the environment' (Clements-Croome, 2006, pp. 22–23). Hence, the seemingly logical response is to focus in on attending to how best to improve the health and psychological satisfaction of individuals through a range of interventions and activities, in Amazon's case an invitation to follow the plastic photoshopped A4 sign of a pool table – which we assume led to a real one somewhere on site. Yet, in reality, it would be more sensible to explore what it is about work that means that 75% of those who do it apparently do not enjoy it. Surely it is a logical human reaction to put both physical and mental distance between oneself and an intrinsically immiserating experience. And, if that's the case, then we might best use our time understanding why work alienates three-quarters of the workforce.

2.5.1.2.2 THE ORGANISATIONAL RESPONSE TO WORKFORCE DISENGAGEMENT WHICH THREATENS PRODUCTIVITY

But what is the organisational response to this? It is a range of reactions with which we are all of us extremely familiar. Weekly fruit drops, yoga classes, personal resilience training, workplace choirs: a wearisome panoply of worthy or fun things to do, to which we are all expected to subscribe. Back in 2017, a journalist revealed how some time into a mindfulness programme 'I began to get the feeling that I might be putting a plaster on a bullet wound' (Garlick, 2017). Off the back of this, other readings and conversations lead us to wonder how much workplace mindfulness programmes are akin to firstly breaking people's legs with busyness and stress and then giving them lunchtime crutch-building classes.

Moreover, of course, not to delight in this scintillating array of activities, that also serve to further blur that much valued boundary between work and life, is perhaps to end up being seen as not quite the 'team player', although what is meant by the word 'team' is more complicated than it looks on the surface and is something we explore later, questioning the assumptions of common purpose and noticing who chooses the 'game', the 'rules', its 'administration', and who is 'playing'. Not being seen as part of the 'team' is one of the most scathing critique that any of us can face in the workplace and also plays into the inevitable psychodynamic of belonging or not belonging, being in the in-group or being other.

Stepping back into the on-the-face-of-it generosity of organisational giving, gracelessness in the face of being presented with what appears to be a selfless gift from one's employer is immediately unappealing according to nearly all social traditions – particularly when all around you seem to be delighting in it. In truth, of course, some may be; many will not be…but organisational silence means that, in most cases, we simply have no idea, and so end up in a state of compliance.

The disparity between what is said corporately and what is actually experienced by the workforce is strongly evidenced when we consider the question of work-related stress. A research report in 2019 highlighted that, whilst there was an increase in organisations taking action in this regard, a third who reported an increase in stress-related absence from work were not taking any steps to address it (Chartered Institute of Personnel & Development, 2019, p. 7). Where there was some response, it did not address the root cause of an overbearing busyness; instead, it tended to be in the area of improving work–life balance, particularly through flexible working, and the provision of employee assistance programmes (Chartered Institute of Personnel & Development, 2019, p. 7).

Again we can see the notion of equilibrium at play in the use of the phrase work–life balance, as if there is some golden mean rather than a relationship of power to be engaged with – it also locates the experience within the individual, seeking to find a personal equilibrium, and decontextualises the social world within which such a reality is seen to exist or not. Meanwhile as a wider public we have become coarsened about what work should look like – on our trip to the Amazon warehouse one of the tour group we were with observed how surprised he was not to see people running as they went about their work. Mark and John saw instead a relentless pace. Our co-visitor saw people having an easy time.

2.5.1.2.3 BUSYNESS AND THE PENETRATION OF WORK-THINK INTO THE HOME

There is some debate around the whole issue of 'busyness', of course. Recent work by the Centre for Time Use Research made much of the fact that we seemed to be spending marginally less, rather than more, time doing work (Gershuny & Sullivan, 2019). However, that observation is underpinned by an historic move towards a five-day week for vast swathes of the salariat (if not those working in care, retail, or delivery of the things we unthinkingly purchase online and expect to arrive at all hours of the day, including quite late on a Sunday evening as both of us can find ourselves doing). It is not so much that we are working more; it is simply the case that the boundaries that we were once able to maintain between our home and work lives are increasingly being eroded.

One critical issue in this regard relates to the development of new information technologies and the ways in which they have been incorporated into our lives, both at home and at work. This leads to what has been referred to as an 'empowerment/enslavement paradox', which is best encapsulated thus:

Most professionals welcomed the introduction of mobile technologies in their companies. They appreciated increased productivity, more flexibility, and more efficient ways to coordinate tasks and people. However, the same tools that empowered them in their jobs in so many ways also took away long-cherished freedoms in others. Besides "less personal time," study participants frequently cited increased work pressure, closer monitoring and supervision, and the inability to separate and keep distance from work. Participants expressed displeasure [at] having to play multiple roles at all times, especially having to constantly switch between family and work roles.

(Jarvenpaa & Lang, 2005, p. 11)

The boundary between being 'on the clock' and 'off the clock' has been dissolved, the zero hours worker may not be working all the time, but they are on-call all the time, responding to someone else's rhythms and priorities. People's lives are increasingly not their own as the rules of work extend more and more into all aspects of daily life. Not having your phone on you and switched on when away from the office, be it during a vacation or a children's sports day, is seen as professionally irresponsible. In another turn to the endless status games played by humans is demonstrating your relative standing by announcing a 'digital detox', which only the impoverished, the outsider, or the very powerful can indulge in. Orwell's 1984 once again comes to mind, when it is a perk of being a senior minister in a police state to be able to escape the all-seeing eye of the visi-screen: 'You can turn it off! He [Winston] said. "Yes", said O'Brien, "we can turn it off. We have that privilege"'.

2.5.1.2.4 THE INTENDED AND UNINTENDED CONSEQUENCES OF ICT

More recently, some researchers undertaking a systematic review developed a model of 'voluntary ICT use', which offers some additional insight into the way in which 'busyness' is facilitated by technologies' capacity to blur the differences between work and home. Broadly and overall, their review acknowledged significant adverse impacts on well-being of this type of work pattern as it sustains the ubiquitous penetration of a surveillance culture. For us, though, the most interesting tension in this whole picture was expressed thus:

A major topic area in existing research was to examine why employees engage in voluntary ICT use. A prominent theme here was the social-normative context, with employees stating that they engage with ICT use because everyone else expects constant availability, thus questioning the "voluntary" nature of ICT use.

(Schlachter, et al., 2018, p. 838)

Writers from a critical perspective such as Paolo Freire, Antonio Gramsci, and others have shown over the years that the exercise of power is at its most all-encompassing when the less powerful find themselves thinking in the same way as the powerful. In popular management texts, self-help books, and movies, the invitation to think and act like a boss as a route to success is ubiquitous, without really unpicking what this means, in terms of the worldview adopted and what gets talked of as 'natural' or 'normal' within the social sphere.

To our minds, all of the earlier mentioned suggests that organisations are talking a talk (although not the talk, as quite what is meant by well-being remains slippery) about well-being in the workplace – but an authentic response to something like stress at work would actually entail taking the leadership foot off of the performance pedal. Only then would it become possible to address the weight of work and work supervision, as opposed to just the supposed balance between work and life and the re-finding of the mythical golden mean of equilibrium. After all, as we've suggested, the contemporary business is constantly benefiting from the neoliberal blurring of that boundary, as more of us end up working from home, or having the needs of work with us at home (which means our home – a precious place for recuperation, personal connection, and living with values that are intrinsic and not imposed from a perspective of efficient utility – is also our workplace).

So the sticky stream of largely pointless, from a task point of view, email traffic slips endlessly through our mobile devices and we find ourselves arranging meetings, thinking about workplace issues, and getting ourselves ready to 'hit the ground running' (or have that all-important Dilbert-esque pre-pre-meeting, before the pre-meeting, before the meeting, because you after all wouldn't just dive into a meeting unprepared. Or do we mean unscripted?). While this slew of constant communication may have little direct value in terms of the presenting work to be done, it plays an important role in ensuring the habits of mind of the workplace and its priorities remain figural in our lives.

But the issue of ICT use reminds us that the workplace is not unidimensional in terms of the way in which we all of us experience power. It is not merely about the ogres of senior leadership conspiring against the rest of us, although their positions in the hierarchies that we allow to persist and grow in significance, means they occupy a significant role in terms of how their behaviours influence those around them in organisations. Workplace power can be subtler and is underscored by two vital elements present in a more nuanced perspective on power: first, the observation that, 'The more powerful power is, the more silent is its efficacy. Where it needs to draw special attention to itself, it is already weakened' (Han, 2019, p. 1); and, second, in terms of achieving effect, 'Not "I have to anyhow" but "I want to" expresses the presence of a superior power' (Han, 2019, p. 2). This is power attained not through violence, according to Han, but which takes place in the soul of the other (Han, 2019, p. 3), where the self is now completely defined in terms of workplace value.

2.5.1.2.5 THE IMPRECISION OF WHAT IS MEANT BY HEALTH AND WELL-BEING

All of which nudges towards an acknowledgement that the very notion of health and well-being, as viewed through the perspective of our working lives, is somewhat imprecise. This is particularly the case in terms of well-being, where there has been a move in the literature towards focusing in on what is called 'subjective well-being' (Diener, 1984). One model designed to encapsulate thinking and practice in respect to employee health and well-being offers three phases: firstly antecedents, those causal elements that nudge employee wellness up and down; secondly, the general idea of how we might consider and recognise people's health and well-being when they present in the workplace, while also acknowledging that satisfaction in life outside of work will also influence this; and thirdly an acknowledgement of both the individual and organisational consequences of wellness (Danna & Griffin, 1999, p. 360).

These authors identify three components of the antecedents, the causal elements, which shape the context for well-being. Firstly, there is the work setting itself, in respect to hazards, working on a deep-sea trawler or with agricultural machinery are notoriously dangerous worlds, never mind the world of unregulated mining and manufacture. Secondly, personality traits make a difference: for those of us of solitary disposition who seek to manage the constant requirement to join in with the sociability of work (be part of the team, one of the gang, join in the fun), it is profoundly wearing and can on bad days encourage the over-enthusiastic use of alcohol once in the semi-privacy of our homes. Thirdly, there is the antecedent of occupation stress. In respect to the latter, we are speaking of the conditions under which people work – in terms, for example, of busyness and the climate in which they find themselves – and their position in terms of role in that organisational setting, encompassing the question of the ease by which they might shape their own roles or move through progression into a new one.

Here again one runs into the fog of bullshit where the language of equality and empowerment (for now we read as a synonym for 'agency' though in this Alice in Wonderland world it is best understood as the power of potent invisibility) co-exists with the workplace micro-management of call centres and Amazon warehouses where people are driven out of the minds and into the world of micro-aggressions through lack of agency. A longitudinal study by a Polish academic identified how workers will, when they have lost the will to go on, damage the bar codes that the warehousing software depends on – a simple scratch is all it takes. It also takes into account the impact that organisational expectations might have in respect to the balance between home and work lives, especially in light of the increasingly complex negotiations that are required in the domestic setting to manage these two sets of expectations and where a sense of precariousness and insecurity makes all parties in the home world anxious about their material security.

To our thinking, the antecedents in this model pretty much all derive from decisions that are made at a senior leadership level in an organisation – where operating models are chosen in collusion with a business school/ consulting industry focused all but solely on the perspective of the senior elite and the budgets they have to spend on them (nearly all the literature produced by this industry has titles to the effect of 'The Executive Agenda' or 'The View from the Top'. Most of the copy-editors would appear to be in the pay of Ayn Rand).

If this observation holds true, then it likely compounds the pressures faced by the workforce by reinforcing their sense of powerlessness in the face of the controls and directions that exist in their organisational context.

This underscores very pointedly the fact that many of us experience work as somewhere in which the senior leadership are so deeply concerned about us that they offer a wide range of initiatives to attend to our health and well-being to go alongside our role as human resources, or labour factors, producing efficient economic outcomes. Perhaps there is some altruism at play therein: we cannot know what motivates all those individuals who lead the firms in which we work. But one literature review in this area very expressly makes an instrumental linkage between what the authors describe as 'healthy workplace practices', employee well-being outcomes, and organisational improvement outcomes, which is offered in the form of a basic and extremely instrumental tabular read across (Grawitch, et al., 2006, p. 136).

2.5.1.2.6 THE ADDICTION TO PERSISTENT, EXECUTIVELY FRAMED, PROGRAMMATIC UPHEAVAL (AKA 'CHANGE')

Notwithstanding the day-to-day aspects of our workplace experiences, there is for us one key feature of organisational life that needs to be acknowledged as being in the control of leadership and negatively experienced by the rest of us – and that is the introduction of disruptive, top-down programmes of organisational change. These programmes might once have been seen as exceptional events – but nowadays they are very much part of 'business as usual', not least because they are seen as one of the few ways in which a senior leader can assert themselves and be seen to be 'impactful'. It is our view that they can only be seen to be impactful in respect to the disturbance that they generate across an organisation and in the lived experience of each and every person implicated in it; they rarely deliver on their stated ambitions – but they create the illusion of leadership control, which is vital to sustaining a traditional notion of what it means to lead a business.

In an ongoing study by John into social activism and the organisational agenda, which has involved a number of people from the world of further education, academics are left bemused by the constant upheaval of their institutions, the churn of the administrative units into schools, then departments and then back again. One senior anthropologist could only make sense of the introduction of constant restructuring and transformational change through the frame of management justifying its existence and high salaries, all underpinned by a sociologically, psychologically, and anthropologically illiterate understanding of the dynamics of groups and society.

At a time when thinking around systems leadership is casting even more doubt on the idea that leadership can be practised as some model of cause and effect – the fiction that the leader acts and something planned occurs – so leaders seek refuge in unleashing large-scale and oppressively directive programmes of change across organisations in order to justify their positions as 'leaders'. Business schools and professional services providers queue around the block to support them in these ultimately harmful practices, pulling their cash and kudos out of the intensified misery of the workforce. And, of course, those same leaders undertake a deceitful sleight of hand by bolting onto these change initiatives a programme of so-called 'employee assistance', where the need for such balm is seen as something ordained by the gods, something beyond human influence, rather than directly arising from forms of senior management behaviour. This invitation to see the decisions of senior actors as being benevolent, or independent of them, evokes for us the insights of Siegfried Sassoon's poem *The General*, where two soldiers slogging up to the front in the First World War pass the General who has masterminded the plan they are about to enact. They notice what a likable fellow he is as they march past him; the kicker in the poem being that it was because of his strategy that they both got killed (along with numerous others).

A pleasant disposition, like good intention, butters no parsnips as the old saying goes. Just because someone has a nice smile, remembers your name, doesn't mean what they're doing will have a good outcome for you.

One case study into this world of programmatic upheaval – based on experience of the introduction of a programme of lean in a division of a US manufacturing company – offers support to this assertion. Helpfully, the authors draw out five variables that are impacted by this sort of transformation effort: Intensity (increase in quantity and quality of workload); autonomy (in terms of greater personal responsibility and less oversight, although we'd put in the rider once again that this refers to visible oversight rather than the worm of insidious oversight that comes from the disciplines of self-policing); skilling (applying skills differently or developing new skills, sometimes in response to process or technology change); teamwork; and computing (that is, increased reliance on IT to do day to day tasks) (Anderson-Connolly, et al., 2002, p. 398).

The findings in this respect are illustrative:

> Overall can we answer the question: Is lean mean? We can claim that intensity is unequivocally harmful for both managers and non-managers. [...] Skilling and teamwork have harmed non-managers while benefiting managers. Autonomy is an advantage for non-managers but not for managers. Computing has benefited non-managers but is largely irrelevant for managers. So the evidence supports our original claim that workplace reengineering is both management by stress and a potentially more humane [way] to work.
>
> (Anderson-Connolly, et al., 2002, p. 408)

On the basis of this assertion, however, we are minded to note that the chief plus for the performers in this organisational context – namely, a greater sense of autonomy – is only ever tentatively (and hence oftentimes temporarily) granted by the leadership. To us this is more than offset by all of the negatives impacting on well-being, and the embedding of habits of mind largely detrimental to the individual in the long term, as their capacity to exercise critical judgement is further eroded by the normalisation of econometrics and self-justifying grandiosity of senior leaders.

In this regard, then, we are mindful of the fact that the initiatives and activities that corporations establish to attend to the health and well-being of their staff are an ideological veil to disguise the fact that it is the climate in the workplace that is generated by the senior leadership that harms people. After all, what sort of generosity is actually involved when the workforce is offered personal resilience programmes in a context that is overly busy, blurs the separation between home and work, and creates what seems like an environment of permanent instability?

2.5.2 Some conclusions about paradox one....

Well-being contra overbearing busyness... 'A fashionable focus on workforce wellbeing initiatives alongside the overbearing corporate culture of busyness'. The conclusions that stand out for us around this faux-paradox are:

* The need for well-being arises from how work is done and is not independent of it, nor of the wider context of contractual/social security and insecurity

- The interests and perspectives of senior leaders are different from the wider workforce – and so their take on well-being initiatives is unlikely to be well-judged in terms of how it will land with others... or they may just be indifferent
- Well-being is a subjective, multi-facetted experience unlikely to be amenable to a simplistic, one-size-fits-all, programmatic response
- Well-being is as much a social as an individual experience and so needs to be understood relationally as much as personally
- Much busyness arises from the needs of senior leaders to demonstrate their significance and justify their existence and standing

2.5.3 *Paradox two: inclusive compassion* contra *heroic control*

A public declaration (particularly in the NHS) in favour of compassionate and inclusive leadership in contrast to a practical adherence to heroic leadership and command-and-control.

2.5.3.1 *In brief...*

The themes we explore in association with this paradox are the:

- Extent to which modern leadership theory distracts from a meaningful inquiry into how power, authority, and hierarchy play out in practice
- Seductive allure of good intentions and idealised norms set apart from the muck and bullets of day-to-day practice
- Persistence of very traditional, archaic practices little changed over decades/centuries
- Allure of taking 'what is' as 'natural', existing apart from context, history and social process
- Confusion around what is discussable in public and what happens in private

2.5.3.2 *The paradox in full...*

We explore the paradox under the following four headings:

- The King is dead! Long live the King! Or so it seems when it comes to leadership practice
- How the traditional model is nourished and constructed – and isn't 'natural' at all

- The addiction to uncritical action – and the social order it sustains
- The distinctive ideology of the new language of leadership

And we begin our argument with the first of these four headings.

2.5.3.2.1 THE KING IS DEAD! LONG LIVE THE KING! OR SO IT SEEMS WHEN IT COMES TO LEADERSHIP PRACTICE

We are often kidded along that leadership in our contemporary context is in some way qualitatively different to the traditional, Henry V at Agincourt type of leadership that once was seen to prevail. The rousing speech that appeals to the primal id, to go 'Once more unto the breach, dear friends, once more; Or close the wall up with our English dead' is dismissed in the face of business logic and economic reason – meanwhile people continue to be drawn into Shakespeare's world of noble Kings and great people. Strangely few would pay to go to the theatre to watch a live performance of the Chair of Unilever reading their statement from the annual report – riveting though we're sure it would be – and filled, no doubt, with appeals to a different form of leading.

As Mark sat to write this section, he perused a hard copy of The Times of London, dated January 14, 2020, to get a sense of the prevailing picture of leadership. The front page that day was dominated by news of Her Majesty the Queen's intervention in respect to two people in her firm who had become challenging towards its agreed vision and purpose (news bulletins the night before had been crowing about the leadership she had shown, how she had demonstrated her authority, shown who was boss).

Thereafter, between the news and sports pages, there were 16 items where it was possible to discern a heroic and extremely directive image of leadership in practice. The language used communicated this very clearly: The Business Secretary, the Transport Secretary, and the Chancellor of the Exchequer needed to 'thrash out' an agreement in respect to regional UK airline FlyBe; in news from abroad, Vladimir Putin had 'seized' the chance to 'shape' Libya, whilst President Macron in France had been forced into a 'climbdown' in the face of strikes; the business pages spoke about Steve Varley preparing to 'hand over the reins' at EY; and, in sport, Barça football club had sacked their coach on the basis of team performance – and that comedy Ur-Boss Jose Mourinho was quoted as saying, 'We're at our limit, it's a difficult' (a slab of corporate boilerplate that could appear anywhere in the paper, to be honest).

This perspective on leadership retains the traditional notions that an individual is invested with the capacity to make things happen: they define their intent – what it is they want to happen, 'close up the wall with our English dead' – and then access means by which that intention will be realised. A perspective that has not changed in millennia as can be seen in the classic work from the beginning of the twentieth century, The Golden Bough, which draws out the persistence of archetypal myths around those who have power (or gods)... in the end sometimes the King needs to be killed, for instance, to make the rains come (Frazer, 1998). The language of the contemporary record referenced earlier tells us all that we need to know: Putin has it in his gift to 'shape' a sovereign state out of the one that he is notionally elected to lead. That verb 'shape' speaks of two hands working together on raw material to produce a representation of something imagined in the sculptor's head, which in turn has echoes of intelligent design and the power of gods to create the world in their fashion.

Certainly, the Russian leader can meddle in the affairs of Libya; he might well influence events in that country. But to suggest that he can 'shape' it is patently absurd – as countless examples from around the globe testify. Assessing the recent history of Iraq should underscore for us all the simple fact that, however much someone might like to 'shape' the future, it consists of myriad elements, all of which combine into a material more like unset jelly than clay. People may have the intention to shape the world as they would like it to be, but their impact is never the same as that intention.

Meanwhile, in the world of global football, the failure of a leader to 'shape' the world around them in the way expected sees them being unceremoniously 'sacked'. The King is killed not to bring rain, but to win points and accelerate the speed of recovery of some injured star. As an anonymous management guru wrote: 'We'd [John & the anonymous guru] met a few days after Kevin Keegan had been reappointed as manager of Newcastle United. "How is Kevin Keegan going to transform Newcastle in a few weeks? We love the idea... we know it's a fantasy and [we] love it"' (Higgins, 2009, p. 70).

The message is clear: the corporate context relies on the idea that a single person can fashion the world in the way that they desire – and, if they are shown in practice not to be able to achieve that, then they are sloughed off without so much as a second thought. To a large extent, the ignominious nature of the dismissal of football managers mirrors the experience of a good many Chief Executives, particularly in the specific instance of the National Health Service. Just a few years ago, the Chair of NHS Improvement – a regulatory body for NHS providers –

> ...railed against the 'firing squads' that sack [NHS] chief executives and chairs when things go wrong. He was also critical of the focus on short-term targets rather than long- term improvements in care. He urged national leaders and NHS boards to lead work on improvement and to see money and quality as two sides of the same coin.
>
> (Ham, 2016)

2.5.3.2.2 HOW THE TRADITIONAL MODEL IS NOURISHED AND CONSTRUCTED – AND ISN'T 'NATURAL' AT ALL

The traditional model of leadership is nourished and maintained by every-one: we all of us carry around the historic and largely unevidenced ideal that a 'leader' occupies their position – and the trappings that attach to it, such as a notional sense of authority and a chunky six-figure, sometimes even seven or eight figure, salary – on the basis that they have a capacity to 'do' things, that is, through their unique and singular effort, they make things happen. Increasingly, cracks are beginning to appear in that shib-boleth. And senior leaders themselves – particularly CEOs – prop up this image of leadership, despite – no doubt – a day-by-day recognition of its lack of grounding in reality. In a publication based on interviews with 12 NHS CEOs, it was noted that

> Several remarked upon the loneliness of the job, that suddenly the buck stops with you. "I am not sure anything can really prepare you for what it's like to be a chief executive," Ben Gowland said. "It is so different from being a director".
>
> (Timmins, 2016, p. 23)

Such commentary often gives a natural feel to things that had to be constructed – and which need to be maintained – by human thinking and practice. The role of CEO is lonely because we allow our picture of the world to be structured around the pyramid of hierarchy and allow people to step into roles where they take on 'godlike characteristics' (Higgins, 2009, p. 133), as was observed by a recently qualified psychoanalyst working alongside a business executive during a major banking merger in the 2000s. Similarly, it is impossible to prepare for the role because it is manufactured in such a way as to be impossible to do by any single human being. We have chosen for it to be 'different' to the role of Director – but, in reality, it does not need to be, unless we all of us conspire to render it so. Put simply, the very idea of the Chief Executive is something that collective human thought and the practices of business in a capitalist society have conjured into existence, and the disciplines of psychoanalysis and psychology have developed within this specific historical period – but, as Marx reminds us, all that is solid can very quickly melt into air, particularly where we choose actively to engage critically with how things are in the here and now.

Leadership, then, is a construct, something that is created out of our understanding of the world, the assumptions about power and authority that arise from that and what becomes seen as an all but 'natural' phenomenon. In its traditional manifestation, as outlined earlier, it hinges on hierarchy, individual presence, decisiveness, and an assumption of linear cause-and-effect, where action A begets outcome B, as surely as night follows day. Anyone with a passing acquaintance with the reality of leading in an organisational context will know that this is something of a fantasy, and yet – as our skimming of The Times seems to show – it is a notion that persists, despite the fact that a lot of conversation around the practice of leadership suggests that we have moved beyond this model, to a situation of transformational, collective, inclusive, dispersed, and compassionate leadership. These perspectives hang loosely like a beaded curtain, through which it is difficult to peer and behind which the real and hard-edged practice of leadership persists.

Hence, notwithstanding all of these variants on leadership, recognised over the years where this practice is studied, from early on (Stogdill, 1974) through to a more contemporary focus (Rost, 1993), all of which get referenced in business contexts and which John taught as part of the Ashridge Leadership Process from 2012 to 2017 before outing himself as being in the fashion business when it came to promoting this or that school of leadership theory, the debate remains underpinned by an archaic vision of the practice. As Prime Minister Boris Johnson dances to the tune of Dominic Cummings, the unelected yet overbearingly influential ideologue at his shoulder, we are confronted with news stories where Ministers of the Crown are instructed that '…they must focus all their energy on developing policies for post-Brexit Britain — or face the sack in a wide-ranging cabinet reshuffle within weeks' (Helm & Savage, 2020). The complexity of their focus and their work reduced to linearity, with a penalty underpinning it, following on from the spirit of Tennyson's poem *The Charge of the Light Brigade* and its hymn to the suicidal military advance by the British cavalry into the teeth of the Russian guns in 1854.

This is leadership as we understand it at a deep level, despite what business books and schools might try to argue.

To some extent, we all choose to reinforce these traditional notions — and, by so doing, endlessly reproduce the overwhelming image of leadership that prevails. This is especially the case amongst our current leaders, particularly those who occupy senior positions where leaders find themselves copying the behaviours of Keynes' bankers in the 1930s where it was better to be wrong and the same as everyone else, rather than killing your career by challenging the orthodoxy. For many in such roles, we might argue that they do not know how to lead in a different way — and, even if some of those leaders do have an inkling of a different type of approach, they sense that those around them (especially those who are deemed in the model as being followers in this context) will expect them to be leaders in that traditional mould. In terms of personal ethics and recognition of wider expectation, these leaders seem to feel the need to justify their positions at the top of the pyramid and the outsize salaries and remuneration packages associated with those locations by defaulting to traditional practice. To say you are a non-Transformational leader these days would be the kiss of death. To admit to being an old school hero who really likes telling people what to do, while often being the case, is frowned upon during the selection process — and so the dance of dissimulation goes on.

2.5.3.2.3 THE ADDICTION TO UNCRITICAL ACTION: AND THE SOCIAL ORDER IT SUSTAINS

What, then, does this look like in practice? It sees these leaders prompted — especially by business schools and their promotion of idealistic, normative models and through their perusal of the endless (and often mindless) checklists attached to business press articles, never mind the thick books from the Heathrow Academy – to be seen to be 'decisive' and committed to action. It is this, of course, that leads people in work meetings to remind themselves to 'stop talking, and start doing something', even when the 'talking' is, in fact, a vital and useful form of 'doing' in the context of human organising. It takes for granted that non-verbal action of any sort must be good and creates what has been referred to as the 'Free Market Taliban' (Binney, et al., 2017, p. 27), where constant upheaval is the only value to be added by a senior leader. It works on the assumption that life in a business setting can be condensed to a simplistic formula of cause and effect, where there is a linear relationship between a leader's action and its anticipated outcome – which, of course, deliberately neglects the fact that these leaders are faced by complexity in so many instances.

And it fetishises the notion that the leader needs to connect with people to make them 'followers', a model that cannot but feel condescending and mechanistic. It is striking how many inherently qualitative and expressive human experiences are presented by social scientists and business school academics through the medium of an equation, even Trust is presented as the functional outcome of a series of seemingly objective variables, whose pseudo-scientism sees complex and subtle, value-laden constructs reduced to a series of letters to be added together... and then divided by another. While outwardly appealing in its capacity to present a complex human experience, it is insidious in the dance it performs to the great god of mechanistic causality – a dance now playing out in the perverse misapplication of the agile software development methodology to human organising, without its bounded primary task and disappearance of power.

The practice of mechanistic thinking sustains relationships of great hierarchical distance, with agency located around the top of the hierarchy – and this is how the language of empowerment hides in plain sight the reality of belittlement and infantilisation that so bedevils so many large organisations. Empowerment is the language of the Parent talking to the Child, who is being conditioned into the value of compliance in return for the sweeties of a bit more choice around which Peppa Pig episode to watch, locking in place roles and relationships shaped by positional authority. In a recent (presently unpublished) study for the NHS London Leadership Academy (2019/20) into the experience of the most junior employee bands, John was left speechless with rage as he heard story after story of capable, mature adults stripped of meaningful dignity in a world built around hierarchy and imposed control. Meanwhile the NHS Leadership model espouses a way of leading only a Buddha or Christ figure could actually practice.

2.5.3.2.4 THE DISTRACTIVE IDEOLOGY OF THE NEW LANGUAGE OF LEADERSHIP

Yet festooned around this orientation towards leadership with which we are all too familiar are, as indicated earlier, all manner of leadership models to which obeisance is paid. There is an ideological content to these developments, such as they are, insofar as they owe much to our attachment to the idea of Enlightenment, an idea created and espoused by the very top (or rather most dominant group) of society. Keith Grint offers a really helpful schematic along two axes, one being time and the other being rationality: the upward arrow connects the early 'Great Man' notions of leadership through to the apparent world of distributed leadership (Grint, 2011, p. 10). This, however, reveals discursive development not practical engagement, reifying ideas of how the world might be (through the lens of one social group). This is rather than paying attention to the activities and practices within which people, from a diverse set of lived experiences, are going about their lives and engaging with those who claim to the right to exercise dominion (and/or define what dominion means).

Leaders nod sagely at this Enlightenment trajectory, from the fierce individualism of someone like Henry V at Agincourt through to the Uriah Heep like conceit of servant leadership (which might be helpfully be seen as a paradox in and of itself, a wonderful piece of conceptual evidence of the diversionary tactics used by those who exercise power to distract attention from social power's actual interests and habits). Meanwhile leaders' practice – and our day-to-day experience of it – remains largely the same, in terms of command and control as an orientation and a tendency to cleave to the directive rather than the meaningfully conversational.

Rather than tear down the ideological shrouds that wrap around leadership – the accretion of models over time, each as enthusiastically advocated as the one that preceded it – leaders need to take a sledgehammer to the tacit thinking and quotidian practice that sits at the core of their leadership, despite their public obeisance to new ideas. This is not so much a paradox: it is more about the persistence of a leadership that simply has no legitimate currency in the contemporary context (if, indeed, it ever truly did), where the world is too massively complex, unknowable and unpredictable as a social system to be meaningfully amenable to the will of a sovereign individual. What we believe is being, or needs to be, cried out for is for us to dismantle this way of knowing and embrace what David Bohm spoke to decades ago: '... the thing which has gone wrong with thought is basically... that it does things and then says or implies it didn't do them' (Bohm, 1996, p. 24).

Thought has created how we currently experience leading and being led, and it's for us to come together and explore through critical thought new ways of actually being a leader.

2.5.4 *Some conclusions about paradox two*

Inclusive compassion *contra* heroic control... 'A public declaration (particularly in the NHS) in favour of compassionate and inclusive leadership in contrast to a practical adherence to heroic leadership and command-and-control'. The conclusions that stand out for us around this faux-paradox are:

- Little has changed in practice in terms of the underlying habits of individualised, top of the pyramid thinking
- Much of the debate around supposedly emerging models of leading serve to distract and confuse from the blunt realities of social power and self-interest served by the status quo
- Idealised, individually focused frames distract from relational dynamics and how they play out in hierarchical settings of gross economic and social inequality
- Senior leaders play into the expectations of those around them, these include employees, peer groups, and external advisors (especially business schools and management consultancies)
- To change requires a brute, collective assault on much that is taken for granted in the way people think about and go about their ordinary day-to-day work

2.5.5 *Paradox three: diversity of voice* **contra** *enforced homogeneity*

An emphasis on diversity – particularly of voice – in organisations alongside the cultural totalitarianism of values alignment, with its orientation towards enforced homogeneity.

(Willmott, 1993)

2.5.5.1 *In brief...*

The themes we explore in association with this paradox are:

- How the terms of debate are set by management consultancies who establish norms lacking rigorous understanding of how humans respond to difference in others
- Why the 'bleeding obvious' of executive diversity checklists are anything but 'bleeding obvious' and hide taken-for-granted habits of mind
- How instrumental, reductionist approaches to diversity are unlikely to make a generative difference to people's lives in the round
- Why alignment and standardisation have been, and continue to be, the organizing watchwords for organisational life
- How the economic axioms of our day sustain a tension between ongoing identity and commercial relevance

2.5.5.2 *The paradox in full...*

We explore the paradox under the following five headings:

- How McKinsey occupied the way organisations think (and not in a good way)
- Diversity seen through a mechanistic lens of supporting creativity and innovation
- Critiquing what is taken to be 'bleeding obvious'
- The 'Just Organisation' in a 'Just Society'... values in conflict
- Freedom on a short leash... the lure of totalitarianism

And we begin our argument with the first of these five headings.

2.5.5.2.1 HOW MCKINSEY OCCUPIED THE WAY ORGANISATIONS THINK (AND NOT IN A GOOD WAY)

One can always be clear that something is afoot in the business world when the dreary mega-corporations offering so-called 'professional services' leap on an idea and start trumpeting it, as if it was something that they have originated. And you can always guarantee that, no matter how liberal and humanistic that notion might be, they will always orient towards economic growth, productivity, and organisational effectiveness. Diversity is a prime example of this trend, as can be seen by a cursory glance at the output of those companies over recent years.

Let's begin with McKinsey, perhaps best considered as the ur-management consultancy, in terms of both longevity and wider impact. The latter is achieved by both billable intervention in organisations and by its wider influence through what passes as thought leadership (rather than hegemonic group-think). Hence, in respect to the latter, it is possible to discern considerable impact by the firm in terms of concepts such as the so-called War on Talent and – in the UK – health care privatisation (O'Mahoney & Sturdy, 2015). It is also argued that the way in which recruits are inculcated into the McKinsey way and a high level of churn amongst a workforce that is worked oppressively hard means that companies across the globe are peppered with graduates of McKinsey now occupying senior management positions, which thereby extends the influence of this mega-corporation's thinking and practice (O'Mahoney & Sturdy, 2015, p. 8). In this respect, a case can be easily made that the intellectual weight that anchors neoliberalism is not derived from academic thinking and research but from the thought leadership and day-to-day practice of McKinsey and the firms that seek to ape it and its prescriptions, which generates a clear hegemony.

In respect to the issue of diversity, then, we can see McKinsey occupying their role as agenda setters in respect to managerial imperative. Their thought leadership work in this area pivots on the way in which diversity supports improved performance. They argue that there are five struts to this (Hunt, et al., 2015). First, it helps to win the 'war on talent' with its questionable conceptual roots which assumes that 'talent' is a scare resource to be found in individuals (in terms of Historians, this equates to the 'great man' school of historical analysis), a recursive observation that calls to mind the ouroboros, the curious historic image of a snake consuming itself, as firms all gear up to chase the same, elusive and scarce/sacred individuals who meet the corporately approved definition of 'talent', and especially the holy grail of scarce 'diverse talent' – and so create exactly the scarcity reported in the beginning.

Second, it helps companies to position themselves better to a market that is now recognised as diverse, whereas marketing might previously have simply been homogeneous in terms of targeting – although the spread of standardised thinking about what constitutes diversity might well be a factor creating global cities that all look alike and where you can buy a McDonalds, or automobiles that are nominally different in terms of brand while strikingly the same in terms of components and engineering. Third, *it is argued that diversity increases employee satisfaction and reduces intraorganisational conflict*, which is a bold assumption when one looks back at the persistence of inter-group violence and the well-established habits of people in creating in-groups and out-groups. Human-beings response to people seen as 'other' is notoriously fickle and in conversation with a gay, Jewish memorial candle (a candle being a person whose parents survived the camps) they are less than optimistic about how the world is unfolding in its attachment to gay rights and opposition to anti-Semitism. Much of the espoused optimism around diversity reflects a simple/simplistic progressive view of History, where the human race is on the way to a better, more desirable world for all. Or as we prefer to describe this perspective: Benthamism for Dummies.

Fourth, *'Diversity fosters innovation and creativity through a greater variety of problem-solving approaches, perspectives, and ideas…[D]iverse* groups often outperform experts' (Hunt, et al., 2015, p. 9). *Lastly, it shores up your brand, by enhancing the image of the company* in respect to legal requirements and the wider agenda of corporate social responsibility and business ethics.

2.5.5.2.2 DIVERSITY SEEN THROUGH A MECHANISTIC LENS OF SUPPORTING CREATIVITY AND INNOVATION

The paradox we are exploring in this chapter focuses in on the fourth of these observations, regarding the value of diversity of voice in terms of supporting organisational practice that is creative and innovative. Before that, however, it's worth calling up the McKinsey prescription for doing this sort of work through the prism that they use to explore the issue. This – as is so often the case with the work of professional services companies, business publications, and management schools – pivots around what looks very much like a checklist for the busy executive and can be seen as being profoundly instrumentalising in practice if not in espoused intent.

This instrumentalisation, as with so much management practice, explores diversity as a thing that exists outside of the dynamics of lived relationships, it is something that is approached as a function of two independent 'I's coming together rather than inter-dependent human-beings who exist as a 'We' in the first case (Dalal, 1998). This is a way of thinking about the world which locks us into an individual framing of leadership and persists in overlooking relational and systemic thinking – and the new forms of social understanding and meaning of agency this opens up.

In this context of a busy executive checklist, it plays out in a fourfold way: it requires people to commit to and then cascade this belief in the creative benefits of diversity, flowing from your top team down, once again reflecting an unproblematic view of communication as bits and bytes to be perfectly sent from one core processing unit to another – a more sophisticated understanding of communication understands that sense making is a relational and contextual experience that unfolds over time, where meaning cannot be made on behalf of others and words are slippery beasts!

Part two of the checklist, recommends you link your inclusion and diversity initiatives to your growth strategy, using a data-driven approach, once again taking a very reductionist view of what counts as 'data', or certainly not opening the pandora's box of the multiplicity of forms and truth traditions that come into view once you ask the question: 'What counts as data? And who makes this judgment'? The entire framing is also firmly stuck with what Gareth Morgan describes as the machine metaphor (Morgan, 2006) as can be seen through words such as 'link', which carry with them all sorts of causal assumptions drawn from the world of mechanical engineering.

Thirdly the recommendation is to craft a portfolio of interventions to land in your company, which assumes that an 'injection' of diversity will change what happens, once again privileging an 'intelligent design' view of the organisational world, where wise and disinterested leaders can manufacture a climate of innovation through diversity training. Sure, interventions can make a difference, but less so when delivered by powerful leadership teams who don't see how their relational dynamic with others is the context within which difference will flower or not. Lastly tailor the impact by taking a global perspective with an expectation of local delivery, whatever that means (Hunt, et al., 2018, p. 27) – a boilerplate phrase straight out of the football manager Jose Mourinho's playbook, a man we've referenced before, and available for use anywhere, anytime.

2.5.5.2.3 CRITIQUING WHAT IS TAKEN TO BE 'BLEEDING OBVIOUS'

As a checklist without our critical commentary you might think that there is not much to argue with there – a rather expensive case of 'stating the bleeding obvious', if one hasn't the turn of mind that is curious about what lies behind what makes the 'bleeding obvious' bleeding obvious. It reflects something akin to thought, but offers very limited insight into leadership practice, because it is so cut-off from any rigorous understanding of how organisations organise (which is through relational practice rather than structures and codification). That's particularly the case if you turn your attention away from the debate as shaped and interpreted by a company like McKinsey and look at the reality of economic life. Once you do that, something that might kindly be referred to as a paradox of sorts quickly becomes apparent, as the Financial Times reported in 2019:

> There is a strange anomaly in the consulting industry. Many of the largest firms have long been vocal advocates of greater gender diversity at the top of the world's biggest companies. Their logic is simple: more diverse teams perform better. Yet data submitted to the UK government over the past 12 months strongly suggest that consulting firms have not followed their own advice. All of the largest consultancies operating in the UK have reported significant gender pay gaps, both in terms of the average hourly rate received by women at the firms and the average bonus gap.
>
> (Marriage, 2019)

More recently, it was reported that the management consultancy retained by the BBC to address the corporation's gender pay gap actually had a gap twice the size of that of its client (Stefano, 2020).

The shortcomings of the consultancies notwithstanding, we return to the way in which companies see diversity as a means of enriching conversation across the organisation, facilitating creativity of thought in that context, and enabling the sort of innovation that firms need to develop what they provide and how they come together to offer that good or service. The critical question at this juncture is quite simple: to what extent is this how people in the workplace experience their organisations, in terms of celebrating voices at the margins and giving licence to people to articulate and test new ideas.

John works with a colleague Dik Veenman through a firm called *The Right Conversation*, which has a strong focus on speaking truth to power in work contexts. One element of that work is the *Speak Up Index*, a survey-based instrument that allows organisations to gain a snapshot of how confident and comfortable their people are to use their voices there. Crucially, that approach ranges across four key concerns in regard to speaking up: psychological safety; the flow of expression up and down the hierarchy; the extent to which people are invited to use their voice; and whether senior leadership acts meaningfully and in a spirit of openness in light of what they hear (The Right Conversation Ltd, 2020).

It reminds us that there is often a disconnect between a public commitment to people openly speaking about their ideas to improve the ways in which they work and an organisation's failure to create the circumstances where people can articulate those ideas and find ways of testing them out in practice. As part of the development of the Index they worked closely with a UK Police force and ran into the most basic of problems, namely that it's hard to speak up when there's no one to speak up to, nor any relational context. The Chief Constable was fighting hard to get his senior leadership to prioritise the habit of hanging out with staff as they went about their work (there are of course lots of pressing and important priorities on senior people's time, for good and bad reasons). He had the obvious and often ignored insight that unless people were used to having small conversations with each other, about ordinary things, then there was no habit in place for the big conversation to happen. Being listened to is not a social habit that can be switched on and off, it has to be part of the ordinary day-to-day of how people rub along together – and it certainly can't be substituted by the heavy-handed corporate set piece, which simply reminds people of how silenced they are the rest of the time.

The first apparent contradiction of interest to us is the seeming corporate acceptance of the importance of diversity of voice, in respect to its positive impact on creativity – and the need then to manage diversity in the organisational context. There is an argument that a positive orientation towards diversity – whilst enabling a polyphony of perspectives and ideas, which support enhanced performance through innovation practices – may inadvertently fragment the cohesion upon which organisations feel that they depend (Bassett-Jones, 2005).

2.5.5.2.4 THE JUST ORGANISATION IN A JUST SOCIETY... VALUES IN CONFLICT

Certainly, anyone seeking to undertake informed and comprehensive work in respect to inclusion and diversity in an organisational context will quickly reveal a complicated field in which to be working. We invariably labour under the liberal democratic conceit that our lives in companies and agencies is in some way insulated from the wider concerns in society at large. Yet, realistically, we must recognise that there is no impermeable membrane between the social and the economic. Hence, a serious piece of work that looked at evidence around inclusive leadership for the NHS recently made this prescient observation: 'For true diversity, organisations need to do more than acknowledge the value of a more heterogeneous workforce, it requires active engagement with policies and practices founded on principles of equal access to opportunities, social justice, fairness and human rights' (Bolden, et al., 2019, p. 14).

This entirely legitimate focus on diversity, in terms of working towards a truly inclusive society and encouraging people to express themselves in the workplace, can be seen to collide with the way in which organisations use culture – as an homogenised notion of how things get done around there – to manage the workforce, not least through ensuring consistency of thinking and behaviour (Ray, 1986). One key feature of this is the attempt to enforce the alignment of people with the corporate values, whether they are seen as noble or otherwise. The work of Milton Rokeach – from the late 1960s onwards – offers insight into the nature of human values; on that foundation, collaborators explored the issue of values in an organisational context, where it was baldly asserted that 'Leadership effectiveness is directly related to [the] degree of value consensus between leader and followers' (Connor & Becker, 1979, p. 78).

In their deliberations, these authors offer a definition, which is useful as part of our consideration of how they play out in corporate settings: '[V]alues may be thought of as global beliefs about desirable end-states underlying attitudinal and behavioural processes' (Connor & Becker, 1979, p. 72). Alongside this psychological orientation to the issue, there is a rich seam of thought that applies anthropology to (in particular) organisations and their culture, which openly reinforces the early observation of the formal and informal structures that coexist in organisational settings (Wright, 2004). Given the definition and its capacity to encompass both the individual and collective and the observation that we all, as employees, occupy both a formal system (which relates to our role, our position in the wider structure, the accountabilities and responsibilities that run up and down that structure) and an informal one (where we connect systemically with others in this context but not necessarily with the public image of the organisation), it seems self-evident that there is a potential for values to be in conflict in the work context.

Later in this book, as we explore the stand out myths that seem to us to most influence management and leadership thinking, we will look again at the idea of values as a means of binding workplaces together. However, the extent to which the wearisome boilerplate that is produced in this respect is truly observed in practice by even the senior leaders and the organisation in general remains a moot point. Take, for example, the example of Boeing, managing a crisis in which two 737-MAX planes crashed and it is apparent that people within the company had grave concerns about the safety of that model. The dissembling that the corporation has undertaken in light of all of this patently runs directly counter to a key corporate value to which they supposedly subscribe: 'Safety – We value human life and well-being above all else and take action accordingly. We are personally accountable for our own safety and collectively responsible for the safety of our teammates and workplaces, our products and services, and the customers who depend on them. When it comes to safety, there are no competing priorities' (Boeing, 2020). Apart from the duopolistic business battle with Airbus and the ever-present profit motive, of course.

2.5.5.2.5 FREEDOM ON A SHORT LEASH… THE LURE OF TOTALITARIANISM

Elsewhere, the promise of a truly all-encompassing diversity of voice in an organisation context can be seen to have dramatically unravelled in the face of the corporate expectation of tight alignment and compliance when we consider the recent case of Google. As a piece in the Financial Times explained in January 2020 noted, 'The freedom given to workers has turned into a liability as tension between management and staff has grown. The tools used to generate cross-company collaboration have become instruments of unrest in the hands of workers opposed to some of the company's more controversial projects, such as its artificial intelligence work for the US military and a study of whether to launch a censored search engine in China' (Waters, 2020). The openness that defined the company from the beginning – and which drew people to it – has been drastically constrained in light of the voices starting to say things that the company finds unacceptable.

Similarly, Zappos, everyone's favourite holocratic organisation, is seen to be exemplary in terms of its removal of management layers and the dispersed nature of leadership across that seemingly flattened structure. Yet the diversity of voice in that context is dramatically limited by the company's somewhat totalitarian sounding cultural precepts, summarised in what it calls its 'oath of employment'. It articulates this on its website in a style that suggests that, any minute now, some functionary of the company (not, of course, a manager, because they don't exist) will invite the employees to line up for their delicious cup of Kool Aid:

> Welcome, my friends, to your Zappos Oath of Employment. This will evolve, change, and grow over time but we wanted to get the most important stuff in here first: our Core Values. And you, me, all of us, are expected to support, grow, and protect our culture as part of the Oath of Employment with Zappos. By reading, studying, and understanding this Oath of Employment, you agree to enact each item and agree to embrace each item in energizing your roles and in your decision making.
>
> (Zappos, 2020)

Chairman Mao, late of the Chinese Communist Party, in his mandarin collar and jaunty red star cap stands admiringly offering his applause at such a bald statement of Party management and support for right thinking (a habit now taken on by his successor President Xi and the extent to which people have learnt how to repeat 'Xi Thought' when faced with pressing challenges). At a recent Organisational Development networking event we both attended on March 10, 2020, we heard someone describe their personal take on being invited to spend three days having a 'Next Jump' experience, another firm filled with the power veiling language of holocratic sociocracy (we're sure that in the right hands these framings can be a force for good, but not to our taste). In the room was someone who had grown up in South Africa in the apartheid era; John's note of her exasperated outburst at one point reads: 'I grew up in a Police state and know one when I see it'.

The Google example helps us to appreciate that this is not in truth a paradox. These two apparently conflicting ideas are merely one subsumed by another: diversity of voice is an ideological overlay to the expectation in organisations that everyone will ultimately toe the line. Where this reaches anything like a crisis point – such as where the employees take that licence to speak out at face value and explore the chance to say even that which might ordinarily be felt to be unsayable – then the brute foundational aspect will assert itself. Employees are granted a voice in a company setting but there is ventriloquism of sorts at work: they are permitted to say what the firm finds acceptable – but transgression will see that voice taken back.

The tension that organisations need to hold between change and stability, between the need to innovate and keep abreast of what is going on in the market, alongside needing to get on with the day-to-day work and firm up the underpinning foundations of what the organisation does, is a regular topic of chin-stroking business school deliberation. But this reflects the imperatives of the capitalist system (namely, innovate or die) and the closing of the corporate mind, in that realistically these are not in any sense mutually exclusive.

Diversity precedes the vitality of difference in that context – and creates the conditions where there can be a free exchange of opinion and ideas. Without that openness of mind, the options and possibilities in organisational contexts are tightly constrained and ideas that might be said to be lying outside of the homogenous mainstream cannot then become part of the wider conversation about how best to organise.

2.5.6 Some conclusions about paradox three...

Diversity of voice contra enforced homogeneity... 'An emphasis on diversity – particularly of voice – in organizations alongside the cultural totalitarianism of values alignment, with its enforced homogeneity' (Wilmott, 1993). The conclusions that stand out for us around this faux-paradox are:

- Most of the focus around diversity and voice in the workplace is in the service of economic performance and has little connection to notions of human rights to be heard or treated justly
- The practice of workplace diversity and voice has shallow roots and is poorly understood outside of the economic imperative
- Much of what passes as diversity of voice is performative, it is a display to be gone through and not a deep-rooted engagement with difference
- You can be different and diverse so long as you are different and diverse in the right way i.e. that fits with the ideology as practised (and sometimes even espoused) by those who hold power

2.5.7 Paradox four: authenticity contra part of the superstructure

An invocation that leaders should be their authentic self in the workplace juxtaposed with a constant organisational drive for performance, which — for middle managers — merely renders them an element of the superstructure that manages the delivery of output and outcome.

2.5.7.1 In brief...

The themes we explore in association with this paradox are:

- The extent to which regimes of inspection and control squeeze out the opportunity for people to show up except in ways that are made visible through these regimes
- How much the notion of an independent, authentic individual has been overwhelmed — hi-jacked even — by the demands of the authentic group/organisational identity
- How being in the middle of the organisation, neither working directly on the primary task nor setting the strategic context, strips people of the opportunity to be anything other than defined by their role
- The way relative power, especially in terms of economic power, sets the terms of trade as to what counts as an authentic identity worthy of the price
- The role that habits of classification and inspection play in shaping authenticity to be an expression of an externally imposed, measurable, and comparable yardstick

2.5.7.2 The paradox in full...

We explore the paradox under the following six headings:

- The discipline of the observed self (in a crowd)
- The failure of the authentic self to be other than a tool of a system
- Validating the authentic leader at work
- The market economy of authenticity and its truth
- Can the watched ('hailed') self ever be authentic?
- The silencing of the unedited voice

And we begin our argument with the first of these six headings.

2.5.7.2.1 THE DISCIPLINE OF THE OBSERVED SELF (IN A CROWD)

Mark is often asked to facilitate sessions for people who have undertaken a 360-feedback exercise as part of their leadership development. Interestingly, with very few exceptions, most of the people with whom he works have a clear sense of where they are most competent and the areas where they might usefully think about doing things differently. Yet, in this context, their voice is only really validated if it resonates with those of the people with whom they work. To an extent, this chimes with the wider notion of the surveillance society, although oftentimes this notion is fixated on our interactions through information technology rather than the common-place, day-to-day technologies of social control in all its forms (Surveillance Studies Network, 2006).

These 360 feedback instruments are panoramic, of course, seeking a view of the individual on the basis of the myriad perspectives of those around them, so long as they fit within the trope of the observable – a sure fire recipe for encouraging performative behaviours and a disassociation between subjective internality and the (pseudo) objectivity of the exter-nal. Implicit in this type of activity is the sense of permanent scrutiny by everyone around you in the workplace, with little inquiry into the scru-tinising mindset of the scrutineer, or of the scrutineer's scrutineer. Such instruments have been described as a 'democratic panopticon', wherein – in Foucauldian terms – 'Being observed by others forces people to observe themselves, which is supposed to lead them to improve their self-control' (Bröckling, 2016, p. 161).

In Mark's experience, almost every leader with whom he has worked on this has been anxiously concerned about what the feedback says about them – and, in many of those instances, how they are viewed by their direct reports, in terms of management and leadership of that group. But the expectation that their staff will be positive about their management and leadership and the grim realities of the day-to-day life of a middle manager, in particular, invariably collide in a way that sits uncomfortably for the candidate. Often, the feedback will draw attention to the way in which the leader is seen to be a mere instrument of the key management imperatives despite the obeisance they might be seen to be paying to the idea of attending to the human needs of the people with whom they work. This, of course, is the plight of what has been usefully described as those seeking to work in the 'torn middle', dancing to the tune from the room above and encouraging a frantic dance amongst those in the room below (Oshrey, 1994). So the theme of the systemic being framed individualistically plays on.

2.5.7.2.2 THE FAILURE OF THE AUTHENTIC SELF TO BE OTHER THAN A TOOL OF A SYSTEM

The lived experience of these people is an embodiment of this tension, where managers are nudged towards being 'authentic' in the workplace when – to an extent – they are cast in the minds of those above them as mere channels for the transmission of their expectations. We will pick up on this question as to what convinces people that this sort of direction is effective and indeed desirable when we turn our attention to the management myths that constrain leadership in our current context. But, for now, we attend to this apparent paradox, which – as ever in our discussions here – is less a genuine contradiction and instead reflects the overlay of a veneer of progress and positivity onto the hard kernel of organisational expectations in terms of getting things done.

In one unattributable conversation John listened in on, it was agreed by the participants (who were informed and senior enough to know what they were talking about) that within the NHS a reputation for 'getting things done' trumps everything else and will see you rewarded and promoted, hence the presence of so many at senior levels who patently don't match with the espoused (and endlessly parroted) organisational values. Performance is all, everything else is window-dressing and 'authenticity' just another part of the obfuscatory dance that hides the harsh realities of the workplace, where the impossible expectations of customers/patients collide with the demands for increasing profit margins and/or delivering more with shrinking budgets. The challenge thrown out to the universe in one of John's recent interviews was along the lines of: 'You want your ready meal lasagne to cost 59p? And you want it to be produced ethically? Just don't ask how it was made if that is what you paid'.

So, what is meant by authenticity in regard to leadership? A 2011 review of the provenance of this notion and the literature that has burgeoned around it opened by making the following statement:

> Spurred by deep-rooted concerns about the ethical conduct of today's leaders based on chilling examples of corporate and government malfeasance, popular leadership authors such as former Medtronic CEO Bill George and leadership consultant Kevin Cashman called for a new type of genuine and values-based leadership — authentic leadership (AL).
>
> (Gardner, et al., 2011, p. 1120)

The work undertaken by these authors leads them to conclude somewhat mawkishly that, 'truly authentic leaders must lead, but they must do so in a way that honors their core values, beliefs, strengths — and weaknesses' (Gardner, et al., 2011, p. 1142). As with so much writing about how power and authority happens within the workplace, it takes on the qualities of secular prayer, seeped in a humanistic stew of 'niceness' that would have Machiavelli spinning in his grave, if it wasn't so absurd as to make it funny.

But this throws up the question of how one reconciles one's 'true' self with the range of corporate demands that prevail upon us, especially when we are seeking to manage and lead in this sort of context. We might rhetorically ask as to what trumps what in this regard? And, of course, we know the answer: our organisations expect us to serve what is jokingly referred to in the current fashionable vernacular as its 'purpose'. This is argued by the sophists of the business world to be the means by which an organisation works to operationalise its vision, values, and objectives, and is seen to embrace both the staff and its customers (Reyes & Kleiner, 1990).

This is where our earlier discussion around values alignment springs to life once again. If authentic leadership is about being true to one's values, then the corporate response has been to seek to replace those personal values for the organisational ones. It is, as Wilmott persuasively argues, the sort of organisational act that carries markings that are remarkably similar to those found in totalitarian systems (Willmott, 1993) with ethics turned into assertions of truth by those who have power, or bland statements of the obvious and never as a troublesome, ongoing inquiry into what 'good practice' looks like and who has the right to claim authorship. Totalitarian systems don't welcome conversational inquiries which might deviate from the Party line.

2.5.7.2.3 VALIDATING THE AUTHENTIC LEADER AT WORK

How then might we assess the quality of our authentic leadership? The first obvious reaction to this would be to say that this would be a deeply personal judgement, based on reflection of the extent to which one could be honest and true to one's values in a leadership context – and how much individual values can ever exist apart from social values co-created in the hurly-burly of a variety of inter-personal relationships. But that's never quite enough in contemporary business: it needs in some way to be quantifiable and externally validated, which immediately denigrates/disappears the qualitative and subjective experiences of life. That, after all, is the purpose of the panoply of assessment instruments, such as psychometrics and other evaluative tools, that clutter organisational life – privileging the sound of the crowd, the external world judgement over the lived personal and subjective experience.

They let us put a number, a cluster of letters, a colour, or some other arbitrary means of distinguishing between people onto individuals, so that we are better able to define the normal in the workplace – and hence those who sit outside of that definition, so may be in need of close supervision and remediation. And these exercises are shrouded in a patina of scientism, the better to reassure us all this is meaningful in an absolute sense and not merely ideological. John recently was invited to contribute to a conversation about MBTI and its underlying rigour on LinkedIn, and he found that he stopped himself from expressing his overwhelming concern about the ideology of classification. This came from his sense that this was a debate unsuited to the casual passing of likes and comments between people with no relational connection. The psychometric and diagnostic industry, of which he has been a part for some years, privileges a profoundly superficial conversation, of traits and habits – in practice it turns into a substitute for sustained inquiry into what the good life means to each and every one of us.

In the case of MBTI this comes to a perfect hurt for him; the instrument is loosely based on the work of Carl Jung, whose extensive insights informed the work John went through with his psychoanalyst over many years. Their work together, peaking at four times a week, unpicked the fissile complexes wrapped up in the well springs of his relationship to love and power and of course SEX (any discussion of which is erased within the workplace, which might be why so much workplace PASSION and PURPOSE seems so empty, lifeless, and dry). John would ever so humbly suggest that the MBTI

16 box typology is a gross perversion of Jung's subtle, mystic, poetic, and sometimes downright odd/batty body of study.

The ultimate absurdity in this regard for us can be found in a method that is meant to give a measurement to our authentic leadership. There exists an Authentic Leadership Questionnaire and an associated Authentic Leadership Inventory, which many authors in the field have been eager to promote (Neider & Schriesheim, 2011). As ever in business, things only really matter if they can be measured and quantified in a way that others can scrutinise and from which they might make judgements about you on that basis. It is, then, an exercise in sorting the authentic from the inauthentic. This clumsy instrument – in its efforts at categorisation – develops for us all at large an understanding of what is normal (that is to say, acceptable in the business context) and that which lies outside of that definition, and thence in need of, at best, improvement and, at worst, remediation.

The thin-ness of this form of inquiry was highlighted for John after talking with a Business School Tutor who sat in on a Programme at one of the Oxbridge business schools. Alongside the normal barrage of models and personality tests, participants were invited to take part in a traditional Oxbridge tutorial in one of the colleges with a renowned Philosopher, where the text they would work with was Plato's Cave. All who took part were, so John's witness told him, blown away by the quality of the conversation and insight they garnered.

The problem is, of course, that with our fixation on speed, measurability, and scalability we have all but eliminated this quality of reflective, guided, learning experience. We dismiss it as uneconomic, rather than working from the idea that our economic framing should be in the service of this form of profound educational opportunity – rather than dictating its pale simulacrum to be found in the on-line learning resources so beloved of the new learning industry. As John's witness to the Oxbridge tutorial observed, this is a model tested and refined over centuries which has been through all sorts of technological 'transformations' (such as the development of the printing press).

2.5.7.2.4 THE MARKET ECONOMY OF AUTHENTICITY AND ITS TRUTH

Modern corporate life – and the associated neoliberal ideas of socio-economic life – applies a distracting veneer to this dichotomy of schooled, normed, and measured authenticity. It offers up the exciting sounding notion of the 'entrepreneurial self', often popularly rendered as the development of 'Me Plc'. The authentic self only exists in terms of market economics, which is predicated on commensurability and price reflecting value in the eye of the buyer of your services. Value and authenticity only exist in the eye of the beholder, the subjective has been rendered irrelevant and invisible.

With further regard to the glibness of 'Me Plc', it carries with it the idea that people can take control by recasting potential employers as 'clients' to whom the individual can market themselves, which conveniently disregards the social and economic relations that are intrinsic to capitalism, where they who have the gold set the rules (Ebbage, 2000). Less eruditely we're reminded of the movie 'Deliverance', where one of the poor, lost urbanites is in the end invited to be the 'Me Plc' of 'I bet you can squeal like a pig'. Elsewhere, glitzy training providers offer courses on 'Me Plc', heading up the publicity for this initiative as follows: 'By intentionally creating our own personal brand, we consider how we want to be perceived by others. When we do this, we manage relationships better and become more aware of our own behaviour' (Mind Gym, 2020). Once again identity and our understanding of authenticity is stripped of relational context and the power hierarchies which permeate our market society. We wonder why what we're left with is a muzak version of anything by the Sex Pistols, Noel Coward sings Johnny Rotten.

In his analysis of the development of the 'entrepreneurial self', Bröckling notes that this does not merely encapsulate rules of conduct, although that is patently there; it offers up '...the forms of knowledge in which individuals recognize the truth about themselves, the control and regulation mechanisms they are subject to and the practices by which they condition themselves' (Bröckling, 2016, p. 21). Hence, this 'management of life' that is expected of the neoliberal subject is only actually interrupted by death itself (Bröckling, 2016, p. 32). Part of this requires us constantly to remake ourselves, off the back of our supposed awareness of self. And that permanent reconstruction pivots around our engagement with developmental opportunities, based upon needs that we identify through a range of panoptical instruments and our incorporation of those observations into our existence. Within the world of professional developers, we are drawn to those who ask the question: 'What do we mean by development'?

'Development in whose eyes'? It is very easy to fall into an assumption that development must be good, that it is a technocratic term – when it is as value laden a term as they come.

2.5.7.2.5 CAN THE WATCHED ('HAILED') SELF EVER BE AUTHENTIC?

The extent to which this sort of attitude of constant remaking – and personal approach to the presentation of self in our contemporary context – sits comfortably with the idea of authenticity seems questionable. Can we truly speak about being authentic where we find ourselves in a surveillance regime, where the knowledge that we are being 'watched', whether directly through information technology – as was the case with systems introduced at Barclays Bank to ceaselessly scrutinise what their employees did minute by minute whilst at work (Jones, 2020) – or via the managerial technologies of appraisal, talent management, psychometrics, and 360 feedback tools?

What are these tools and regimes reporting, beyond our capacity to play a role that will be found pleasing by those who oversee the regime? Who in turn are also overseen by regimes of inspection that invites them to 'play-up and play the game', a phrasing we deliberately use to echo the language of the British Public (i.e. very Private) school system, which produces the excellent hollow men who so dominate senior roles in so many private and public sector institutions. What the inspection of the self shows is that we know how to be an inspected self – and we're assuming that the inspected self is not the same as an authentic self, free from playing the inspection game, an insight schooled out of much of the British elite (and probably elites around the world).

The myth of the authentic subject cannot be sustained in light of what we know of the ways in which the very act of being watched (or, to use a specific term, 'hailed' by another or others) serves to generate our human subjectivity: the argument goes that, if someone calls across the street to me with the phrase 'Hey, you there'!, then

> ...the hailed individual will turn round. By this mere one-hundred-and-eighty-degree physical conversion, he [sic] becomes a *subject*. Why? Because he has recognised that the hail was "really" addressed to him, and that "it was *really* him who was hailed" (and not someone else).
>
> (Althusser, 2008 [1970], p. 48)

This is all compounded by the withering expectations that sit on those lodged in the middle of the hierarchy, as we noted earlier. If we crudely calibrate our organisations as performers, managers of performers, and managers of managers, the central tier can be seen purely as a somewhat dehumanised instrument. People therein are merely conduits through which the strategic designs of the senior leadership are operationalised through oversight of those at the frontline who produce the good or deliver the service.

It is our view that those people are so tightly defined by the structural expectations that prevail upon them that it denies them the opportunity to be authentic. They are 'hailed' in the workplace through demands to deliver in respect to key performance indicators and appraisal objectives over which they invariably had very little control – and which inevitably have a profoundly negative cultural impact for our organisations and on the people therein:

> The proliferation of measures, coupled with the perceived need to monitor and rely on them for decision-making, makes it difficult to keep track of, and utilise, performance information in a meaningful way. If management effort is widely dispersed across everything that can be measured and controlled, the really important signals get lost in a frenzy of measurement activity. Thus, paradoxically, increasing your reliance on measurement renders effective decision-making more, not less, difficult.
>
> (Gray, et al., 2015, p. 35)

Enmeshed in these measures (where – to a large extent – those managers will not have contributed to a conversation about the why, what, and how in respect to the construction of those metrics) and often merely being expected to respond positively to the commands that issue from above, the managers of managers wistfully imagine an authenticity to which they aspire but which is denied to them by the weighty expectations upon them. They have become all role, without agency. This organisational subjectivity simply precludes the opportunity to be one's true self in the workplace, there's nowhere for people to go where they can step out of the performance the organisation requires of them.

2.5.7.2.6 THE SILENCING OF THE UNEDITED VOICE

It is organisational glitches like this that leads John and his collaborators to look so intently at the whole question of speaking truth to power (Reitz & Higgins, 2019). After all, the ultimate authenticity must surely be to feel unthinkingly able to give voice to issues that might concern us and ideas that will improve our experience, the experience of those with whom we work, and the experience of the people for whom we do that work. The unedited voice able to speak without fear.

The denial of this sort of authenticity, of course, must surely impact on the wider issue of performance and its management by managers. The former creates the circumstances where work will be safer and improved in terms of process because it is the gift of the speaker to give voice to what matters to them and share their particular understanding of a situation. Yet management heavily privileges the notion of tight control – it is actually seen to be intrinsic to the very idea of management in industrial society – not least so as to justify the two tiers that sit on top of the 'performers' who actually get things done on a day-to-day basis. Many of us accept management simply because we are managers. And management persists, even when capitalist organisations engage in the fiction of being post-bureaucratic and flat in terms of structures; it is merely buried away in the warp and weft of their quotidian practice, with a heavy emphasis on the whole workforce being compelled to 'manage' (without the reward ordinarily associated with that practice and its associated status). Hierarchy, it is argued, has a remarkable tendency to persist, even where the stated aim is to rid ourselves of it (Child, 2019, pp. 128–129), it simply relocates from the formal organigram into the informal shadows and more insidiously into our synapses.

2.5.8 Some conclusions about paradox four...

Authenticity *contra* part of the superstructure... 'An invocation that leaders should be their authentic self in the workplace juxtaposed with a constant organizational drive for performance which – for middle managers – merely renders them an element of the superstructure that manages the delivery of output and outcome'. The conclusions that stand out for us around this faux-paradox are:

- Like buying a Ford car at the beginning of the twentieth century, where you could have any colour so long as it was black, you can be any form of authentic self you want so long as people will want to buy you

- As well as having to be this purchasable identity, you must be able to describe your authentic self using the yardsticks and framings approved of by those to whom you must appear purchasable by
- Within the workplace the overwhelming priority given to performance and especially measurable, comparable performance squeezes out the capacity to notice and pay attention to the unique and particular experiences of people
- The authentic self, should such an identity be possible, is so hemmed in by custom and practice and the technologies of observation that even those aspects of yourself that feel authentic remain unseen because they will be disappeared by the rules of observation (and we are left with a reframing of the philosophical conundrum concerning the unseen, unheard pine tree in the forest. Does the authentic self, if never seen, actually exist?)
- There is also the matter of whether or not an individual's authenticity can exist outside of the relationships of which they are part – that authenticity is always authenticity-in-relationship rather than an essentialist quality of individual identity

2.5.9 *Paradox five: all to be heard* contra *the privileging of extraversion*

The invitation in a corporate setting for all voices to be heard yet the continued (and encouraged) dominance of an extraverted culture in this context, where thoughtfulness, reflection and quietness is ascribed an otherness in contrast to the dominance of decisiveness, action and noise that is privileged in nearly every organisational setting.

(Cain, 2013)

2.5.9.1 In brief...

The themes we explore in association with this paradox are:

- The extent to which belonging, being present during conversations and meetings, has significance and weight in its own right... indeed belonging to a conversation without responsibility has its own form of pleasure
- The role hierarchy plays, whether tacit or explicit, in the form of an over-seer or as a self-disciplining habit of mind, sustaining the context within which forms of speaking up and being heard happen

- How personal preferences and social labels shape the capacity to have a voice
- How woke-washing, and associated social fashions, does and doesn't sustain a lived experience of having a voice and being heard
- The historic roots of silencing some groups and privileging others

2.5.9.2 *The paradox in full...*

We explore the paradox under the following six headings:

- The work of meetings (or meetings, bloody meetings...)
- The pleasure of exercising power and/or belonging
- The curse of thoughtfulness
- The silencing effects of hierarchy – and its subversion
- Let's talk about gender and ethnicity
- Woke-washing and the inclusion game

And we begin our argument with the first of these six headings.

2.5.9.2.1 THE WORK OF MEETINGS (OR MEETINGS, BLOODY MEETINGS...)

There are myriad internet memes and Dilbert-style cartoons that lampoon our corporate fascination with meetings. Many of us in organisational life glance at our calendar for the coming week late on a Sunday afternoon, because the workplace disciplines are now so entwined in the rhythms of the domestic, and release a weary sigh as we see how our days have been populated – invariably by others, using the access we all have to one another's electronic calendars – with meetings. On many occasions, we will stare at the block of time – with its uninspiring meeting title, grossly inflated list of expected attenders, and soul-sapping attachments to be waded through in advance – and ponder what on earth is meant to come out of this congregation. A survey of 182 senior managers in a range of industries found 65% of the group saying that meetings kept them from completing their work...when meetings are, of course, meant to be one of the ways in which we actively do that work (Perlow, et al., 2017, p. 65).

In fact, Patrik Hall at Malmo University argues that the growth of meetings in this way actually reflects what we were speaking about at the end of the last segment of this chapter, namely the expansion of the manage-rial caste. Their work is meetings, rather than doing concrete things. And that contrast – between being expected to be seen to do something in the world, in terms of the modern notions of what leadership and management involves, and spending most of one's working life sitting in meetings – is suggested to lead to two things, namely a burgeoning sense of frustration and a therapeutic reliance on those 'coming togethers' (Malmo University, 2019).

Research that explores the link between satisfaction with meetings in work and overall job satisfaction finds a linkage and makes the following crucial observation:

> [O]rganizations that see the value in maintaining and promoting employee morale and job satisfaction should not take meeting experiences for granted. Meeting satisfaction matters, not only for those with frequent meeting activity, but also those with moderate levels of meeting activity. It follows that organizations should regularly assess meeting satisfaction.
>
> (Rogelberg, et al., 2010, p. 167)

The ubiquity of the meeting – by which we mean a formalised commit-ment of time wherein a number of people are expected to come together, either face-to-face or via communication technology, to have an exchange in respect to a topic of organisational significance – means that our work-ing days are dominated by this sort of event. They vary, of course, in terms of levels of formality, although the pre-planned quality in this regard is important in terms of trying to think critically about working lives. They may involve some people in a work group coming together or someone in a particular work group reaching out to personnel in other work groups. They may be highly formal, in terms of regular frequency and responding to particular governance challenges in a business context: this might range from 'task and finish' groups through to regular committee meetings.

2.5.9.2.2 THE PLEASURE OF EXERCISING POWER AND/OR BELONGING

So, why do we endure this rigmarole when – for most of us – we recognise it as an absurd performative activity that delivers little in terms of practical-ities? In John's work as part of The Right Conversation, on more than one occasion when reviewing the quality of a particular group's conversational dynamic, what came out was that this group ceased to have an organisationally purposeful function some years before.

The following critique, drawn from a book published in 1976, still seems to us to resonate:

> Even inadequate meetings and conferences serve the needs of people to feel powerful and included. The designated leader can feel proud and powerful in his [sic] devotion to the task, and these feelings may compensate for all the frustration he [sic] experiences. As he uses his position and power to bring the meeting to the end he desires, the leader is viewed with respect and admiration, attitudes which strengthen his self-image. Power, authority and status are a heady mixture, even though stress – 'keeping the meeting on the beam' and controlling aggressive and recalcitrant members – is the price that is paid. For members there are a number of values that may outweigh frustration, anonymity, and lack of power. Being a member provides the individual with a feeling of belonging without paying the price of responsibility. Belonging – whether to a group, committee, or association – means that some others do not belong. Self-identity develops from many factors and one is the recognition that one belongs. Meetings may also provide the latest information and gossip. In meetings, a self-serving remark judiciously camouflaged can appear as a contribution to the decision. And meetings can interrupt the routine of dull work.
>
> (Bradford, 1976, pp. 15–16)

In practice, then, meetings in organisational contexts – today as much as might have been the case over 40 years ago – are merely leadership sandpits, where the chair or the person who is in possession of the HIPPO (the Highest Paid Person's Opinion), get to play with power and bolster themselves professionally and personally through this practice. Meetings can be said to reproduce the hierarchical relationships that exist in our companies and agencies. But they also define for the members – through the way in which they sit in a mesh of power – normalcy and otherness; being 'in' the meeting is the preferred place, because it places you in the mainstream. The lines written by Oscar Wilde in The Picture of Dorian Gray can be repurposed – in the original it runs 'There is only one thing in the world worse than being talked about, and that is not being talked about'. In the case of our world of meetings and belonging this can read across as: 'There is only one thing worse than being in a meeting, and that is not being in a meeting'.

Our compliance with this regime requires us to assume a level of docility that in any other circumstance we might not be content to display. Meetings are very often pointless and soul-destroying in terms of dullness...and yet we prop them up by endlessly taking part in them and never once really challenging them, because we fear being evicted from this tawdry Eden.

2.5.9.2.3 THE CURSE OF THOUGHTFULNESS

All of which is intensely amplified by the fact that there are so many people in corporate life whose introversion (for want of a better word – and making no judgement in terms of types and psychological make-up that might be lazily drawn from the use of this term) means that meetings are oppressively complicated to navigate – and do not bring out the best in those people. As an introvert with a reflective bent, Mark speaks about the way in which he has negatively experienced meetings over the course of his 40 years in the workplace: sitting pregnant with a contribution but never finding an opportunity to offer it, as the conversation whizzed amongst the more powerful and more forthright in the room; hearing the contribution that he had been nursing latterly delivered by one of the blowhards in the room, to universal approval; offering a faltering and quiet interjection to a sea of faces impatiently waiting for him to stop so that they could offer their opinions without even acknowledging what had just been said; and having his quietness in these arenas adjudged as an indication of a lack of confidence or of something to see in terms of the crucial business of the organisation.

In the early stages of the Corona virus mayhem of spring 2020, John lent his ear to a friend caught up in the chaos of an organisation trying to work out what to do. An all-hands meeting was called on-line and John's friend both valued the contribution of colleagues who were able to fizz with expressed ideas in this mass gathering, while also resenting how silenced they in turn felt. It was only in the peace of their conversation with a trusted professional friend such as John that they felt able to explore their experience and give voice to the insights they had inside them.

The generalised critique of the idea of 'meetings' in organisational sittings enjoys widespread currency, notwithstanding the specific issues faced by introverts in this arena. Research in this regard observes the following:

> [L]ess than half of participants' comments about meeting effectiveness are positive; practical improvements are clearly needed. The contrast between positive and negative comments is mainly one of function (positive comments) versus structure (negative comments). Positive comments generally contain the theme that meetings are important for organisational purposes — not only to achieve work objectives (e.g. focused on goals, solving problems etc) and to disseminate information, but also to maintain both commitment to goals and a collectivistic/ team-based culture. Negative comments, on the other hand, emphasise more structural problems in terms of poor organisation — for instance, poor planning, lack of an agenda, and a content of low relevance to attendees' work. In addition, many negative comments note the perceived lack of impact of meeting attendees, as manifest in the form of unproductive discussions or a lack of consideration of attendees' input.
>
> (Geimer, et al., 2015, pp. 2022–2023)

2.5.9.2.4 THE SILENCING EFFECTS OF HIERARCHY – AND ITS SUBVERSION

We know that human organising requires us to come together to speak about the focus of that work. But we are equally of the mind that current structures for meetings do not achieve that essential expectation around connecting and conversing. And this is compounded by the oppressive presence of hierarchy, whether tacit or explicit, internalised or externalised, in these settings. Mark recalls someone speaking with him about their experience of attending a key Board committee in their organisation, where they were responsible as part of their day-to-day work for the production of a great deal of the material that these meetings considered as part of their standing agenda. However, whilst they were expected to attend each and every meeting, they were not permitted to speak in that setting: only their manager could 'speak to' the papers that had been produced – and their author was expected to sit in silence, merely capturing the elements of the exchange.

In truth, this looks to be a performance rather than an authentic exchange between human beings. We suspect that it would be unclear even to those taking part in this dreary activity what purpose it was serving, beyond inculcating across the organisation an expectation of how people should conduct themselves, who should be heard, and how they should be heard. It serves to inscribe the stultifying effects of hierarchy into the culture of the organisation, tacitly defining those who are allowed to give voice and those who should expect to be gagged. We work on the assumption that the organisation in question would not embarrass itself by publicly subscribing to the idea of diversity of voice – but, were it to be the case, it would not be altogether surprising, given our experiences of corporate life.

Writing of the experiences of the American factory worker in the post-war period, a study made mention of the monthly safety meeting that employees were expected to attend. In this context, they observed, that,

> The workers are exhorted to bring their complaints to this safety com-mittee. To stimulate worker's participation, they appoint three shop workers as the first rung of the safety committee. Thereafter the com-mittee consists of the company engineers and personnel.
>
> (Romano & Stone, 1947, p. 68)

Most of the 30 minutes would be dedicated to a speech from a foreman, whilst the last few minutes were open to the floor. Insignificant issues raised were indulged; general antagonism amongst the workforce present would see the meeting briskly adjourned.

The authors capture some of the reactions of the workers to these meet-ings. For instance, one response was simply, 'Oh boy, another half hour to rest' (Romano & Stone, 1947, p. 69); others dozed during the event or sniggered together. Lastly, in a prefiguration of today's apparent altruistic concern for employees' well-being, the workers observed the following: 'The foreman and superintendent always say: "The men [sic] are negligent and don't cooperate with the safety committee". You are told to get enough sleep, not to drink, and to eat the right foods' (Romano & Stone, 1947, p. 69). Like the committee meeting mentioned earlier, where the writer of papers was denied the opportunity to speak, this meeting from the early 1970s simply reinforces the power relations in the organisation and under-scores the hierarchy. Plus ça change... especially when it comes to people's capacity to be slyly subversive.

As part of John's research with Megan Reitz into speaking up they were told the story of a town-hall meeting at a manufacturing company within the last few years. The senior leader turns up, in his suit, to address the factory workforce, in their overalls. After his speech extolling the virtues of the company and its strategic plan, he is bombarded with questions and the meeting rolls well over the allotted time. The senior leader is bowled over after the event by the enthusiasm of the workforce. The counter-narrative offered to John and Megan, but not to the senior leader, was that being in a nice warm meeting room and being paid to be there sure beat the hard graft of being out on the factory floor.

2.5.9.2.5 LET'S TALK ABOUT ETHNICITY AND GENDER

This whole matter is overlaid, of course, with issues of gender, as well. Not only do these meetings reinforce power in its widest possible sense, they also carry with them the oppressiveness of patriarchy (and it's fair to observe that these two are intimately related, in corporate life as well as in wider society – one recent observation John came across in his research travels was that patriarchy predates capitalism by a considerable margin, so capitalism has gender oppressiveness deep within its foundations). Hence, the very fundamental idea of a diversity of voice is undermined by the organisational practices in which the vast majority of us engage. Research on this illuminates the conflicting attitudes of men and women on this issue. For the former, there is a sense that women fail to speak up loudly enough and do not express strong points of view; for the latter, in contrast, it was observed that it was difficult for them to get a word in and that their confidence in these settings is an issue (Heath, et al., 2014). The meeting format that most of us experience at work privileges men's voices and thereby inhibits the voices of women in those settings.

The authors of the study intimate that it is entirely possible that the negative effects they highlight could equally apply to people from ethnic minorities and to what they describe as more reserved men (Heath, et al., 2014) – work by Carol Campayne (www.differentwomen.co.uk/) presents compelling evidence that in the women she researched it was their ethnicity that was the most defining factor in their experience of being othered and silenced. This observation has the subtle effect of normalising those who dominate our meetings and casting as the Other those who find it difficult to speak up and be heard in this context. As is so often the case with the sort of 'business school research' that the *Harvard Business Review* showcases, there is an innate conservatism at work: the context and the ways in which we have been doing things is left unquestioned – and the focus falls instead on fixing those who are unfairly limited by those circumstances. In John's research into the experience of women in hospitality (Moody-McNamara & Higgins, 2020), the focus on 'fixing the women' was strikingly present, systemic inquiry was frequently not that welcome because that might well threaten the status quo and shine a light on patterns of unacknowledged voice advantage.

2.5.9.2.6 WOKE-WASHING AND THE INCLUSION GAME

As we have seen, there is a strong emphasis on the issue of inclusion in the workplace – and on supporting diversity of voice in that context. As with all the paradoxes we have highlighted here, this one represents a valued business custom and practice – privileging the noise maker, who is oftentimes speaking in a masculine register, with their specific style and orientation towards action – wrapped in an ideological cellophane that says that diversity of voice – of women, of BAME members of staff, of introverts – is part of their corporate raison d'etre. Both sides of the political spectrum are minded to call this out as 'woke-washing', the mobilisation of attitudes and positions that have wider resonance in a social context in order to build the brand and plump up the bottom line.

Hence, Owen Jones, writing in The Guardian, explains it from the progressive perspective thus:

> Whether you think it's "woke-washing", or companies raising and mainstreaming important issues, this is a phenomenon that is not only here to stay, but will keep on growing. Capitalism has proved its ability to adapt: at a time when so many younger people quite legitimately feel that the economic system doesn't work for them, big business appealing to their sense of idealism is a savvy move.
>
> (Jones, 2019)

Meanwhile, Toby Young comes at this from the other perspective yet lands at pretty much the same conclusion, when writing about what he calls the 'woke corporation':

> Crackpot ideas that used to be confined to neo-Marxist professors in grievance studies departments have been enthusiastically embraced by the giants of capitalism. Apple, Amazon, Facebook, Goldman Sachs, Coca-Cola are all on board and anyone who publicly challenges this

new orthodoxy is not merely endangering their chances of promotion, but at risk of being fired.

(Young, 2019)

Elsewhere, in the UK magazine *Private Eye* during 2020, you could find stories of companies with seemingly strong public stands on social issues whose practice leaves a good deal to be desired: we have a large sportswear company chasing the cheapest labour rates from country to country around the far east – and a supermarket with a significant shareholder located in a country that condones and supports slavery.

As we have just seen, both poles of political opinion take a very similar view in respect to the idea of large companies embracing progressive positions in relation to issues of social justice. Such attitudes merely become an accoutrement, designed to prettify the corporate profile. The brand must prevail, even when a significant number of people seem to be turning their backs on capitalism. After all, such people remain consumers of goods and services, such as Nike trainers and Gillette razors; even as they occupy Wall Street, they unwittingly occupy the status of both producer and consumer of the boundless goods and services that our unthinkingly growth-oriented system churns out. Companies persist – and are not above momentarily clothing themselves in apparently radical perspectives if it keeps the brand at the forefront of the supposedly enlightened mind and shifts a few more units every quarter.

Companies pay obeisance to the notion of diversity of voice, in order to be seen to be altruistic and in tune with contemporary social challenges. And yet, behind that gleaming pretence of enlightenment, there remains a commitment to business practices that inhibit voice. Moreover, if we explore the disparity between public pronouncements in respect to voice and the day-to-day experience of many who work in the corporate world, where they are silenced (or silence themselves in face of organisational expectation), then the whole question becomes even more risible. Here, then, is much talking of the talk that leaders think that the world wants to hear, but little walking of the walk that would see their organisations turned upside down in order to make them a richer human experience for those who work there.

2.5.10 *Some conclusions about paradox five*

All to be heard *contra* the privileging of extraversion... The invitation in a corporate setting for all voices to be heard yet the continued (and encouraged) dominance of an extraverted culture in this context, where thoughtfulness, reflection, and quietness is ascribed an otherness in contrast to the dominance of decisiveness, action, and noise that is privileged in nearly every organisational setting (Cain, 2013). The conclusions that stand out for us around this faux-paradox are:

- Unacknowledged and pervasive patterns of hierarchy, both externally imposed and internally owned, create contexts of expectations about whether or not we expect to be heard at work
- Personal preferences make a difference – with taken for granted habits of interaction effectively silencing those who would feel able to speak up in a different social dynamic
- The need to belong to a conversational context trumps the frustration at not being able to have a voice and be heard
- The fashionable adoption of particular stances, around including the voices of people who are traditionally not heard, makes little difference to the lived experience of those used to being at the margins
- Not speaking up, or speaking up in a subversive way, is its own rich reward in a world where the rules of the game are stacked against you

2.5.11 *What lies beneath... some conclusions about paradox in the workplace*

The substance of this chapter has been an exploration of workplace experiences which are often presented as paradoxes, or a continuum of contradictions to be managed. This coda looks to synthesise and pull together all that has been covered, while at the same time wanting to point out that this synthesis is in itself part of the obfuscatory dance of our current world of truth-power. We are playing this game by meeting the world where it is in its belief that everything can be reduced to a bullet point, that a magical essence can be distilled from an argument – because we don't have the time to participate in the process of argument.

A particularly harsh colleague brought this into sharp relief for John when he worked at Ashridge Consulting/Management College. John was busy copying a paper he'd written to share with a group; John recalls the colleague saying: 'Ah! Sharing our effluent are we'? What lay behind the comment was the insight that it is the writer of a paper who gets the most from it, as they are the one who has had to struggle with the sense making experience. With that in mind, we still think a bit of a synthesis can be useful as a reflective invitation! And in the case of John's colleague, there might have been a bit of an envious attack playing out as well.

2.5.11.1 *In brief... as an overview of the review of the five paradoxes*

Cutting across all these paradoxes are some North Star assumptions, towards which management practice orientates itself, and which lead us to conclude the following (which point largely due South):

- There is no golden mean or equilibrium to take away the reality of contradictory priorities, interests, and experiences
- Paradox is one of the ways in which power gets hidden by a veil of obfuscation (and so made all but undiscussable)
- Unexplored paradox inhibits even the possibility of fresh thinking and action
- Making sense of the paradoxes of organisational life can feel like wrestling mist, or trying to grapple a greased pig, so elusive is its linguistic turn (and the obfuscatory purpose it serves)
- Our thoughts and thinking create this world, coming together to think differently and see the world anew is our way out of the reality we currently create together
- Money and our current approach to wealth are not side order issues, but lie at the heart of how we think and create the world (don't disappear context!)

2.5.11.2 *In brief... an overview for each paradox*

The themes and conclusions for each paradox are:

Well-being contra overbearing busyness – a fashionable focus on workforce well-being initiatives alongside the overbearing corporate culture of busyness.

- The themes in summary are…. We go along with, willingly or not, the extension of workplace logic and rhythms into all parts of our lives. Meanwhile what is meant by wellness remains indistinct

- And in conclusion… Well-being and working practices are two sides of the same coin, they are not independent of each other; immiserating work immiserates. And what counts as well-being is an ethical not a technocratic consideration, it is much more about the question of 'What is the good life'?, rather than the number of steps walked today (although that could be part of it).

Inclusive compassion contra heroic control – a public declaration (particularly in the NHS) in favour of compassionate and inclusive leadership in contrast to a practical adherence to heroic leadership and command-and-control.

- The themes in summary are… the way modern leadership theory distracts from the persistence of very traditional, archaic practices… and the divide between what is discussable in public and what happens in private
- And in conclusion… little has changed in terms of individualised, top-down leadership practice… the realities of social power and self-interest served by the status quo are hidden by being supposedly past their sell by date

Diversity of voice contra enforced homogeneity – an emphasis on diversity – particularly of voice – in organisations alongside the cultural totalitarianism of values alignment, with its orientation towards enforced homogeneity (Willmott, 1993).

- The themes in summary are… the role norms, checklists, and instrumental thinking play in stripping diversity of its generative capacity… and how the economic perspective trumps all
- And in conclusion… diversity in practice is about economic performance and social justice is a nice to, not a need to (within the limits of enforceable legal limits)… you can be diverse and different, so long as you do it in the right way

Authenticity contra part of the superstructure – an invocation that leaders should be their authentic self in the workplace juxtaposed with a constant organisational drive for performance, which – for middle managers – merely renders them an element of the superstructure that manages the delivery of output and outcome.

- The themes in summary are... individual authenticity is in thrall to group identity and the need to express identity in a commercially attractive and comparable way
- And in conclusion... authenticity is always authenticity-in-relationship... and you cannot separate out a personal identity from a role identity... technologies of observation and classification also serve to drive out, or make ignorable, deviant authenticity

All to be heard contra **the privileging of extraversion** – the invitation in a corporate setting for all voices to be heard yet the continued (and encouraged) dominance of an extraverted culture in this context, where thoughtfulness, reflection, and quietness is ascribed an otherness in contrast to the dominance of decisiveness, action, and noise that is privileged in nearly every organisational setting (Cain, 2013).

- The themes in summary are... belonging to a conversation, even if you say nothing, can be its own reward... having a voice and being heard is enmeshed in the social games all groups and societies play to privilege some and quiet others
- And in conclusion... pervasive hierarchical patterns create expectations around who and what is heard... woke-washing does little to disrupt habits of marginalisation and encourage news of difference which might upset the status quo

2.6 A concluding commentary

Whilst we have opined throughout these chapters on the organisation, the company, and the firm, these are mere synecdoches for the aggregated lived experience of all who work in those spaces – and, in particular, for the way in which those in formal leadership positions choose to relate to and speak about their places of work, that is, the shape they seek to give to the way things get done in that space. It is people who have to make individual decisions regarding all five of the issues/paradoxes about which we have spoken in this chapter. They are not mere reeds in the wind, buffeted by breezes blowing in opposite directions.

All of which means that those leaders who know this – all too well – are assuming public positions that to many seem to run counter to the day-to-day experience of the people with whom they work. And if they do not know this, then they are not worthy to be called leaders, as they lack the insight and critical capacity to assume that role. In essence, then, we began by referring to these as paradoxes, but, in reality, they are not: they are a persistence of miserable practice that ends up being shrouded by the public adoption of principles that seem enlightened but do not impact on people's lived organisational experience.

This is not a conundrum to be considered and carefully navigated, as the overall question of leading through complexity can be seen to be. It is, instead, an ideological choice on the part of leaders – and, to some extent, for those of us in organisations. Leaders sustain the grim practices of our organisations, whilst espousing positive positions that serve to disguise them. But the choice is open to them to lead changes in the way in which our organisations function – and stop indulging the deceit of publicly suggesting that things are different.

This observation in respect to complexity helpfully reminds us of the need to acknowledge presence in a system:

> Almost everyone using the complexity sciences in relation to organizations stresses the importance of interaction and relationships, just as almost all natural scientists working in the field of complexity sciences do. However, just as with most natural scientists, management complexity writers emphasise individual agency. Individual agents form the relationships rather than the relationships forming the agents.
>
> (Stacey, et al., 2000, p. 164)

That agency exists but endures some systemic limitation, of course.

Following on from this, we are eager to underscore the idea of choice in this regard, in order to help people to recognise that notwithstanding the fact that they have capacity to make a difference to the way in which things are constituted, it remains the case that our individual ambitions to act differently are subtly limited by the discourse in which we reside. How might this work? Here, the concept of *habitus* – drawn from the work of French sociologist Pierre Bourdieu – is helpful in terms of helping us to balance the social constraints on thinking and action that exist and our own sense of human agency (Maton, 2014). Our understanding of this notion draws on the example of a football game: players have freedom to play the match as they choose, although – outside of the radical elegance of 'total football', a notion worthy of exploration from an organisational context (Siregar, 2018) – the position in which they play alongside the rules and practices of the game overall will determine how they engage as footballers.

These so-called paradoxes cloud our capacity to engage critically with the reality of our lived experience. They inhibit our capacity to think differently about the world – and, through that reimagining – to exercise our agency, initially individually and latterly using the power in the collective, in order to reshape that experience for us and for the others with whom we find ourselves in the workplace. This challenges us to tear down the shibboleths, the better to cast light on what has been described as the 'darker side of interorganizational relations', which encompasses '…processes and behaviours which can leave members feeling disempowered and isolated, creating suspicion, conflict and distrust and being pressured into behaviour they do not fully support' (Brown, 2019, p. 133). This, then, is the challenge of liberated leadership: to deny these paradoxes; to recognise the choices implicit in day-to-day practice and its ideological veneer and to have the courage to make them explicit, and to openly acknowledge the ideological obfuscation in which we have all become complicit.

References

Althusser, L., 2008 [1970]. Ideology and ideological state apparatuses (Notes towards an investigation). In: L. Althusser, ed. *On ideology*. London: Verso, pp. 1–60.

Anderson-Connolly, R., Grunberg, L., Greenberg, E. S. & Moore, S., 2002. Is lean mean? Workplace transformation and employee well-being. *Work, Employment and Society*, 16(3), pp. 389–413.

Bassett-Jones, N., 2005. The paradox of diversity management, creativity and innovation. *Diversity Management, Creativity and Innovation*, 14(2), pp. 169–175.

Binney, G., Glanfield, P. & Wilke, G., 2017. *Breaking free of bonkers: How to lead in today's crazy world of organizations*. London: Nicholas Brealey Publishing.

Boeing, 2020. *Vision – A foundation of innovation*. [Online] Available at: www.boeing.com/principles/vision.page [Accessed 5 February 2020].

Bohm, D., 1996. *On dialogue*. Abingdon: Routledge.

Bolden, R. et al., 2019. *Inclusion: The DNA of leadership and change*, Bristol: Bristol Leadership and Change Centre, UWE.

Bradford, L. P., 1976. *Making meetings work: A guide for leaders and group members*. La Jolla, CA: University Associates, Inc.

Bröckling, U., 2016. *The entrepreneurial self: Fabricating a new type of subject*. London: Sage.

Brown, K., 2019. A darker side of interorganizational relations. In: W. Thomas, A. Hujala, S. Laulainen & R. McMurray, eds. *The management of wicked problems in health and social care*. Abingdon, Oxon: Routledge, pp. 133–147.

Cain, S., 2013. *Quiet: The power of introverts in world that can't stop talking*. London: Penguin.

Cave, P., 2009. *This sentence is false: An introduction to philosophical paradoxes*. London: Continuum.

Chartered Institute of Personnel & Development, 2019. *Health and well-being at work*, London: CIPD.

Child, J., 2019. *Hierarchy: A key idea for business and society*. Abingdon, Oxon: Routledge.

Clements-Croome, D., 2006. Consciousness, well-being and the senses. In: D. Clements-Croome, ed. *Creating the productive workplace*. Second ed. Abingdon, Oxon: Taylor & Francis, pp. 14–24.

Clements-Croome, D., 2013. The nature of consciousness. In: *Beyond environmental comfort*. Abingdon: Routledge, pp. 17–46.

Connor, P. E. & Becker, B. W., 1979. Values and the organization: Suggestions for research. In: M. Rokeach, ed. *Understanding human values: Individual and societal*. New York: The Free Press, pp. 71–81.

Dalal, F., 1998. *Taking the group seriously: Towards a post-Foulkesian group analytic theory*. London: Jessica Kingsley Publishers.

Danna, K. & Griffin, R. W., 1999. Health and well-being in the workplace: A review and synthesis of the literature. *Journal of Management*, 25(3), pp. 357–384.

Day, A., 2020. *Disruption, change and transformation in organisations: A human relations perspective*. Abingdon, Oxon: Routledge.

Diener, E., 1984. Subjective well-being. *Psychological Bulletin*, Volume 95, pp. 542–575.

Ebbage, A., 2000. *How to build the brand 'Me Plc': Start treating your boss as your client*. [Online] Available at: www.theguardian.com/money/2000/apr/15/jobsadvice.careers4 [Accessed 21 February 2020].

Frazer, J. G., 1998. *The golden bough: A study in magic and religion.* Oxford: Oxford University Press.

Gardner, W. L., Cogliser, C. C., Davis, K. M. & Dickens, M. P., 2011. Authentic leadership: A review of the literature and research agenda. *The Leadership Quarterly*, 22(6), pp. 1120–1145.

Garlick, H., 2017. *The madness of mindfulness.* [Online] Available at: www. ft.com/content/9b8c0c6e-e805-11e6-967b-c88452263daf [Accessed 14 December 2020].

Geimer, J. L. et al., 2015. Meetings at work: Perceived effectiveness and recommended improvements. *Journal of Business Research*, 68, pp. 2015–2026.

Gershuny, J. & Sullivan, O., 2019. *What we really do all day: Insights from the Centre for Time Use Research.* London: Pelican.

Grawitch, M. J., Gottschalk, M. & Munz, D. C., 2006. The path to a healthy workplace: A critical review linking healthy workplace practices, employee well-being, and organizational improvements. *Consulting Psychology Journal: Practice and Research*, 58(3), pp. 129–147.

Gray, D., Micheli, P. & Pavlov, A., 2015. *Measurement madness: Recognizing and avoiding the pitfalls of performance measurement.* Chichester: Wiley.

Grint, K., 2011. A history of leadership. In: A. Bryman, et al. eds. *The Sage Handbook of Leadership.* London: Sage, pp. 3–14.

Mind Gym, 2020. *Me Plc.* [Online] Available at: www.uk.themindgym.com/topics/me-plc/ [Accessed 21 February 2020].

Ham, C., 2016. *Real trust rather than regulated trust should be the foundation on which improvement in the NHS is built.* [Online] Available at: www.kingsfund. org.uk/blog/2016/03/trust-improvement-nhs [Accessed 14 January 2020].

Han, B.-C., 2019. *What is power?* Cambridge: Polity.

Harvey, F., 2019. *Antibiotic resistance as big a threat as climate change – chief medic.* [Online] Available at: www.theguardian.com/society/2019/apr/29/ antibiotic-resistance-as-big-threat-climate-change-chief-medic-sally-davies [Accessed 14 December 2020].

Heath, K., Flynn, J. & Davis Holt, M., 2014. *Women, find your voice.* [Online] Available at: https://hbr.org/2014/06/women-find-your-voice [Accessed 17 June 2021].

Helm, T. & Savage, M., 2020. *Johnson to cabinet: shape up or I'll sack you within weeks.* [Online] Available at: https://www.theguardian.com/politics/2020/ jan/18/boris-johnson-warns-cabinet-shape-up-or-be-sacked [Accessed 17 June 2021].

Heywood Thomas, J., 1957. *Subjectivity and paradox*. Oxford: Basil Blackwell.

Higgins, J., 2009. *Images of authority: Working within the shadow of the crown*. London: Middlesex University Press.

Hunt, V., Layton, D. & Prince, S., 2015. *Diversity matters*, London: McKinsey.

Hunt, V., Prince, S., Dixon-Fyle, S. & Yee, L., 2018. *Delivering through diversity*, London: McKinsey & Company.

International Labour Organization, n.d. *Workplace well-being*. [Online] Available at: www.ilo.org/safework/areasofwork/workplace-health-promotion-and-well-being/WCMS_118396/lang--en/index.htm [Accessed 8 January 2020].

Jarvenpaa, S. L. & Lang. K. R., 2005. Managing the paradoxes of mobile technology. *Information Systems Management*, Fall 2005, pp. 7–23.

Johnson, B., 1996. *Polarity management: Identifying and managing unsolvable problems*. Amherst, MA: HRD Press, Inc.

Jones, O., 2019. *Woke-washing: How brands are cashing in on the culture wars*. [Online] Available at: www.theguardian.com/media/2019/may/23/woke-washing-brands-cashing-in-on-culture-wars-owen-jones [Accessed 12 March 2020].

Jones, H., 2020. *Barclays installs 'Big Brother boxes' that monitor when staff have breaks*. [Online] Available at: www.metro.co.uk/2020/02/20/barclays-installs-big-brother-boxes-monitor-staff-breaks-12272711/ [Accessed 21 February 2020].

Kets de Vries, M. F. R., 1995. *Organizational paradoxes: Clinical approaches to management*. 2nd ed London: Routledge.

Lewis, M. W., 2000. Exploring paradox: Toward a more comprehensive guide. *Academy of Management Review*, 25(4), pp. 760–776.

Luscher, L. S. & Lewis, M. W., 2008. Organizational change and managerial sensemaking: Working through paradox. *Academy of Management Journal*, 51(2), pp. 221–240.

Malmo University, 2019. *Work meetings have an unwarranted bad reputation*. [Online] Available at: www.mau.se/en/news/work-meetings-have-an-unwarranted-bad-reputation/ [Accessed 2 March 2020].

Marriage, M., 2019. *Big consultancies struggle to close the gender pay gap*. [Online] Available at: www.ft.com/content/c8118e14-143e-11e9-a168-d45595ad076d [Accessed 29 January 2020].

Maton, K., 2014. Habitus. In: M. Grenfell, ed. *Pierre Bourdieu: Key concepts*. Abingdon: Routledge, pp. 48–64.

Moody-McNamara, J. & Higgins, J., 2020. *How to unlock potential and created a talented pipeline of senior women leaders*, London: Brilliant Women/Gameshift.

Morgan, G., 2006. *Images of organization*. Thousand Oaks, CA: Sage.

Mowles, C., 2015. *Managing in uncertainty: Complexity and the paradoxes of everyday organizational life*. Abingdon, Oxon: Routledge.

Neider, L. L. & Schriesheim, C. A., 2011. The Authentic Leadership Inventory (ALI): Development and empirical tests. *The Leadership Quarterly*, 22(6), pp. 1146–1164.

Surveillance Studies Network, 2006. *A report on the surveillance society – The full report*, London: Information Commissioner's Office (ICO).

O'Mahoney, J. & Sturdy, A., 2015. *Power and the diffusion of management ideas: The case of McKinsey*. [Online] Available at: www.orca.cf.ac.uk/73610/ [Accessed 29 January 2020].

Oshrey, B., 1994. *In the middle*. Boston, MA: Power + Systems.

Perlow, L. A., Noonan Hadley, C. & Eun, E., 2017. Stop the meeting madness: How to free up time for meaningful work. *Harvard Business Review*, 95(4), pp. 62–69.

Ray, C. A., 1986. Corporate culture: The last frontier of control? *Journal of Management Studies*, 23, pp. 287–297.

Reitz, M. & Higgins, J., 2019. *Speak up: Say what needs to be said and hear what needs to be heard*. Harlow: FT Pearson.

Reyes, J. & Kleiner, B., 1990. How to establish an organisational purpose. *Management Decision*, 28(7) pp. 51–54.

Rogelberg, S. G. et al., 2010. Employee satisfaction with meetings: A contemporary facet of job satisfaction. *Human Resource Management*, 49(2), pp. 149–172.

Romano, P. & Stone, R., 1947/1972. *The American worker*. 3rd ed. Detroit: Bewick Editions.

Rost, J. C., 1993. *Leadership for the 21st Century*. Westport, CT: Praeger.

Schlachter, S., McDowall, A., Cropley, M. & Inceoglu, I., 2018. Voluntary work-related technology use during non-work time: A narrative synthesis of empirical research and research agenda. *International Journal of Management Reviews*, 20, pp. 825–846.

Siregar, C., 2018. *What is Total Football? Famous tactics explained: the clubs, countries & players to use it*. [Online] Available at: www.goal.com/en-us/news/what-is-total-football-famous-tactics-explained-the-clubs/w5yd-5dzofn4p17ewmav4atk2b [Accessed 13 March 2020].

Smith, K. K. & Berg, D. N., 1987. *Paradoxes of group life: understanding conflict, paralysis, and movement in group dynamics*. San Francisco: Jossey-Bass Publishers.

Sorensen, R. & Sainsbury, M., 2020. The number of unknown paradoxes. *Philosophy*, 95(372), pp. 155–159.

Stacey, K. & Romei, V., 2020. *US and UK hospitals vulnerable to surge in virus cases.* [Online] Available at: www.ft.com/content/effdodae-655f-11ea-b3f3-fe4680ea68b5 [Accessed 14 December 2020].

Stacey, R., Griffin, D. & Shaw, P., 2000. *Complexity and management: Fad or radical challenge to systems thinking?* London: Routledge.

Stefano, M. D., 2020. *BBC under fire over consultancy hired to tackle gender pay gap.* [Online] Available at: www.ft.com/content/79354020-386d-11ea-a6d3-9a26f8c3cba4 [Accessed 30 January 2020].

Stogdill, R. M., 1974. *Handbook of leadership: A survey of theory and research.* New York: Free Press.

Stutzer, A. & Frey, B. S., 2004. *Stress that doesn't pay: The commuting paradox,* Bonn: Forschunginstitut zur Zukunft der Arbeit/Institute for the Study of Labour.

The Right Conversation Ltd, 2020. *Speaking truth to power.* [Online] Available at: www.therightconversation.co.uk/speaking-truth-to-power [Accessed 30 January 2020].

Timmins, N., 2016. *The chief executive's tale: Views from the front line of the NHS,* London: The King's Fund/NHS Providers.

Waldman, D. A., Putnam, L. L., Miron-Spektor, E. & Siegel, D., 2019. The role of paradox theory in decision making and management research. *Organizational Behaviour and Human Decision Processes.*

Waters, R., 2020. *How staff came to question Google culture.* [Online] Available at: www.ft.com/content/86b00e9a-33a1-11ea-a329-obcf87a328f2 [Accessed 7 February 2020].

Willmott, H., 1993. Strength is ignorance; slavery is freedom: Managing culture in modern organisations. *Journal of Management Studies,* 30(4), pp. 515–552.

Wright, S., 2004. Culture in anthropology and organizational settings. In: S. Wright, ed. *Anthropology of organisations.* London: Routledge, pp. 1–31.

Young, T., 2019. *The rise of the woke corporation.* [Online] Available at: www.spectator.co.uk/article/the-rise-of-the-woke-corporation [Accessed 12 March 2020].

Zappos, 2020. *Zappos 10 core values.* [Online] Available at: www.zapposinsights.com/about/core-values?utm_campaign=newsroom&utm_medium=about-us&utm_source=what-we-live-by&utm_content=our-core-values [Accessed 7 February 2020].

3

THE SIX MYTHS OF MANAGEMENT (THINKING)

The key themes of this chapter are:

- How we think about the world shapes our actions and to find better actions means paying attention to our taken-for-granted habits of mind
- How we have thought about the organisational world, and its management and leadership, in recent decades will not help us address the consequences that thinking in this way has brought about
- Our thinking has for the most part become overly-simplistic, persistently mechanistic and reductionist when it comes to understanding how people create and experience the reality of their working lives
- Our management 'common sense' has become management 'nonsense' as we've disappeared power and stripped out the subjective, emotional, and relational experience of working life – much of the edifice of managerial thinking is consequently built on impersonal sand
- Because managers and leaders in health and social care believe wholeheartedly that their work is guided by good intentions, they go about

DOI: 10.4324/9781003035015-3

their work believing their impact must be good (which doesn't necessarily follow)

- The scientific method of thinking has been applied to aspects of human life where it doesn't apply such as the ethical, personal, inter-personal, and social

In terms of the alternative recommendations for how people think and act at work we identify the following areas:

- Slow down and inquire more... and cut back on the rush to premature advocacy and superficial solutions
- Stop senior people from thinking they know best and running into the familiar arms of the above... embrace the frustrations and messiness of collective inquiry
- Dial down the cult of measurement... and question the use of the word 'objective' every time you or others use it
- Work with the realities of power and hierarchy rather than wishing them away – they play out whether you want them to or not
- Engage with the unique challenges presented by working with sick and vulnerable people – and the existential challenge of facing into the reality of mortality every day

In terms of the key sources of analysis and thinking we have drawn on, the following are important touchstones when it comes to identifying the current situation and what an alternative way of leading and being might look like. You won't go far wrong by tracking them and/or their work down:

- Paul Watzlawick... who offers us a way out of the stuck thinking that plays out in simply doing more of the same sort of thinking that has got us stuck in our current intellectual cul-de-sac
- David Bohm... and what it takes for us to step away from the tyranny of advocacy and embrace the possibility of knowing the world differently when we let go of our attachment to our rightness
- Ron Heifetz... who provides a framing that provides a constructive challenge to our attachment to overly mechanistic thinking in complex and dynamic social settings

- George Binney... and his reports from the frontline of healthcare deci-sion making and how the behemoth of formal change management has grown out of control in a world shaped by decisions mired in the blood and guts of Politics
- Kathleen King... who is out there trying to get people to take relation-ships seriously and step out of the excesses of individual agency and a belief that people can exist outside of the relationships they are part of
- Alison Reynolds... who has re-popularised the notion of the 'tyranny of the tangible' and how our ways of measuring and knowing the world lock us into a very impoverished, and at times actively mislead-ing, understanding of how the world works
- Megan Reitz... and her work into speaking truth to power, how senior leaders are not as well informed as they'd like to think they are and how they curate what does and doesn't get said to them, especially when they are unaware of how scary others may well find them to be
- Amy Edmondson... who pulls at a loose thread of much modern man-agement theory which advocates chaotic and relationally destructive actions without stopping to count the cost in terms of psychological safety (and which might explain why the learning organisation is rarer than the fabled unicorn)
- Reg Revans... the father of Action Learning, who is the forgotten guru sitting on the celestial side-lines as the world continues to pour resources into largely useless set-piece programmes, designed and delivered apart from people's day-to-day realities
- Lars Volmer... who called out much of what goes on in modern work-places for what it is, play acting... people performing in the theatre of business

3.1 Setting the scene for the six myths and why challenging them can be unpopular

... telling people who are devoting their lives to improving care that action and improvement does not work... [it's] a tough sell.

(Anon, December 2019)

John presented an early iteration of the myths at a workshop attended by the person who subsequently sent him an email from which the

earlier-mentioned quote comes. Challenging these myths and their individual and collective shortcomings results in an unsettling assessment of
how fit for purpose our current habits of thought are, because however
much John wants to sugar-coat the message, the conclusion is bleak – or at
least it is for those who are invested in the intellectual and organisational
status quo, who have spent much of their working lives assuming that what
they are doing is of use.

Those who have devoted their lives to taking action within the current
frame of reference (with the emphasis on being seen to 'do' something and
not taking too long, or thinking about the wider system) and whose intention
is to improve what gets provided to people across the health and social care
world, often see themselves as part of a noble, self-sacrificing tradition. This
has much in common with the heroic Stakhanovite movement of the early
years of the Soviet era. To question the purpose or meaningfulness of such
enormous endeavour might well be too much to bear, as TS Eliot has put it
in Burnt Norton: 'Humankind cannot bear very much reality' (Eliot, 2001) and
facing into the futility of well-meant effort might be an unbearable truth.

There is also an entire industry that has grown up around the myths,
that give them a sense of rightness and 'truthiness', justifying the long
hours, bureaucracy and hollowed out lives away from work that result.
This industry sustains considerable levels of busyness and activity and may
on occasions result in people experiencing glimmers of light. Often these
glimmers may be phantasms, but people still like to go along to the endless
awards ceremonies and celebrations of 'transformational' work – hiding
their eyes from the possibility (even probability) that much of their work is
now no more than the theatre of business (Vollmer, 2016), where everyone
is doing a second unpaid job of 'managing other people's impressions of
them, showing themselves to their best advantage, playing politics… hiding their uncertainties' (Kegan & Lahey, 2016, p. 1).

People can sense they are living a lie; they know that so many things in
human affairs are literally beyond our control but are having constantly to
pretend that – and to be seen to act as if – they all are. Holden Caulfield, the
anti-hero of Catcher in the Rye, delighted in his adolescent angst to condemn
those around him as phonies – and yet that is precisely what we have
become in contemporary society.

As part of a research study into the experience of the most junior people in the health system, John came across a project about to be launched

addressing the under-representation of black and minority ethnic (BAME) staff at senior levels. The project had gone through the standard project planning process, found itself a sponsor, and was in the process of identifying the drivers of the problem and the measures to be tracked. A knotty, deeply rooted social pattern, with links into generations of discrimination, imperialism, and persistent patterns of in-group/out-group identity formation reframed into a mechanistic root-cause analysis diagram. The project has good intentions, but we are willing to bet it will achieve little when framed in such a simplistic and mechanistic manner – much as well-intentioned public policies to eliminate all forms of discrimination achieve only glacial rates of social change. This imposition of structure reassures people, especially senior leaders and those charged with taking 'action', that something is being done. Meanwhile such approaches end up distancing the project from the lived experiences of those involved, turning rich human voices conveying emotional stories into dreary and gratingly mechanical 'analyses' that meet the criteria of the tools in question.

This naivety, whether deliberate or not, reflects a lack of philosophical rigour within the management tradition especially when applied to the setting of health and social care. Workplaces are littered with trite assertions of how things need to be done and an unproblematic advocacy of particular world views which try and avoid ethical contention. Yet, as Reynolds et al. seek to show, ethical statements should provoke a sense of tension, of something that needs to be held and grappled with, not resolved or turned into generic statements of general niceness – which is what most statements of organisational values and purpose turn into (Reynolds, et al., 2020).

At the same time the ahistorical nature of much workplace analysis strips it of any breadth or depth of understanding of the situation being grappled with – whether it is to do with how people deal with knowledge of their mortality, which is beyond our capacity to cope with when looked at directly (Becker, 1997), or the way that women have been demonised by western culture for millennia, as explored by Mary Beard in one of her recent pieces (Beard, 2018). Simply making public statements of 'zero tolerance' achieves little except pushing the problem underground – or being a manifestation of the problem in the first place. Making a hectoring and inflexible statement of 'zero tolerance' towards bullying and harassment simply demonstrates the bullying culture in action.

Meanwhile the ground breaking work by Isabel Menzies Lyth from the 1950s (Menzies, 1960) keeps being lost, rediscovered, and lost again as intellectual rationalism tries to disappear the all but impossible emotional burden being carried by those who work in organisations in general – and within health and social care in particular. We live in a time when there is a general expectation that the NHS CEO who meets the husband and son to tell them that their mother did not die because of her illness, but because the ventilator wasn't switched on for nine minutes, will move smoothly on to their next management appointment soon afterwards[1].

Then there were the meetings of staff involved in dealing with the grief of treating desperately ill premature babies and their distressed and distressing families; meetings where chairs were being thrown around and it was initially hoped that such unprofessional behaviours could be resolved by some basic 'agenda management'. Step forward the legion of consultants who offer 'facilitation' skills to dampen down such issues on behalf of managers, by adopting best practice for meetings, as developed in sectors where the work lacks such charged human factors (Lubitsh & Higgins, 2001). If it works at Tesco's surely it must be relevant to the premature baby unit of a major hospital? Please note that last sentence was written with heavy sarcasm, which might not always come across.

Never mind its prevailing emotional and relational illiteracy, the management tradition has been very poor at looking at the thought processes that create the world we experience, instead preferring to focus on a seemingly unproblematic external world which exists outside and apart from ourselves, which we have no responsibility for bringing into being and which has a life independent of our participation in it. As noted in the citation offered at the beginning of this chapter, David Bohm attempted to challenge all of the above back in the 1960s, briefly re-popularising the importance of paying attention to the headwaters of our thinking, but to date his recommendation has had little impact.

Asking people to pay attention to the headwaters of their thinking is not a popular activity, it is dismissed as impractical because it doesn't fit within a world view which views all situations as amenable to a simple diagnosis and rapid solution, which is why staying busy dealing with the downstream consequences of headwater thinking feels so much more satisfying. In fact, satisfying in this instance is without doubt a misnomer; it might be better to declare that it is rated *satisfactory* (given a four out of five star rating) within the realms of a generalised corporate culture – discernible across the globe from Berlin to Beijing – wherein action is privileged specifically where it can be seen to be 'measurable'.

Or it is written-off as theoretical – because we have lost the discipline to notice how our lives are lived through a lens of unacknowledged theory. We would argue that everything is praxis, an interwoven world of practice and theory. To those of us of a social constructionist bent what counts as real, what we notice in the world as worthy of attention comes about through an encultured and learnt habit of mind not because of an 'objective', external reality. Whenever you read something or hear someone use a word like 'natural' when describing human habits, be aware some ideological belief is being hidden in plain sight.

The vast majority of the management consulting industry does not work with this social constructionist bent and instead works with the world of the apparently external, socially independent data. Insight in that benighted industry typically starts by the formulation of a testable hypothesis, a methodological trick that repurposes the scientific method used to study chemicals in a laboratory into the social world of contested ethical and epistemological perspectives. It ignores, or wishes away, a social world where '..."society" is not an objective reality – period. It is a reality created by all people through their consciousness' (Bohm, 1996, p. 88).

In this chapter we will explore what we see as the headwaters of our collective thinking about organisations which we claim lock us into largely trivial busyness and serves the needs of those who live for busyness and profit from it – even at the cost of their soul (or humanity for those of you uncomfortable with such enduring but intangible notions). If we don't pay attention to these headwaters, we will be condemned to a frenzy of dealing with their downstream consequences, getting busier and busier, with busyness becoming an end in itself. An insight which led at least one group of sober academics to subtitle their latest book 'How to lead in today's crazy world of organisations' (Binney, et al., 2017). They gave it this particular, provocative title 'prompted by a chief executive who, in a candid moment, told us that his job was to work with the "bonkers" – to make sense of an insane world; to do a good job against the odds' (Binney, et al., 2017, p. 1). Within the health and social care sector this busyness has a particular pathology, with a focus on endless measurement, a giant and critically unquestioned addiction to endless audit, based on a heroic belief that more inspection (in a largely pseudo-scientific form) is always the answer.

Paying attention to headwaters is also unfashionable within the literature on leadership. When we approached a more traditionally pragmatic publisher with our proposal the feedback suggested that work of this nature was popular ten years ago – they also suggested that it also only really sold well when promoted or endorsed by a celebrity. Sadly, our attempts to entice Ed Sheeran and one of the Kardashians (any of which would do, in the cultural quagmire in which we find ourselves) into becoming our co-authors fell on stony ground. Maybe we should have gone for Taylor Swift.

It is hard work to prevent everything being turned into a simplistic 'how-to' book that such exemplars could endorse. These books are full of top tips and key messages. One author we both admire was deeply frustrated by how her intention not to write a 'how to' leadership book, slowly morphed into just that over the life of its writing, editing, and marketing. When it comes to incorporating subtle and sophisticated insights even Doctoral students fear what is expected of them and what might come of their work. When John was working with a Turkish student keen to incorporate his Sufi practice into his corporate leadership, the student remained fearful of how he might trivialise it, how it could be taken out of context and turned into yet another management fad in the style of the Tao of Leadership (Heider, 2015).

3.2 What are the six myths that create the seemingly unbreakable boundaries of our management and leadership thinking?

We consider there to be at least six myths making-up the headwaters of management thinking that create these unbreakable boundaries – and they are:

- **All is fixable** – we live in a consequence free world, where solutions to all situations exist, where pills and modern medicine, technology, the market, new so-called 'thought leadership', and a battery of management techniques, will be a *deus ex machina* (or *deus ex McKinsey*) stepping in to make everything better. This fictional certainty encourages leaders to ignore the messy complexity of the here and now and instead focus on the dream of a visionary tomorrow. Advocacy dominates inquiry. Action, especially fast action, trumps understanding.

- **Perfection is the only state worth pursuing** – idealism and the pursuit of 'world class' operating models dominate the leadership discourse. 'Good enough' and contextual realities have been abandoned in the face of an ideal which is being permanently recast. Perpetual revolution and reinvention have become the new normal. We are consumed by the 'innovator's dilemma', yearning for that breakthrough in terms of newness that will disrupt our markets and catapult us into the lead (Christensen, 2000). Perfection co-exists, of course, as a part of fixability: it can only truly be fixed if it's seen to be perfect.
- **There is just one true way of doing things** – bleeding through from the (Newtonian/Material) scientific method is an unfortunate belief that social systems can be reduced to a mechanistic model of cause and effect, where a single approach to knowing the world can be identified as an 'objective' truth. This is further fuelled by a belief that all approaches need to and can be scalable and replicable – resulting in local realities being trashed and everything being recast in terms of the lowest common denominator of what can be seen as the same. This bleeds into the game of piloting, where the pilot is an experiment that tests a hypothesis and if, in the precise moment of piloting there is a positive outcome, then the hypothesis is proven and the steps of the 'experiment' become a process or a method for delivering that outcome. Most of which is unsupported by our day-to-day experience of the lived world. Commensurability is all and that which is non-commensurable irrelevant.
- **Metrics reflect an objective reality** – modern management is in the grip of the 'tyranny of the tangible' (Reynolds, et al., 2020) and now lives with the consequences of reporting systems which have little connection to the lived experience of customers, patients, and employees. Measurement has become a lousy master rather than a useful tool. Metrics prevail because they allow management practice to ape the so-called 'scientific method'. They also create a simulation of reality wherein those measurements can be bent and stretched into shapes that seem, to those who buy into this fiction, to show the fixability, perfection, and speed of change that corporate life craves. Changing the numbers is always much easier than engaging with the complexity of meaningful workplace reconfiguration.
- **Values bind the organisation** – they don't. They may bind the executive team and keep their competitive instincts in check. For people

involved in the primary task of an organisation abstract values have little meaning in comparison to the lived experience of what actually gets valued in the here and now. However, the corporate values encroach upon them as hoops through which they are expected to jump: job applicants are asked to demonstrate their understanding of an organisation's values and their individual and entirely hypothetical capacity to apply them in practice as part of the selection process. That process offers no space or opportunity for a candidate to outline the values – individual or social – that motivate them as a human being; it is solely about whether they can absorb the Orwellian Newspeak of the companies' carefully crafted values.

• **'We're all in this together'** – workplaces are political systems where individuals and groups have distinctive priorities and interests. The excessive advocacy and policing of compliance to a single narrative fuels an underground culture, where difference is fought out in the shadows and cannot be acknowledged, sustaining the chasm between espoused and actual experiences of leadership. This myth allows people to indulge the illusion that resistance has evaporated from the workplace, when more diligent and thoughtful writers seek to remind us that it persists, even amidst the idea that organisations are more akin to 'happy families' than spaces in which we constantly contest our positions (Fleming, 2014).

We are mindful of the observation of one systems thinker from the late 1960s that the whole business of management is itself a myth, particularly when we allow ourselves to consider who might be thought to be a 'good' leader, when so much in life is complex and contingent (Churchman, 1968, pp. 17–29). But we are more interested in the ways in which the myths we outlined earlier shape and constrain thinking and practice. Let us now explore them in turn in a bit more depth before moving onto our suggestions as to what an alternative form of understanding would make possible.

3.3 The first myth: all is fixable

There is no situation, no problem, that cannot be made better. In the mid 1990s John found himself working in New York and was fascinated by a series of TV ads for some medicine or other. They spoke of the two traditional aspects of the human condition that none of us can avoid, namely Death and Taxes… the smooth talking, purposeful male voiceover said with a definitive, downward voice-trained inflection that 'We're working on the first one' i.e. death is optional, a conceit that has already been nicely skewered (Gray, 2012). This sense of boundlessness is played out in popular culture, with everyone being urged to live the dream of being what they want to be. There is no condition that can't be sorted out by pills, free markets, or technology.

When it comes to health, there are the repeated press images of people protesting outside children's hospitals when those derided experts are seen to be wilfully refusing to use the miracle of modern medicine to 'save' some dreadfully ill child. Those parents and families being ill-served by the ideology which has promised them nothing is beyond being managed, but the terrible reality of their experience runs counter to this. It is small surprise, in light of what was promised – that they felt denied access and so ended up in hostile demonstrations which alienate them from those who would do what they could to help them.

Health technology keeps pushing on, drawing out the half-life that many elderly people have to stumble through – an experience that left John in a sustained state of impotent fury, as he watched his mother die slowly over 19 years, following a series of strokes and related conditions. His brother, a vet, would have been struck off if he'd allowed any other sort of animal to endure the suffering that the miracle of modern medicine put their mother through. This is not to deny that older people have a right to enjoy their twilight years, but it does challenge the notion that consumes most of us that longevity, in and of itself, is to be a sought-after state – and that it ought magically to be guaranteed for us all, regardless of the condition in which we find ourselves.

Meanwhile we struggle to integrate this popularised expectation of a consequence free life with the existential crises that loom larger and larger, be that in terms of carbon emissions fuelling manmade climate change or the unregulated use of penicillin leading to a growing reduction in the efficacy of anti-biotics and the return of health risks thought to have been consigned to history. The writing of this book has also taken place in the shadow of the return of the global pandemic, perhaps the most profound jolt to the belief system that we have allowed to achieve dominance in the period since the end of the Second World War. It has starkly shown us that the 'fixability' upon which we have built our modern lives is illusory;

neither technology nor present medical knowledge was able to 'fix' it in the way we have come to expect, although regimes of treatment are markedly improved and vaccines have been rapidly trialled – ahead of what will inevitably be not so much a roll-out of a product guaranteed to 'fix' things as the myth suggests but more akin to a global trial.

Patently, this frame of mind undergirds society at large – and so is obviously to be found in our organisational lives. The application of some method or understanding is seen to allow us to fix a range of problems, such as illness and death. The present COVID 19 crisis illustrates this exceptionally well, with myriad reactions built on a sense of incredulity that this blight cannot merely be 'scienced' away. Denial and resistance have appeared as key reactions to the fact that we have finally run out of road with the great fiction of everything yielding to the God-like power of humankind. As one anarchist commentator so pithily expressed it,

> The Black Death or bubonic plague of 1348–1350 was perhaps the worst pandemic in history, killing up to a third of Europe's population, and possibly more than that in Asia and North Africa, where records are lacking. It was not the first pandemic, and Covid-19 will not be the last. Psychologically, this one may be the worst yet – we are better at denying our mortality than our medieval ancestors were. The omnipresence of unpredictable death forces us to remember that we're all mortal.
>
> (Martin, 2020)

And leaders reproduce this fiction that there is always a ready solution to whatever the world throws at us in their organisational practices.

What lies unexamined is the thought, the habit of thinking, that has created this world; how the language of being able to 'fix' things is rooted in a mechanistic world view or metaphor (Morgan, 2006). It also plays out in terms of two approaches to how people engage with and understand the world around them – firstly it results in people seeing the world and how to change it as a technical exercise, to use the language of Heifetz who distinguished between simple technical change and the more socially complicated adaptive change (Heifetz, 1994). In the realm of technical change, the world can be changed as easily as replacing a SIM card. Everything is plug and play, as in the film *The Matrix*, where knowledge and skill are things that can be downloaded at will – a model of learning now playing out more widely in many classrooms and corporate online curricula where the contextual nature of most learning is disappeared in place of simplistic, right-answer, content.

Secondly, and wrapped up in seeing the world as a machine which can be technocratically managed, we become stuck in a particular form of what has been described as Type 1 change, where the only approaches to management and change that are acceptable are those that fit within the consensus of what passes as 'common sense' (Watzlawick, et al., 1974/2011). We can therefore only address the negative consequences of mechanistic, technocratic thinking by thinking about them in a mechanistic, technocratic way. To think about them in any other way is wrong, according to the institutionally approved ways of going about management work. There is a need for people to step out of this self-limiting bind of Type 1 thinking by embracing Type 2 change, which involves engaging with the world in a way that seems non-sensical according to the reason of the prevailing, Type 1 orthodoxy (Watzlawick, et al., 1974/2011).

The idea of 'fixability' prevails in every corner of human existence – and has inveigled itself into our day–to-day practice through our diminished capacity for critical thinking, for paying attention to not only what we think but how we think about our thinking. It originates in the ideas bundled together under the general title of 'Enlightenment' thinking, such as an inescapable progress based on the application of reason. While these two notions of 'progress' and 'reason' share the same point of origin they now appear to confound one another: initially, reason offered us scientific development, which in turn was seen to lead inexorably to social progress... but now we are left with science without reason, which looks more like a religion – and a religion not subjected to any form of critical thought. The ideology seems simple: humankind conquered the world – and so will continue to do so. Progress is inevitable: we just have to sit back and wait for it.

Consequently people feel content to disregard all of the public health messages we're all familiar with around diet, managing your relationship with alcohol, and not smoking, not because they don't recognise how bad choices in these regards will impact them but on the basis of a delusion that the heart attack, the stroke, or the 'vulgar little tumour' that Uncle Monty describes as his likely nemesis (Dickinson, 1987) will be fixed by medical science. This has led to a medical defensiveness – Mark vividly recalls the

15 minutes that an ophthalmologist spent with his 80 year old father, out-lining statistical possibilities arising from a cataract repair on the basis of obtaining 'informed consent' – and to the upturn in litigation that we have seen in health care, where those that aren't fixable demand compensation for the fact that fixability has turned out to be a fiction – or that attempts at fixability did not deliver or, indeed, made things worse.

This attitude bleeds into our economic lives. Business leaders have actively embraced this notion, in part to justify their own position and merit. If we concede that not everything is fixable, that each and every challenge in a business context cannot be managed in the way the manage-ment consultancies, business schools, and technique peddlers would want us to believe – then we need to rethink what is meant by corporate man-agement and leadership. But those in such positions resist this by retreating into a defensive position. After all, how does one justify drawing down a comparatively eye-wateringly large salary if you can't show that the actions you take impact and improve upon the challenges faced in organisations on a day-to-day basis?

What then happens is the telling of a complicated story which bears a passing resemblance to the reality of our workplace existence but is not meaningfully linked to it. This reproduction of our supposed experience is generated by the interaction and mutual reinforcement of a wide range of artefacts, embracing corporate visions, missions, objectives, values, strate-gies, operational plans, project plans, key performance indicators...and all the other ephemera with which the management class busies itself in order to sustain the story and their central role in it. In something akin to a *folie a deux* or, less charitably, a wilful attempt at hegemony by the managerial class at large – this is the only way in which organisations are allowed to be understood or through which ideas about organising can be expressed.

It is in this ideological space that the myth of fixability sustains itself. A clerk can change a cell of a spreadsheet from amber to green and add some fabricated commentary to validate that action. Anyone who has cheerlessly worked through a risk register will know this action; it can even be supplemented by a corollary of putting some sort of score or rating against it, drawn from a carefully crafted matrix. Hey presto, the risk is 'mitigated' – and the leaders in the organisation can be reassured that by their action something in the organisation has been fixed. In this case, we can see the supposed capacity to initiate or engender change merely as an act of hubris, or narrative inflation, with the author of the story promoting themselves into a leading role.

3.4 The second myth: perfection is the only state worth pursuing

'Let's start with a blank sheet of paper' is an invitation to imagine a perfect world. It seems such an uncomplicated suggestion and yet it is riddled with assumptions, the most notable of which is that there is such a thing as a 'blank sheet of paper'. It invites people to disappear those aspects of the current reality that will persist and which shape how the world will play out, in particular it hides how power in all its forms will inform what gets written or drawn onto the blank sheet and what is going on underneath the blank sheet. Hence, the paper is supposedly blank – yet the invitation to start writing carries with it a sense of somebody assuming a directive role, requesting people to make their mark on the sheet.

Moreover, in so many instances where this exercise is used, the pen is held by one person: sometimes it's the person in the group who is seen to be the most powerful; occasionally, that powerful person transfers their power to someone deemed to be neutral, such as a 'facilitator'; sometimes it is a person in the group who wants to assume the mantle of power; and there are instances when everyone in the group is seemingly invited to 'share' the pen, sketching things out on post-its or something similar, which are then appended to a blank sheet of flip chart paper.

The blank sheet is also an invitation into a world of the Platonic ideal, with the assumption that there is some world outside of the one we know which speaks to a more permanent and enduring truth. The world of organisational writers and practitioners is filled with such ideas, with the heroic idealisation of one form of structure over another, in recent years this has included 6-Sigma management, the Teal holocracy, and the Deliberately Developmental Organization (DDO). These are, of course, grand narratives built around something akin to a utopian vision. They tend in that sense immediately to bisect their audiences into those who object to this direction of travel and those content to quaff the Kool Aid. But, as poststructuralist thought has helpfully revealed for us in its analysis of political ideologies, the reality of the realisation of those utopias can often be the creation of a hell on earth.

Some might say that these shifts in the way in which organisations seek to shape themselves in a way that embraces the idea of progress can be seen to be disingenuous – but also might be argued to be politically prefigurative, in terms of intimating at a deeper level what real human organising might look like. In exploring what this double-coding looks like in practice, the following important observation is made: 'Organizations, from cutting-edge innovators to military bureaucracies, appear increasingly paradoxical – at one embracing self-managed teams and visionary leadership, while also grasping for ever-wider control over every feature of an organization, particularly its employees. It is in this grey area of control and autonomy that we suggest the insights of anarchism might have the most potential' (Wierman, et al., 2020, pp. 36–37). These authors also helpfully steer us past the hyperbole of these supposedly new organisational forms and outline people's experiences of their significant limitations and obfuscations.

This was very personally revealed to us both at a presentation offered by a colleague about their experience of an organisation that had embraced the idea of the DDO – and taken it to some uncomfortable and to us disturbing conclusions. She described the company Next Jump (which we have already had a stab at exploring), a capitalist concern that revelled in a culture that reeked of Maoism. Building on the popular but largely conceptual notion of the growth mindset (Dweck, 2017), Next Jump's interpretation of being a DDO appears to involve offering employees stretch opportunities (which looked to us like exploitation in terms of extended workload and expectations of a commitment to the company far in excess of what might ordinarily be expected); establishing electronic means of real-time feedback delivery on every worker by those with whom they work (which looks like a super-surveillant system that would not look out of place in a totalitarian political regime); and remediation of performance shortcomings through coaching or training (an approach that calls to mind the re-education efforts so warmly embraced throughout the history of the Chinese Communist Party).

Next Jump put what looks at first glance to be a lot of 'warm and fuzzy' sentiments on their website about being a DDO, to the extent that it is difficult to work out what it is that the company actually does in the economy other than promote the notion of DDOs (Next Jump, 2020). It boils down to physical, emotional, mental, and spiritual 'training' opportunities, the listing of which looks to suggest something more like a cult than a company, as perhaps suggested by the employee responses captured on the Glassdoor website, which have been used to develop the critique of the firm offered above. Just 31% of those respondents would recommend the company to others – and, on the basis of 184 responses, the company was given an overall star rating of just 2.3 out of 5 (Glassdoor, 2020). To our minds, the commentary offered by respondents to be found alongside these metrics makes particularly depressing reading.

Looking at the pursuit of perfection as a form of personal heroism, those who are judged by popular opinion (or in their own eyes) to be successful organisational leaders, from Jack Welch (Slater, 1999) and an offer of 'insights and secrets', to Richard Branson offering a grindingly dull 600 odd pages of brazen self-promotion, replete with leonine wind-swept portrait on the cover (Branson, 2011), their biographies and auto-biographies are held up as exemplars of the perfect form of organisational leadership, perfect heroes. A specific critique of this narcissistic and indi-vidualistic form of heroism has already been helpfully rehearsed (Higgins, et al., 2017), although that work falls into the trap of replacing one form of narcissism with another one, in this case something more humanistic. However, whilst 'thought leaders' offer checklists and templates, the dei-fied entrepreneur or corporate leader uses their own life story as a model for others to marvel at and possibly emulate. They offer something akin to a vision of a perfect way of being in the specific context of business – and the idea of an individual reflexively finding their own way through their own life course is overshadowed by the idea that there is a perfect map to be unquestioningly followed.

Meanwhile the industry of benchmarking frequently assumes some form of progression towards an ideal form, the perfect business or oper-ating model towards which all should aim. As a consequence, whatever is going on in the here and now is seen through a deficit lens, defined in terms of how it is not perfect, how it is not as good as it should be. By focusing on the ideal form, the reality of the present gets dismissed or is only understood through what is missing. A recent commentary on corporate life highlighted what the authors called the Moscow 1935 effect (Binney, et al., 2017), where anyone seeking to navigate the city had to rely on a combination of the map of how the city would look when it had achieved its perfect design (then predicted for 1945) or what it used to look like prior to the revolution in 1917, an analysis that drew on a rich analysis of Soviet culture (Brooks, 2000).

This escape into the idealised future is also a mechanism for disappearing the current political reality, the power politics of existing organisational practice. Because in the future all will be for the best, in this the best of all possible worlds, there is no need to pay attention to how power is currently being exercised to privilege one group or way of knowing over another. The dictatorship of the proletariat was subtly appropriated by the old Soviet regime, much as the end of history in the perfection of liberal democracy was erroneously predicted (Fukuyama, 2020). Moreover, that state of perfection, the utopia promised by a McKinsey-type model, or by a dense dollop of business school 'research', or a pilot success that must be disseminated, or by the life history of some titan of industry – can be eternally deferred, thereby preserving the status quo whilst promising jam tomorrow, if only the right approach to fixability can be designed.

It might be reasonably suggested that these two myths – the idea of fixability and that of the pursuit of perfection – could be seen as both complimentary and in dramatic tension with one another. Can something be fixed without a perfect solution? Or will the constant striving for the most elegant solution to an issue simply allow for fixability to be deferred? We suspect they feed on one another and constrain a more critical way of thinking about our challenges: there is no problem that cannot be fixed...and there is likely to be a perfect method for doing that, even if that status is only temporary. The next big thing – as promoted by whomsoever – assumes the mantle of perfection until such time as a new big thing appears.

We are not arguing the perfect solution is being tested and found wanting in practice. For us the case is that perfection does not exist in the real world but solely in the febrile atmosphere of business thinking and policy design. The perfect solution never gets implemented but it does get supplanted by the new perfection, rarely does it disappear by being applied in real life and found wanting. Hence leadership thinking and practice is fiercely bounded by the notion that everything can be fixed – and that the only possible response to something that needs to be fixed is perfection. This pincer movement of mythology denies the leader any outlet for thinking and experimentation that extends beyond these conceptual precepts.

In all of this, what gets disappeared is how what counts as an ideal future is in turn created in the image of the prevailing truth-power conventions, that we can only see what we have been conditioned by our past and present to see. For idealists who disagree with this idea of the co-existing relationship between past, present, and future, the ideal future is seen as existing apart from the present and the past, which in turn creates a highly problematic challenge when people begin to plan how to move on from the benighted present. Since the present is to be discarded as less than perfect, and the past as simply a forgettable journey now completed, so there is no continuity between the present and the future and there is little to be built on or valued. It is a wholly achronological approach to the warp and weft of lived human experience and the social construction of knowledge through its course. To an extent, it also speaks to our contemporary obsession with 'newness' and the supposed significance of novelty in all that we think and do.

Within a world of ceaseless technological advancement, and where organisational form is overly influenced by a technocratic-mechanistic frame, the challenge of perfectionism also plays out at the pace of the latest gizmo or technocratic dream. In the current era the Secretary of State for Health and Social Care (Mathew 'Appcock' as he is referred to by those who experience him on a regular basis) sees all the ills of the NHS, and the citizens it serves, being resolved by new Apps and other technologies. In private conversation with a member of the Digital Transformation group that works with the Secretary of State on such matters, it was revealed that the group never questioned his belief in the perfect application of technology – although they did manage to slow its rollout, knowing as they did that it was barely fit for purpose. The life and times of Comrade Stalin are with us still with powerful people pointing us towards an unrealisable, perfect future which their followers sustain by shielding these powerful others from the unreality of what passes as their knowledge.

No wonder the powerful are so confident of their rightness, that Politicians instruct their staff to 'sweat the data until it gives me what I want' (Higgins & Reitz, 2019), when there is no one around to challenge them... except after they retire, as so often happens with senior leaders in health and social care.

3.5 The third myth: there is a right way of doing things

The assumptions that have created and sustained a belief in there being a single right way of shaping organisations come from many directions and are also a particular expression of the second myth of perfectionism i.e. there is a perfect way to achieve the perfect result. In the case of the managerial tradition, it is soaked in an unproblematic commitment to the value of activities such as benchmarking and best practice, where the phrase 'world class' is bandied about as if it is a self-evident truth, something axiomatic and without need of interrogation, where questions around what makes a comparison useful and valid or what context is assumed for best practice to take root, go unasked.

These practices and beliefs come from an uncritical embrace of management as an ahistorical, asocial activity i.e. a set of technocratic approaches that exist apart from specific historical, geographical, and social practices. The disappearing of context, especially relational context, is something that some of us have been trying to challenge, but it is hard going (King & Higgins, 2014). Despite building on the work of the relationally informed schools of psychology as explored by people such as Carol Gilligan (1993) and Joyce Fletcher (1999), the world remains addicted to notions of sovereign individualism and universality. Psychometric evaluation and models of human progression, from a lesser to a greater state, promote the idea that there is an essence to human character that exists outside of and apart from local realities and relational bonds.

When management is seen in this way it creates a comforting sense of order in the world, an order which at best is merely a safety net of reassurance and − at worst − an ideological conceit that merely justifies the way things are. Decisions are being made rationally − where rational is defined as a course of reasoning deemed to be in tune with the orthodoxy of opinion i.e. Type 1 approach to change (Watzlawick, et al., 1974/2011) and can be assessed against what is assumed to be an objective baseline i.e. the one, true way. The 'one true way' is a template that is stretched into more or less every realm of our social existence in contemporary society. For instance, there is the ideal worker, someone that we should all seek to emulate in our corporate lives. They tend to be defined metrically, either in terms of a rating obtained in the course of the overbearing structures of 'performance management' or via a positioning in the ubiquitous nine-box grid of the taxonomic practices of what is questionably called 'talent management'.

Similarly, there is whatever the very latest fad is thought to be in terms of how to get things done. These claim to be the exclusive and only means by which perfection can be achieved in terms of attaining fixability. The world has endured unbridled enthusiasm for methods such as Business Process Reengineering, Lean Techniques, and the ceaseless wheel of new products rolling out of the doors of the professional services firms. When John was a tutor at a business school, he would warn the people he was lecturing that he was in the fashion trade, compelled to produce a new right way every 18 months or so.

Modern management when seen in this way has many of the qualities of a religious sect which shares a set of revealed truths, beyond the questioning of man or woman. There is an unchallenged philosophy in action around the nature of the human condition, one that assumes that there are universal human characteristics, which can be defined as better or worse, more desirable or less desirable, and these exist within relational patterns which in turn can be assessed in terms of their rightness of behaviour. These relational patterns are treated as things that can be configured out of correctly configured sovereign human beings – the relational take that human beings first exist as inter-dependent beings of which 'I' is the singular and 'We' the plural is ignored (Dalal, 1998).

The idea that 'rightness' or 'better-ness' are actually socially constructed norms that reflect the truth-power culture of the moment is denied and much like the Wizard from the Wizard of Oz remains hidden behind the scenes – for the very good reason that it really doesn't stand up to much scrutiny. The arbitrary nature of human norms gets lost when engaged in without any sense of time and place – the relentless focus on the future that the Business Schools and the Management Consultancies advocate, performs a fascinating ideological role (O'Mahoney & Sturdy, 2015), cutting off the world from acknowledging and understanding its roots, why the world is as it is and so how power is being exercised to create a particular truth-power culture.

In his seminal work on the civilising process, the German-English Sociologist Norbert Elias recounts how basic norms of behaviour evolve over time and acquire different currencies at different times in different places (Elias, 2000). What counts as acceptable or unacceptable, civilised or uncivilised, comes and goes around such basic activities as farting in public, using a fork to eat with, or how to greet (or not) someone you know who is defecating in the street. There are no universal rules as to how the sick and infirm should be treated, with many approaches wrapped up in the West around particular religious traditions informed by a belief in the sanctity of human life.

This denial of the essential arbitrariness of social conventions and the belief in the existence of a right way co-exists with two other forms of universalist thinking, with very different origins. Firstly there is the universalism of US national culture (Trompemaars & Hampden-Turner, 2000) with the mythology of the exceptionalism of the US way and its applicability to all contexts – a state of mind associated with nearly all great imperial powers and one that can be seen to be emerging strongly in China at the moment. In the US case this can be seen to be playing out in the US approved tests that govern who does and doesn't get accepted into the great US Business Schools and those Schools which seek to ape them, which in turn sustains a particular right way of thinking about how to manage organisations. These are tests with right answers, where knowledge exists without a context, and individual cognitive recall and manipulative skill is seen as the gold standard of learning.

In the wider world we can see how this plays out in the geo-political sphere, with the sustained investment in exporting the US version of democracy and economics to countries around the world, whatever the national culture it encounters – and however unsuccessful it has been to date in achieving its espoused aim of spreading the democratic ideal (even if it may be achieving other apparently less honourable geo-political goals).

The second source of universalism within the habits of mind that shape the provision of health and social care in the UK is state capitalism, an ideology that informed the thinking and life experience of the founders of the NHS, who wanted to ensure that every dropped bedpan reverberated through the corridors of Whitehall (as recommended by Aneurin Bevan). It is an approach that sports the badge of socialism – but tends towards an illiberal effort to sustain capitalism in the face of its inefficiencies. State capitalism is founded on the command and control thinking that permeated the War Cabinet of the 1940s combined with a belief in the efficiency of centralised, bureaucratic control as a mechanism for achieving fairness and efficiency, which in turn chimed with the production line mentality of the Henry Ford business model – where customers could have any colour of car they wanted, so long as it was black.

In state capitalism, the system was everything, with the assumption being that the provision of human needs was best met through task specialisation and clear role definition, as recommended by Adam Smith and Max Weber, where individual agency and judgement could be eliminated. The system was a perfect machine/bureaucracy, not the complex adaptive one spoken of more recently, designed by superior 'men'. Deming's work in post-war Japan and his focus on statistical management showed this to be an approach not without merit, although it needs to be said that his seemingly central role in that work may have been overstated (Tsutsui, 1996).

In the UK, this surge around state capitalism in the period immediately following the end of the Second World War saw the creation of a monolithic arrangement for the delivery of health and social care focused over the years on engineering the activities of producers of health services to achieve a standardised, universal model. This inward looking, technocratic view of health care delivery can be seen to be alive and thriving in the language used on the signage in Hospitals – meaningless to the ordinary lay person, who doesn't know their phlebotomy from their oncology. It can also be seen in the design of care pathways which reflect the needs and priorities of service deliverers not its users.

A fascinating example of how different healthcare would look like if being patient-centric ever really took hold can be found in some brilliant doctoral work on health care innovation in Denmark (Ingerslev, 2014). In this work the author explores what care pathways would look like if configured from the perspective of people with chronic, complex conditions – who not only had to engage with multiple forms of professional clinical support, but also with local transport realities and their need to keep their day-to-day family and working lives on the road.

At heart, the idea of 'a right way to do things' is formed discursively, wherein the constraints on our own thinking and our openness to fresh ideas and opinions default to the notion that there will always be one generally accepted right answer to any issue. School entrains us with this tightly limited view: even in the humanities, formal education defines the right and the wrong answers – and, perhaps even worse than that, demands that we 'show our working' to demonstrate that we have absorbed completely every element of that 'right' answer.

As we move up the corporate ranks, the same discourse prevails: we are told to write 'option papers', an exercise designed for us to show our working and recommend the 'right way' of doing something. In such work, there is no space for ambivalence, for contradiction, for a more rounded conversation of the complexity that we face, socially and organisationally. And – if we move from being a compliant conformist to becoming a big noise in the workplace – we carry the expectation of 'right way' thinking into our leadership role, thereby further underpinning the discourse. In this setting, the practice of leadership is understood at the most fundamental level to be simply the capacity to quickly and decisively decide on the 'right way to do it'. But this must force us to question whether much of what passes for leadership can really be considered such, when it is culturally measured in terms of creating an air of directiveness and sprinting to conclusions, as opposed to engaging critically with the world and applying thoughtfulness to the challenges that are faced at any given time.

3.6 The fourth myth: metrics reflect an objective reality

My main goal is to... replac[e] the unscientific term 'evil' with the scientific term 'empathy'.

(Baron-Cohen, 2011, p xi)

There is an epistemological battle going on which is perhaps most noticeable in the health economy, where New Public Management still enjoys an overwhelming presence – and in practice the so-called hard sciences have positioned themselves at an epistemological peak, with the scientific method being seen as an unchallengeable gold standard that all other disciplines should seek to attain. In the quote from Baron-Cohen's work above this full-scale assault on other epistemological traditions is made plain – all of human existence can be explained, and explained better, through scientific terminology. Poets, Philosophers, Anthropologists, Qualitative Researchers, and all who practice lesser epistemologies are assumed to speak to a smaller truth than those who practice the so-called hard sciences.

Alongside this hierarchy of method persists a division between the knowledge that is valued and the ways of knowing that are seen to be junior to it, or are adjudged to have no right to assert themselves as knowledge at all. The ways of knowing used by what might be broadly seen as the 'Other' (or 'outsiders', the 'little people') in our societies fall into this category, feeding off the notion of 'rankism', where somebodies know things and nobodies do not (Fuller, 2004). Indeed, they are cast aside from the very process of developing an understanding of the world and made to feel that they have nothing to contribute.

The inherently fluid and charged nature of language is disappeared by the assertion of the scientific method – we sense that Baron-Cohen has never come across the observation that gets attributed to Jean-Paul Sartre that 'words are like loaded revolvers... they always carry a charge' and that 'empathy' is as subjective a term as 'evil', however much it hides behind a numeric diagnostic which in turn rests upon people's subjective response to word-based statements.

In the ordinary world, there is a lot that is taken for granted about the value of measurement. 'Kim', a metaphorical five-star general from the world of organisational turnarounds in the world of health, went to an awards ceremony in Barcelona two years ago, a celebration of the latest practice of all things organisational and developmental. A Partner from a world-renowned, Big Four, consulting firm was making polite conversation on the table at which Kim and their fellow prize contenders were sat. In the spirit of not rocking the boat and staying within the accepted bounds of conventionally approved truth the Big Four Partner noted, with words to the effect that: 'Of course, what gets measured gets managed'. A statement of the seeming obvious that left 'Kim' without words – to challenge this statement, which she knew to be as objectively untrue as its possible to be in a subjective world, was to open up a whole world of intellectual inquisition and pain.

In Kim's experience measurement was a game. She would be parachuted into an organisation deemed to be failing and told to turn it round, usually in some heroic timescale of months, certainly less than a year. Kim knew how to manage the numbers to create the necessary impression of success – they also knew that this manipulation of the symbols had made no difference to what was going on, on the shop floor; making a difference to established custom and practice is a long-term endeavour and enmeshed with the ubiquitous world of power and the truth it creates and is created by. What Kim's politically astute sleight of hand made possible was to give people in the organisation sufficient headroom to get to grips with what was really going on. By giving Head Office the reports it needed, with the necessary data for it to back off, the organisation could free up the vast resources currently dedicated to being scrutinised and do something with the territory of the workplace, rather than the map that represented it.

'What gets measured, gets managed' as a statement of the obvious stands as a totem for our modern management culture, a visible symbol for what is taken for granted, what is seen as the starting point for discussion rather than a point of discussion in itself. When we go the other way, when we turn our attention to the ground on which that axiom stands, what is revealed is a mass of unquestioned thinking which is creating a world increasingly unfit for human endeavour. Measurability is fetishised in our society, not least because it plays a central role in creating taxonomies of the world that seek to enforce an order on it that simply does not exist without it. And – as we've already noted – Eliot's axiomatic line goes a long way to explain that: in fact, humanity finds reality so insulting to its sensibilities that it seeks to imprison it. In this regard, it is worth recalling that the space in an Excel spreadsheet is called a cell.

Our sentient qualities – those capacities that many suggest render us possibly the only animal on the globe with a sense of its own mortality – demand that we are seen to be at the top of the tree, in some way different to all other creatures on the Earth and blessed with a unique capacity to shape and direct the world. It turns out that our only contribution in this regard is a destructive one, as is evidenced by climate change and oceans full of sea creatures choking on our plastic. To substitute for an agency that is less impressive than we would like to imagine, one that shows little capability to encompass truly the fact that the world has complex and chaotic elements that cannot simply be harnessed through scientific method, we create an absurd superstructure of metrics, tables, and plans. Whenever a company Board settles to review the acres of physical or virtual papers in front of it, it is worth recalling that this is as closely connected to the world that their organisation physically inhabits as the video game Sim City is to the actual business of town planning.

We will now explore four aspects and consequences of this myth under the following headings:

• The cult of measurement creates a world where the extrinsic is valued over the intrinsic

- The theology of measurement privileges the tangible over the intangible
- The science of measurement hides and distracts from power and its ubiquitous presence
- Measurement fuels a (Useful? Necessary? Unexamined?) fantasy of control

The cult of measurement creates a world where the extrinsic is valued over the intrinsic. Nothing can have value in and of itself, it can only have value or meaning when it can be expressed in some other way – through the lens of measurement. The unique, the non-commensurable, gets lost, because measurement is in the service of comparability. The thing in itself has to be ignored. It can be of little surprise then that so many organisations are forever trying to find the lodestone of innovation, forever chasing after a unique identity or selling point, while all the time simply finishing up with something generic and profoundly imitative. Indeed, in the popular model of this type of thinking, there is an attempt to double down through the demand that innovation needs to be 'disruptive' – and the effectiveness of that innovation becomes measured on that basis rather than on the sheer utility of what might be offered (Christensen, 2000). Most corporate strategies, for instance, are strikingly similar with everyone promising the same sort of stuff using the same sort of words. The same can be said for many corporate values that exist in the world, even those that seek to be self-consciously 'edgy'.

John finds himself increasingly frustrated by the excesses of this corporate 'doublespeak' language, which makes outrageous claims of being 'outstanding' and 'excellent' whereas, in his experience, most organisations he has to deal with would be world beaters if they could simply be a little less crap than their competitors. 'Your call is important to us', we are told as we wait on hold, 'But your time is free, which is to say it represents no cost on our books, so we keep our staffing to the minimum', is the unspoken reality that is left hanging in the air.

To go along with this bind of – frequently lowest common denominator – imitation that an extrinsically focused habit of mind results in, is the desperate attempt to connect with people's sense of purpose. Organisations wish to connect into subjective personal realities but for instrumental reasons and so are doomed to failure. The management journals bang on about how leaders need to engage with people's enthusiasm, but within an unspoken assumption that this sense of purpose can be expressed extrinsically – not seeing how the act of objectification, of turning purpose and personal enthusiasm, into a collective, measurable, and manageable resource cuts it off from the informing intrinsic, felt, personal, subjective reality that is the source of its vitality in the first place.

To borrow from the Medieval Christian writer of *The Cloud of Unknowing*, human vitality (or in theological terms 'God') is a wild animal, an untamed spirit, a Lion – and doesn't sit well in a world which believes in the external containment of such a spirit (Anonymous, 2019). Through the act of measurement, modern corporates want to focus and direct the untamed spirit of people, blind to how the act of containment kills exactly what it is they lust after i.e. originality, energy, and self-motivation. The current management orthodoxy holds that what is impossible is possible when it comes to the human spirit.

The theology of measurement privileges the tangible over the intangible. In recent times we have seen the revival of the notion of 'tyranny of the tangible' reiterating what has been seen ever since the cult of targets and plans took hold (Reynolds, et al., 2020). Modern Western management has sadly looked at one aspect of what brought the old Soviet bloc to its knees and thought: 'We need some of that'!

Throughout the life of the then USSR there was a fixation with heroic targets, tangible ones that could not possibly be faked in the world of 'objective' reality so beloved of Marxist theoreticians. Vehicle production was reported in tonnage, weight being a universal truth that could exist beyond the vagaries of fashion. Soviet lorries were therefore produced with extra lead in their construction, that being the most efficient way of hitting targets which would otherwise be impossible. Within the modern Western Banking industry, in the build-up to the fiasco of 2008 and after, one COO interviewed for another study reported how stretch objectives for increased sales and reduced costs resulted in a world of lies, the budget being the 'biggest lie of all'. This ill-conceived belief in measurement is not without costs, with only the most senior management believing the reports coming from the dealing rooms, as the world's financial dealers played the system as much as they could to deliver the numbers that they'd been signed up to (and on which their bonuses depended).

This belief in the magical properties of a tangible, measurable target created a world of fantasy – where in both the Politburo of Old Russia and the shining temples of Wall Street, senior leaders believed themselves masters of an objective universe, little knowing what a mess of games were being played to deliver the tangible truth they so believed in. This attachment to the theology of the objective results is a philosophically impoverished way of knowing the world, an over-extension of the scientific method into the social sphere, way beyond its field of useful competence in understanding aspects of the material world.

Metrics help us leave behind reality and seek solace in the virtual. Many theorists lurch towards discussing *The Matrix* film franchise when seeking to explore how best to understand the virtual. To our mind, revisiting the precepts that underpin the movie Tron is more helpful, as this analysis helpfully describes:

> In Tron, the hero enters the universe of the video game by literally being "digitalised" by a powerful light beam directly aimed at him. He is thus reduced to small cubicles to be reassembled elsewhere in the game console. The complex machinery we are made to see only has one function, namely to "scan" the body of the hero line after line and reconstitute its virtual double who will eventually materialise as an assemblage of pixels. This operation has three characteristics: first, it is entirely reversible – in the end, the hero reappears in the real as if nothing had happened. The light beam redraws his body in real space, line after line, to an extent that one wonders whether the directors merely played their tape backwards. Second, in both cases it is the machine that captures and reconstitutes the body – the procedure does not require any particular skill, it is entirely automated, one merely has to let it happen. Finally, the hero is absorbed into the video game involuntarily, by mistake.
>
> (During, 2006, p. 142)

The powerful light beam at the heart of our corporate virtual reality is the application of measurability. Our bodies, performance, plans, and practices are captured by the slicing and dicing of that invisible but ever-present beam – but with one crucial difference: reality is not something to which to return but merely a fleeting origin upon which a notionally controllable 'virtuality' is constructed.

Tangibility and objectivity are tossed around carelessly, without people taking a moment to consider the implications of what they are saying. Words such as 'evidence' are used as if it was an unproblematic term – because it is usually associated with the tangible and the visible. The result being a horrible 'rattomorphic' behaviourism, to use Arthur Koestler's term (Kohn, 1993) where human beings are reduced to that which can be seen, little more than Pavlov's dogs responding to the bells of reward and punishment (however sugar coated, they are actually two sides of the same coin). Those who study what is going on in the workplace are now slowly beginning to realise that this is creating a world of fake-believe where the 'theatre of business' has created parallel universes, one of the tangibly observed and the other the subjectively lived (Vollmer, 2016). Hence, the seemingly closely ordered modern workplace can actually play host to subtle yet essential acts of resistance, an area in industrial sociology that is oftentimes sadly neglected in the current climate, where a uniform compliance with nominally generous employers is presupposed.

The science of measurement hides and distracts from power and its ubiquitous presence. When inviting people to understand the role of power in the workplace, our mutual friend Ben Fuchs starts by reminding people of that widespread Physics experiment many of us will have done at school. A magnet is put under a piece of card and then iron filings are sprinkled on top – and in no time arrange themselves according to the organising force of the magnet. The same can be said to be seen at work. Whatever is introduced in terms of new working practices and policies, they quickly fall back into place to fit within the established social hierarchies (the denial of hierarchy and the advocacy of the 'flat' organisation being another fascinating example of trying to disappear a social reality that is hiding in plain sight).

Measurement is often presented as objective fact, when it is actually a subjective construct which is an expression of who has power and authority within the social system of the workplace. Behind a measure lies a series of assumptions about what matters within the workplace and what is of importance to pay attention to. Wrapped up in this is who has the right to set measures and interpret them, who are the in-groups and out-groups when it comes to the measurement game.

At the top of the corporate tree is the endless tussle between Executives and Non-Executives, the former keen to lock in easy to hit targets that will deliver their usually outsized rewards, while the Non-Executives try and set the bar a little higher. At the bottom staff have targets set for them, often by people who have little understanding of the nuances of the task they do. As a result hospital cleaners are often unable to do a job that meets their criteria of doing a good job, because there is a standard algorithm in place that has fixed the work schedule and rate of pay. No surprise that hospitals have become ever more dangerous places to be, as outsourced cleaners are hurried along and well-done cleaning takes second place to financial imperatives.

In setting the measurement and evaluation criteria, so the rules of the social game are set – with only those who are powerful enough free to ignore them (such as Jess Staley, the still-CEO of Barclays, who saw fit to play fast and loose with the anonymity promised to those who used the Barclay's whistleblowing process) or interpret as they see fit. In the Prison sector a standardised model of prison design is assumed when it comes to inviting people to tender to staff and run them. The ex-Governor of a Prison, now famous for its recent years of barely controlled anarchy, spoke of how he submitted a bid to continue the public sector staffing of his complex and historic prison. His bid was dismissed as over-manned. The private sector rival came in with a much leaner offer, based on what it took to run a modern super-prison with clear lines of sight. Context was ignored and the private sector took over and within months of the new regime, with its fewer, less experienced staff, so the riots began. The mother of one guard in a similar situation spoke of the fears she had for her son, as dangerous men were under-escorted through dark alley ways and around blind corners.

In time this reinforces an all but para-military approach to prison guarding, with staff taught from the earliest stage the basics of physical restraint. In the Swiss system guards are trained for a year before they go on the wings, experts in mediation. The seeming science of measurement, when it comes to selecting who is fit to take responsibility for incarcerated citizens, leads to the creation of dangerous boot camps of violence and sustains a de-facto ideology of punishment and brutalisation over rehabilitation. Measurement in social systems is always in someone's or some group's interest – it is never neutral, never objective, never 'true' in and of itself. Metrics are like the Sartrean loaded revolvers already mentioned, they always carry a charge – and often not the one expected from them.

Measurement fuels a (Useful? Necessary? Unexamined?) fantasy of control. This fixation with the tangible and the pseudo-objective can be seen to meet a particular need, rooted in the classical machine metaphor of life and so loved by FW Taylor and the whole school that sees the production line as the wellspring from which organisational life should flow – and in Taylor's case might have been compensating for his own lack of physical stature (Beart, 2014). In a market tradition that privileges continual upheaval, unmediated by potent movements that exist to sustain social continuity, organisational leaders are forced to operate in a wider world of sustained creative and destructive destruction. A context in which we have what has been referred to as 'the Taliban of the free market' shaping our lives, fuelling our sense of individual and collective insecurity (Binney, et al., 2017).

This linear, cause and effect model, allows people to have a sense of control over what are largely uncontrollable circumstances. This is of course well known and documented, with authors exploring management and organisational life through the lens of complex-adaptive systems for some decades BUT its implications have not taken root (Stacey, et al., 2000). Instead, what persists is this boundless desire to ignore the inter-dependent, acausal, and multi-causal nature of much human activity – a habit of mind that has allowed the notion of externalities to be taken as common sense, and which is an essential feature of humankind's toxic entwinement with the biosphere of which it is part. The wealth of thinking in respect to systems (Carson, 1962/2002; Meadows, et al., 1972; Capra, 1997) seems unable to nudge us out of our poisonous mind-forged measurement manacles, despite its eloquence and apparent persuasiveness.

As the consequences of our civilisation's established way inexorably play out (our particular reading of the work of the *Cambridge Centre for Existential Risk* [www.cser.ac.uk/] is that they have basically written our civilisation off, despite their overall positive orientation) so we cling to the only language we know, measuring those things we feel we can control – the drunk under the lamp-post as the storm rages in the darkness. Maybe this is what lay behind Kim's silence at that awards dinner in Barcelona, quite simply he was left dumbfounded in the face of once more hearing the tired old saw of 'What gets managed gets measured'. This time from the lips of someone others turn to for making sense of the world. Instead, that management consultant merely worked to constrain the abilities of their clients to see the world properly and interact with it meaningfully.

3.7 The fifth myth: values bind the organisation

In around 2014 John was researching into the workforce's response to an ongoing managerial restructuring at a London hospital. The Chief Nurse gave him some advice in the canteen, words to the effect of: 'Remember John, most people here earn less than £21,000. At the end of their shift they're tired and want to go home. They don't care about all this leadership shenanigans'.

The people most attached to 'leadership shenanigans', of which organisational values statements are a part, would seem to be the Executive Team and the Board i.e. those who are most invested in the identity of the institutional unit and whose power and authority is most directly framed by the position they hold within the managerial hierarchy. The act of creating and upholding a set of values tied specifically to the organisation per se can be seen as reflecting their need to create some coherent, and legitimising, principles around which they come together, and which gives them a felt sense of authority. This naturalises the positions they occupy – for them and, in principle, for those who work on their behalf in an organisational context. Importantly, this cohesion – so vital to the persistence of the organisational constructs that currently prevail – actually serves to limit significantly the capacity of the senior leadership to move and adapt to the circumstances that they face. Hence, we are better able to make sense of the recent research that indicated that NHS Chief Executives had no real impact on the quality or financial performance of the organisations in which they work (Janke, et al., 2018).

This need to find legitimising authority could be seen to come from their distance from the primary task of the organisation, which informs how most people outside of the managerial power game get their felt sense of worth. This reasserts the obvious observation that the unspoken (and unspeakable) primary task of the organisation is not about sustaining the self-worth of the managerial elite; this perspective adds a power slant to Harold Bridger's useful conceptualisation of the double-task (The Bayswater Institute, 2017). Hence, the formation of values is an internally hegemonic act that effectively offers ideological cohesion to the siloed and fragmented uppermost levels of the organisation, as Poulantzas intimates in respect to ideology and the fractionated ruling class (Poulantzas, 1978); in this respect, it may actually be the appearance of cohesion that creates a discursive impact up, down and across all who work within that organisational setting, rather than the values themselves.

After all, this organisational tic unveils one of our organisational paradoxes, where rhetoric around diversity of voice in firms is countered by the lived reality of encouraging the whole workforce to align to those values. Yet the reality remains that, despite a multitude of efforts to 'manage culture' (with culture, the dynamic expression of relational power, now reduced to an object) through manipulation of espoused values, the vast majority experience these precepts as a laminated presence in various physical parts of the organisation – screensavers, tired posters on the walls, words on staff ID badges, and occasionally decorating staff lanyards – which are rendered largely invisible given the staff focus on the primary task of getting the work done.

This need to establish legitimising managerial authority, through the use of acts such as creating and espousing value statements, can also be seen to reflect the needs of the senior managerial leaders within the wider health and care system beyond the boundaries of any specific institution. These senior players are keen to be able to demonstrate that they are 'managing' the frequently reified thing called the culture of the care and health economy. Within the nested hierarchies of managerial authority that exist at every level and in every institution, value statements and the process of creating value statements create a felt belief that such values matter to everyone in the system and not just to those tasked to administer those systems.

In this managerial echo-chamber there is little challenge to the importance given to these statements – given the unsurprising finding that senior people have an over-estimation of how much people junior to them speak up (Reitz & Higgins, 2019a), people with managerial positional authority are unlikely to have their views about the world and the importance of espoused institutional values challenged. Muted and unexpressed scepticism by the wider, non-managerial, less senior world leaves senior leaders unchallenged in their belief that these statements of values are for the good of the wider institution and not primarily for the good of themselves as members of the executive elite.

Instead, as intimated earlier, the senior leadership sets out on an endless and fruitless quest to 'align' everyone in the organisation to their values, an act which enriches the dominant discourse and, in turn, makes the ideology that coalesces the senior leadership unquestionable – other than through small acts of cultural resistance that take place despite this overbearing organisational structure.[2]

While researching into team resilience in a UK hospice (King, et al., 2018), this breakdown in the perceived value of statements of corporate values was starkly visible. In conversations with a grouping of direct care givers, from a range of professional health disciplines but without any full-time managers, a Physiotherapist talked to his experience of engaging with the corporate values – as approved by the Board of Trustees a year before. The values were 'dumped' (as John recalls him saying) on them to discuss briefly at an Away Day, where serious conversation about them was made all but impossible and certainly avoided. In time these one-word values would be inscribed on the walls and corridors of the Hospice. The Away Day values 'discussion' was also a useful distraction from engaging with the challenging situation the Hospice faced, with growing demand for their services without any growth in funding (the Hospice was being gamed by other parts of the health economy system so that the Hospice became the carer of last resort).

Interestingly, for Mark, this experience reinforces for him his work critiquing current organisation development activity in a capitalist context and how he tries to find approaches to this type of work that is authentically liberating (Cole, 2020). In so many instances, organisations harbour – as suggested earlier – paradoxical gaps between public rhetoric and practical experience; OD, as a practice, often finds itself trying to efface this contradiction through interventions that are nominally humanistic, democratic, and progressive. It shrouds the tensions that prevail in this context – but is yet to find a way to explode them in order that people might move to a more authentic position in respect to human organising around a shared purpose, or given how improbable that might well be, organising around a set of purposes which can be negotiated between them and held in tension.

3.8 The sixth myth: we're all in it together

Let's start with a story based on recent events. An NHS trust is keen to get more of its staff vaccinated against this year's flu. It seems like a win all-round – by having the inoculation staff avoid getting ill, patients will be better cared for as more staff are around and they are less likely to spread the flu virus and on top of that the Trust gets a cash bonus for hitting the target. Yet only a third of staff have the jab, a long way short of the cash bonus or any other target. Little evidence here of everyone coming together for the greater good and little curiosity about why this might be, beyond a shrugging of shoulders.

Around the same time John shares a report based on verbatim experiences of NHS Bands 2 to 4, the most junior levels of the NHS. A relatively senior person reads the piece and sends him a challenging email: Why's the report written in such negative language? Where's the balance? John replied that the report reflected the tone and language of the vast majority of those with whom he'd spoken. As we've said before, senior people often find it hard to hear news that doesn't fit with their world view (Reitz, et al., 2019).

This attachment to assuming that their world view is the right one showed up in a workshop Mark recently ran. A senior leader was dismayed by the anxieties people reported filling in an anonymous staff survey. Exasperated, he exclaimed that: 'There's no evidence for their fear…I'd love to be able to talk to them and ask why they're scared'. He was convinced that he could explain away their fears, show them how misguided they were to feel the way they did. What they felt was a form of false consciousness, which his objective emotional reality could put right. An inquisitive dialogue might just have helped this individual to recognise what prompted their concerns; his heartfelt desire, however, to dispel fears that he felt illusory merely provided additional evidence for them not to engage with an exercise that played the game of valuing their opinions – but actually cast them as dolts because they opted to express their opinions by simply not engaging with the survey.

This lack of attention to the subjective felt reality of others makes sense to John given how the NHS Bands 2 to 4 spoke to him, how ignored, isolated and powerless they felt:

Middle and senior managers shouldn't take silence as a sign that things are okay'… **'If people are not listened to time after time, in the end they ask: "What's the point?"… People start sleep-walking through their job'**… 'I felt I didn't have a brain… the job and my boss made me feel dumb… I felt I had no intelligence or social skills… I couldn't speak up… you are out of conversations'… 'For Bands 2 to 4 to step-up they need to find their confidence and aspiration… in a recent survey we asked Bands 2 to 4 if they felt valued, only 30% did'… '2 to 4s seen as low skilled jobs, not respected… no respect for those who do it well

When people feel forgotten, when they're not performing well, errors happen, patients get the wrong appointments'… 'I became unwell due to stress… knew I was so busy in my job, the amount of work, there was no time to look around… I didn't want to go to my

line manager, she'd say: "You are wrong. You are imagining things"'...
'2 to 4s are just trying to navigate the system, they're not in a position
to make waves... **most of us are in lower income families and don't
want to risk making waves**... problems between staff and managers
and their relationship are deemed to be "personality clashes".

(Higgins, 2019)

This has echoes for Mark of his three-years as an Operating Department
Orderly (ODO) at Bromley Hospital in the early 1980s – and what he recalls
as the '5pm Click'. Between 8am and 5pm, the six young men who worked
in this role were disdainfully treated as the 'Theatre Porters', the brawn
needed to move patients from ward to theatre table – and to reposition them
during their procedures. Little respect was shown to them, occupying – as
they did – the bottom rung of a very pronounced hierarchy: surgeons, who
wore green scrubs, were at the top; nurses, in blue clothing, came next, and
lastly there were the porters in grey. The cut and style of these were broadly
the same, only the colours differed. Mark recalls being torn off a strip by the
Theatre Sister (who distinguished herself by eschewing the standard paper
theatre cap in favour of some wimple-like affair, that had – Mark suspects –
to be ordered in specially) simply because there were no laundered grey
scrubs so, in order to be ready for work at the start of the list, he had donned
the only set that he could find, which happened to be green.

The surgeons had a small lounge to themselves; the nurses had a separate
staff room; and the porters had their own locker room. This is a reminder
that our experience of power – and its reinforcement – derives from a
wide range of different sources, including architectural design. During the
working day, the only interaction between these groups was around the
primary task; there was little social exchange in the course of the com-
pletion of the work, with nurses and porters in close physical proximity
when, for instance, collecting a patient. The relationship between surgeons
and porters was pretty much non-existent. For instance, Mark was once
summoned by buzzer to one of the theatres during a procedure. He asked
the very old-fashioned general surgeon what it was he needed done. The
surgeon spoke to the scrub nurse: 'Tell him to move the light'. She spoke to
Mark: 'Move the light'. Without detailed instruction, Mark moved the light
to and fro, returning it to pretty much where it had been, and proceeded

to ask whether that was right now. 'Is that OK, sir'? asked the scrub nurse. 'Tell him it's fine', came the surgeons reply. And Mark left the theatre.

Whilst the working day saw five or six ODOs at work, after 5pm there was just one porter left to work the on-call, which ran through until 8am the following morning. This work involved finishing off the tail-end of that day's operating list – and then being available for any emergency surgeries during the night. These night times could often be busy – and the staffing across all three groups was of course significantly reduced. Hence, come 5pm, Mark would shift from being 'one of the Theatre Porters' to a valued member of the team, often trusted to undertake duties outside of his actual scope of practice, such as opening sterile packs, helping doctors and nurses to get gowned and gloved, and counting swabs on the swab rack. It was as if the hierarchy flattened at that magical hour – and suddenly Mark's brain as well as his (to be honest, somewhat limited) brawn was being employed. And this transformation literally felt as though it took place at the instant that the minute hand clicked past the hour.

While sometimes senior people can deliberately misuse their rank (as with the old school surgeon in the story mentioned earlier), often their silencing of their juniors happens unintentionally. They have forgotten what it really feels like to have less resources than others, what it feels like to have to be careful around others, and generally feel constrained in terms of personal choice. One ex-CEO from a Third Sector firm was shocked at the palpable sense of fear she encountered at a workshop John was running, where people explored what really helped and hindered them speaking up in the NHS. We suspect that many senior people would simply advocate that these people need to learn how to have 'courageous conversations' – a point of view that disappears their role, as senior others, in creating a felt sense of relationally situated fear. It presupposes a levelling across the organisation, a fiction that senior leaders love to indulge but which does not resonate with the lived experience of most. The marketplace for 'courageous conversations' groans with training products and how-to guides, and would probably not exist were it not for the constant presence of hierarchy (and its denial), which is discernible in organisations that are described by the sophists of the business world as 'post-bureaucratic' (Child, 2019). Often these conversational tools are more about equipping senior people with technical abilities to better manage those who report to them, now that most firms notionally take a dim view of a harsh parental management approach.

Meanwhile, in the NHS, a member of staff who assumes the role of a Freedom to Speak-up Guardian talked to us about the workload of her team and how, despite being out in the community engaging with some of the most challenging families in the city, it was only the Senior Management who were allowed to personalise their workspace and have an office. Everyone else was being hot-desked as the Trust went through endless mergers, consolidations, and reconfigurations (no doubt described by its proponents as 'transformational') – no personal effects or family photos were to be displayed (unlike on the desks of the senior leaders). There was no safe and familiar place for her team to come back to after being exposed to the psychic assault/emotional labour that comes with the work they do.

While the workplace for many has moved towards 'depersonalisation', as suggested in the earlier mentioned example – not least because space costs money and revenue spent on this is seen as 'soft' – the membrane that used to separate our home from our work lives has slowly become eroded. As with the arguments about how school uniform is a way in which to shroud the distinctions that might be discerned between children from rich and poor households, so the workplace – notwithstanding the fetishisation of the corner office and access to the executive washroom – was a practical and uniform resource to which notionally we all had equal access. Now, the 'office' is translocated into our homes: that which was once strictly private, a space for us and our loved ones to build and enjoy a personal life, now belongs to our organisations. Businesses have colonised our domestic spaces and annexed them to their purpose.

We should all by now be very aware of how different the world looks and feels depending on where you are in the system in terms of the organisation's hierarchy (Oshry, 2007), a hierarchy which has been persistently shrouded to give the sense that it has disappeared ever since the notion of the 'flat organization' first materialised (Ghiselli & Siegel, 1972). No wonder those at the top of the hierarchy are confused, they've been told by the Business Schools and its followers that the world is flat, while the workplace is riddled with hierarchies of pay, gender, ethnicity, and so on.

As well as the ideology of flatness which has infected all walks of organisational life, the philosophy behind health provision can be seen as broadly, and uncritically, Benthamite. The goal is the greatest good for the greatest number, without any critical examination of what would need to be in place for such a statement to have meaning. While government tends to segment the population through the application of a wide range of statistical means, when it comes to engaging them in regard to health improvement, they are treated as a homogeneous mass to which it is simply required to 'broadcast'. This disregards the simple truism that our society is not flat and uniform, but is instead riven with fracture, distinctions, and rankings that means that – beneath the surface of rhetoric – humans are not truly born equal, as the second paragraph of the United States Declaration of Independence announces with some delusion. The other myths reinforce this naïve notion, especially the sense that there is an ideal 'good' that exists and that all can agree on. Difference and conflict are disappeared in an instance and the self-interested attachment to particular definitions of what counts as 'good' are seen as noise to be ignored or suppressed, rather than the energising social context within which what counts as good can be debated, established, sustained, and changed.

With a Panglossian assertion that we exist as part of a harmonious whole, the NHS and its associated actors seem to be acting out from the ancient Christian notion of the Golden Chain, where there is an ordered and fixed hierarchy that connects the smallest beast to the Godhead itself (a chain that served the Kings and Queens of Yore well as they wished to establish themselves through the divine rights of Kings). Given the Christian/Chapel-Socialism of many of the founders of the NHS, this is perhaps not a surprising piece of informing mythology.

Meanwhile health outcomes continue to mirror disparities in wealth and social standing, with life expectancy between the richest and poorest boroughs varying by up to ten years (Iacobucci, 2019). Access to health services are unsurprisingly easiest for those rich enough to avoid the NHS queues by taking advantage of the parallel private system – and for those who are wealthy and/or well-educated and/or socially well-resourced and who insist on using the NHS as a matter of principle, well they know how to game the system or use their inter-personal skills to bring about outcomes that serve them better than those who are less well-resourced. While the map we tend to rely upon is (by its very nature as a representation of reality) very much flat (and largely lacks anything like contour lines to hint at the terrain we inhabit), our actual social topography is more like the Lake District than Norfolk.

To embrace a world of conflict and difference, of unfairness, sits uneasily with people who have been uncritically encouraged to believe that the world of health has the potential to be a level playing field. Owning personal and social advantage is hard to do for people who want to think that they deserve to be treated well because of their personal qualities, when in fact they've been winning a game that is rigged in their favour (Fuchs, et al., 2018). Assertions of the common good and shared purpose are always suspicious acts, of course – where the less advantaged are invited to see the world through the eyes of the more advantaged (Freire, 2005). But one thing seems apparent across all of this discussion: we are patently not all in this together, whether we're thinking socially or organisationally...and the failure to acknowledge is not merely an omission or a delusion – it is, in fact, a covert act of aggression. Those who glibly hide behind this conceit (either through blind belief that takes it at face value or because they understand its usefulness) are promoting a deliberate ideological device.

3.9 What are the implications of the six myths... and what can we do about it?

We have touched on at various points in this chapter some alternative ways of thinking and what such alternative ways open up in terms of different action. In the following we explore more explicitly what it is we see as being a better way of thinking which might help us address the unhelpful consequences of our currently taken-for-granted norms.

3.10 The implications of the first myth that 'All is fixable'... and what we can do about it

The 'All is fixable' myth of management can be summarised as: everything can be put right and made better within the existing framework of thought and the actions this legitimises. Seemingly unproblematic phrases such as 'evidence-based management' simply reinforce this legitimacy, condemning management to ever more mechanistic, technocratic solutions to situations and challenges that simply do not fit within that frame. In the first phase of the COVID-19 pandemic, the UK government mobilised the mantra that it was 'following the science', as if there was some monolithic corpus of understanding that one could simply stand behind – and not the multiple sciences that become apparent when taking notions of complexity really seriously.

We will look at reframing the 'All is fixable' myth in four ways:

- Reframe 'evidence-based management' into 'creative-experiment management'
- Put 'Adaptive' and 'Type 2' change at the heart of how we approach engaging with situations we seek to make better
- Stop using language which leads us towards seeing the world through notions of it being 'broken' and therefore 'fixable'
- Focus on slower inquiry rather than rapid advocacy

1. **Reframe 'evidence-based' management' into 'creative-experiment management'.** In theory many organisations understand the value of experiments, in practice most of them try and manage them as if they were technocratic projects, with defined outputs and processes. Often these projects are called 'pilots', a practice some way from the notion of experimentation. Out of this comes an expectation that a positive pilot will be generalisable...which is rarely the case for a number of reasons. Primarily, it is the case that the pilot enjoys the positive focus of the organisation and a significant commitment of resources to it, which tends to allow it to be seen as successful within its own terms. The politics of investment tends to nudge leaders to find positives where they might not truly exist – especially those who have yoked their status and reputation to the pilot having a good outcome. This steers towards a clamour for the dissemination of the successful project across the rest of the organisation: this 'lift and shift' occurs without the positive focus that the original pilot enjoyed – and sees it dropped clumsily into contexts that are often very different. Hence, organisations contrive to create boundless numbers of successful pilots – which falter when then rolled out into other areas of the firm. '... [A] pilot is much more like a dress rehearsal than an experiment. If the performance fails to impress [others], they are likely to adopt the initiative in a perfunctory way, without genuinely integrating the processes within the organization' (Davidson & Büchel, 2011).

Social experiments in particular are messy and unpredictable, where learning comes from noticing whatever happens rather than tracking a specific pre-determined outcome and pivots around a positive re-evaluation of the very idea of 'failure' in organisations, particularly in respect to seeking to function in a complex system (Edmondson, 2011). Much as the work of Ralph Stacey and his collaborators has become fashionable at the level of public presentation and academic analysis (Stacey, et al., 2000), the practice of management continues to operate with an implicit assumption of experimental certainty, where outcomes are pre-defined and the so-called experiments managed to deliver against them. Learning from failure, in terms of not delivering against expectation, is much mooted and little followed – unsurprising in environments where people have their goals set a year in advance and are appraised against them. Whatever the opposite of a learning culture is, our predictive, hypothesis led, outcome managed workplaces are it.

2. **Put 'Adaptive'** (Heifetz, 1994) **and 'Type 2' change** (Watzlawick, et al., 1974/2011) **at the heart of how we approach engaging with situations we seek to make better.** This means avoiding the comforting balm that comes with reaching for familiar analytic tools or expert third parties who promote off the shelf, pre-prepared answers to situations far too subtle, over-whelming and bound up with tacit social practices to resolve themselves through the application of self-interested and self-serving intellect invested in the intellectual status quo. Within the consulting world organisational complexity has been collapsed back into technocratic, Type 1 change which avoids grasping its profound and radical implications by sticking firmly within the world of 'common-sense'. In 2010, McKinsey yoked together one of their people with an academic at a business school to produce a simplistic checklist for the busy executive in an article hubristically titled 'Putting organizational complexity in its place' (Birkinshaw & Heywood, 2010).

Meanwhile, Bain & Co provides another example of intellectual impoverishment by announcing on their website: 'Our battle-tested approach to complexity management has enabled companies in many different industry sectors to capture maximum value using a repeatable model that keeps complexity out while improving profitability and customer centricity'

(Bain & Company, 2020). In one sentence, we are forced to endure both the war metaphors that inexplicably have such traction in the business world, as if every middle manager secretly wishes they were in a foxhole and surrounded by barbed wire and bodies, and also the highly questionable notion that complexity can in some way be excluded from human affairs.

Becoming familiar with the unfamiliar is the new management requirement – seeking to do the opposite of recruiting in your own image, of letting go of the dead-hand of over-engineered competence matrices which doom organisations to recruit for sameness and then expect difference to flourish. In conversation with a 'new techniques' unit of a well-known business school, the then head of it reported that very little new was generated from within the organisation – most of it came from small bands of people who had the intellectual and institutional freedom to test out new ideas and ways of working.

Within the mainstream business literature, it is possible to find pointers as to how people coming together to organise around an idea or action might find their innate drive to work differently amplified by a range of supporting factors. This resonates with a foundational element of our thinking, that there is a vital need to acknowledge individuality in socioeconomic settings whilst never succumbing to the ideology of sovereign individualism, with its inversion of John Donne's poetic observation where rather than no man being an island, we all are islands. Hence, one review of studies around innovation underscores the interplay of individual and contextual factors in respect to encouraging people to develop a meaningful sense of control in respect to how their work is done – and how it might be done in the future (Standing, et al., 2016).

It would be remiss of us not to acknowledge that we really need to be thinking systemically when it comes to creative development of the ways in which we work and what we work on; such thinking brings with it an even greater imperative to collaborate collectively. As one commentator observes:

> Systemic innovation isn't usually under the control of any one organisation, let alone one individual. Part of the reason is that it always involves complementary innovations – the full value of the car depended on innovations around garages, road markings, driving schools, oil refining, and many other things. The full value of the mobile phone has

arguably still not been realised because it depends not just on thousands of apps, but also on changes in existing organisations (e.g. banks allowing phones to be used as accounts, or transport systems allowing them to be used as tickets). The full value of universal integrated childcare depends on linked innovations from employers, legal rights to leave, advisory and mutual support for parents, and so on.

(Mulgan, 2013, p. 9)

Within the NHS it is striking how those institutions that are more informed by 'Technical', 'Type 1' thinking (which sees social change as no more complicated than an operating system upgrade on a computer) win out in the endless rounds of restructuring – unsurprising in a context which values the illusion of control and predictability, over the messiness and happenstance of creativity and innovation. In terms of training and development the focus returns time and again to formulaic workshops and techniques that promise new insight, while delivering the very little that such decontextualised learning is all but doomed to. Reg Revans and all the schools of creative applied learning, from Action Research to Action Inquiry to Action Learning (Boshyk & Dilworth, 2010), don't stand a chance when they are being appraised by people who think new learning can be ordered up like a burger in a well-known fast food joint.

3. **Stop using language which leads us towards seeing the world through notions of it being 'broken' and therefore 'fixable'.** As we have stated several times in this chapter, we very much subscribe to Sartre's notion that words are never neutral. If we start our engagement with the world around us through the lens of it being broken and fixable, we inevitably begin the rush to solution, we lose our capacity to stay with the world as it is and become more sensitive to a richer reality. Fritjof Capra's *Web of life* gets lost with its invitation for us to weave together how mind and matter co-mingle and co-create the world around us (Capra, 1997). Yet the metaphor of fixability is everywhere – a few years ago a colleague of John's was invited to tender for some work for a world renowned organisation that works in the environmental sphere and the Board used the language of the machine, in particular the phrase 'If it ain't broke, don't fix it', without seeing how out of kilter this was with the world and language of ecosystems that the majority of their staff worked with.

4. **Focus on slower inquiry rather than rapid advocacy.** One of the world's most highly regarded and traditionally minded management consultancies fiercely follows the principle of hypothesis led advocacy in diagnosing what needs to be done to its host organisations. Its highly intellectually able, driven partners and their young foot-soldiers arrive with an idea of what needs to change and collect the data to prove it. Drunks looking for keys under the light of the streetlight where they know they never left them but keep returning to because it's the only place they know they can see it. Their back up analytic teams work through the night producing thick packs of power point slide decks, leaving no opportunity for the people who work in the company to join in the sense making (given their day-jobs and family lives). Inquiry invites people to come together at a slower pace, to notice what they notice and how they notice it – to see the world together and anew… and this will be a real challenge for most workplaces, where busyness and speed are the order of the day, even if much that is achieved has all the qualities of a well-known fridge magnet's view on coffee: 'Drink coffee, and do more stupid things faster'.

3.11 A concluding commentary on what can be done with the 'All is fixable' myth

Inevitably the 'All is fixable' myth is rooted in patterns of power and power-relating, which in turn are steeped in ancient rituals that go back millennia. In *The Golden Bough* – a compendium of allegorical stories collated at the end of the nineteenth century – what can be seen playing out in our modern psyche are the self-same habits of mind that are outlined there (Frazer, 1998). Kings need to be killed to make the rains come when the crops are dying in the field, new rulers acquire their status through killing the old one, only to be deposed when one stronger or craftier comes on the scene.

There is always an answer, always something that can be done when the world is not as we would have it. Our modern resorting to succession planning and root-cause analysis often being as arbitrary as the Ancients' belief in the need for blood to be spilt and sacrifices made to the gods (these days played by Hedge Fund operators in chinos). What we have not learnt to do over the years is to sit still, to pay close attention to the culture of the world we are part of – and by seeing our role in the world we are part of, rather than apart from, see what happens when we notice and participate in slightly different ways, a form explored in the work of Adrian McLean and foregrounded by the story of the CEO of a local authority (McLean, 2013).

Week after week, year after year, this CEO does a shift on the reception desk of the Council offices, experiencing first-hand what wants, needs, and complaints walk in the door from citizens indifferent to his institutional status. He is not there to use his institutional clout to resolve problems that would otherwise get gummed up in the churn of the authorities custom and practice, but to experience what the world is like when lived from another place on the institutional web.

3.12 The implications of the second myth that 'Perfection is the only state worth pursuing'... and what we can do about it

The 'Perfection is the only state worth pursuing' myth of management can be summarised as: the future will be right and nothing in the present will be fit for purpose and so can be discounted. Implicit in this is a fetishisation of the new and the endless chase for the optimal 'solution', a pursuit that continues in perpetuity by its very definition. And many will move into a space where they are seen to be offering something new or the provision of a model that can finally crack the problem that is faced (even though, in the course of facing it, it changes and mutates to become something to which a fresh 'antidote' is offered). In the course of the first phase of the COVID-19 pandemic, Mark recalls a parent categorically stating that his child would not return to school until a vaccine or treatment had been developed, which seemed at that time to be a prime example of the way in which the myths shaped our thinking even when our real-time experience of life ran very much counter to the idea that such things could appear.

Seemingly motivational advocacy of a better future, of visionary possibilities, can undermine the quality of the current system because it is only seen through the frame of a glass being half empty. From a perspective of motivation, it denies us all the opportunity to celebrate what it is we do in the present that is broadly getting things right. The present is not a place wherein we practice and deliver what it is that we want to provide: it is merely a stepping off point from which we endlessly launch ourselves (or find ourselves launched) in pursuit of the perfected future. This is the realm of the metanarratives of which Jean-Francois Lyotard spoke, which can often manifest themselves as conceptual certainties where we are making progress and need to endlessly commit ourselves to the notion of better even if those perspectives can be seen to overwrite our knowledge and experience (Lyotard, 1984). It can also lock people into habits of charismatic and heroic leadership cut off from the day-to-day, often resulting in leaders being experienced as delusional rather than visionary. (The overused saw that 'Vision without action is a daydream; action without vision is a nightmare' tends to remind us always to parenthesise the conceit that the job of a leader is to peddle their 'vision'.)

We will look to reframe the 'Perfection is the only state worth pursuing' myth by suggesting people work with the following:

- Start any inquiry into the perfect or ideal future by addressing two questions: 'Perfect in whose eyes?' And, 'What does the focus on the perfect future allow us to avoid looking at in the here and now'?
- Identify what there is to work with in the here and now
- Foster the discipline of looking into the mirror of current reality, warts and all
- Pay attention to how what is noticed gets noticed

1. **Start any inquiry into the perfect or ideal future by addressing two questions: 'Perfect in whose eyes?' And, 'What does the focus on the perfect future allow us to avoid looking at in the here and now'?** Exercises where people explore a possible future need to pay close attention to two realities – firstly perfection is not an absolute in organisational life and even if achievable will tend to be perfection in the eyes of specific individuals and groups. The ideology of 'shareholder value' within the private sector has created an entire industry to explain the prefect alignment of interest, with echoes of theological logic rooted in the argument of the Great Chain of Being (Boethius, 1999). Secondly, and also part of the 'Great Chain' where all have their place in the hierarchy, the exploration of the perfect future takes place within the context of existing power-relations, where what can be talked about or considered acceptable as perfection exists within the context of what current power-brokers are willing to contemplate.

A further consideration in regard to the perfect future is to acknowledge the complexity of the context in which we ordinarily find ourselves. If we recognise that we work (and have perhaps always worked) in complex adaptive systems where directable cause and effect is a fleeting epiphenomenon, then our understanding of leadership needs a root and branch overhaul, as some have started to do (Uhl-Bien, et al., 2007). Once this perspective is embraced, so the futility of pursuing a single 'future', let alone a perfect one, becomes obvious and attention shifts to working with possible scenarios.

The challenge is that leaders today still cling to a Shakespearean version of Henry V, where the eponymous hero asserts: 'In peace there's nothing so becomes a man as modest stillness and humility; but when the blast of war blows in our ears, then imitate the action of the tiger; stiffen the sinews, summon up the blood, disguise fair nature with hard-favor'd rage' (Henry V, Act III, Scene I). Business and many other spheres remain addicted to warlike and heroic metaphors, with middle managers and their executives enticed into being like a big cat in the jungle – when, in reality, they will appear more like Steve Coogan's comic character Gareth Cheeseman announcing 'I'm a tiger' to the mirror of his Travelodge-style hotel bathroom (Coogan, 1995).

2. **Identify what there is to work with in the here and now.** From a Gestalt perspective, any individual, group, or organisation can only become more of what it is – the future, so to speak, already exists in the present and not as some abstraction that exists 'out there', defined by its otherness rather than its familiarity. At its best this attention to the present is part of the practice of Appreciative Inquiry (Cooperrider & Whitney, 2005), which when it doesn't collapse into the dead hand of methodological application in a corporate context is a discipline for seeing the world not only for what is missing but for what is there.

3. **Foster the discipline of looking into the mirror of current reality, warts and all.** This staying with 'what is' is often undermined by the escape into the perfect fantasy and the magical thinking it invites. Certain observational, critical and defensive routines kick-in to different degrees, leading to a refusal either to see anything that is good or bad in the present – a habit of splitting where all good and all bad are attributed to one state or another, so the present is either all good

while the future is all bad, or vice versa. Within the context of the myth of the perfect, the judgement tends to deliver against there being anything of worth in the current reality.

To look into the mirror of what is can be hard when for many of us, personally and organisationally, the preference is for us to look away and not own what we really are, especially when we want to buy into our myth rather than our reality. One of the most popular ways of avoiding this in-depth self-examination is to reach for the comforting balm of comparative analysis, or rush into quick fixes and busyness. Sustained inquiry, which looks to invite multiple voices and perspectives, is at the heart of John's work with the Ashridge Doctorate into Organizational Change (King & Higgins, 2014). Until we learn to stay with what is, nothing new can happen, because for new to happen it has to have its roots in the material and social reality of the current order.

4. **Pay attention to how what is noticed gets noticed.** The earlier mentioned point is about the discipline of reflection, of really seeing the world with close attention. What also needs to happen is the practice of reflexivity, to pay attention to the lenses through which the current world is being known. This is working from the perspective of social constructionism (Burr, 2003), that sees our experience of reality as a creative act, in which we construct what passes for real through the ways that we engage with, make sense of and engage with reality. Our perspective announces a caveat in respect to this, which is to ensure that this thinking also invites in a rich discussion of power – and, in particular, the Foucauldian notion of disciplinary power, with its nuanced mixing together of power and knowledge i.e. the two co-exist and co-create each other – and don't really exist apart from each other (Foucault, 1991). This invites us to see some categories and types of knowledge being privileged over others according to the social and political rules of the game.

In many instances we are confronted by a dominant discourse that intimately shapes our thinking and practice, what counts as 'common sense', and is able to render other forms and types of knowledge junior to it, or even irrelevant and so open to being disregarded or dismissed. Those who want to work with these junior/minor forms of knowledge are invariably defined as being the 'Other', part of an out-group defined by its at-the-edge relation to the normalcy approved of by the dominant discourse – and often pathologised as a result.

Hence, for us, part of the challenge to the whole myth of perfectionism, is to challenge the perfection of particular ways of knowing and in particular the privileging of the scientific method into areas of life where its assumptions and practices are unhelpful. This means letting go of the language of objectivity when applied to the functioning of social communities, where 'good' is a subjective value statement, not some truth that exists outside of that community's codes of practice. The discipline of 'critical subjectivity' comes to the fore, with its focus on how to notice our subjectivity in action, rather than disappearing it in the perfect epistemology of the natural sciences.

3.13 A concluding commentary on what can be done with the 'Perfection is the only state worth pursuing' myth

Life can only be understood backwards, but it must be lived forwards.

(Kierkegaard, 1843)

The headwaters of perfection ensure that we see our current world as being a shadow of something better; it leads us to undervalue the here and now and also to create a divide between the world as it is and the world as it should be – and because we see the world this way any attempt to change, to move towards something better, becomes impossible because it has no roots and has no connection to the social process through which the negotiation between what is and what could be happens. In the world of ideal futures, the messy reality of existing social processes and all its power and politics gets disappeared.

This reflects the implicit dangers of indulging in what is sometimes called Utopianism, deriving from a powerful human desire to move briskly from what is perceived as a negative present to land in a future – a desire that owes more to wishful thinking than experience (Sargent, 1994). Imagining a future that serves to avoid the present, without reference to lived experience to date, represents a leap into idealism and a proposed social structure that is developed ideologically rather than organically. Ideologically imposed structures have a habit of requiring people to subscribe to a particular set of abstract concepts in a relatively unthinking fashion. At its most extreme it is possible to discern from history what can happen – such as the coming to power of the Khmer Rouge in Kampuchea in the 1970s – where Utopianism forcefully colonised specific organisational settings with truly tragic and grisly results (Clegg, et al., 2012).

From a perspective of social constructionism there can be no perfect social process, because social processes are dynamic expressions of a lived philosophy, soaked in the realities of people's social relationships which are in turn wrapped up in how power and truth gets created.

The major reframing required to the myth of perfection is to replace it with the world of the good enough, a language which draws on psychoanalytic work and the concept of the good enough parent (Winnicott, 2005). It also embraces the possibility that comes from the observation of the writer Samuel Beckett, that the best we can do is 'fail better'. In a world that is made up of flawed people, going about their lives in often barely understood contexts, where technologies and the wider environment seem to be more random than predictable, this more modest understanding of our relationship to the future is both more practical and more hopeful – assuming of course that we view these as being a 'good thing'!

3.14 The implications of the third myth that 'There is a right way of doing things'... and what we can do about it

The 'There is a right way of doing things' myth can be summarised as: there is an objective reality that pervades organisations and the systems within which they operate and any deficiency in performance can be seen in terms of a gap between what is going on and what should be going on. The evaluation of performance is not seen as problematic and is understood to be a largely technical exercise which allows for organisations and people to be readily graded against a universal set of criteria. The criteria chosen are not the focus of debate or challenge.

How might we look to reframe the 'There is a right way of doing things' myth?

- Start by critically engaging with any form of comparative analysis between your organisation and any other – pay attention to what needs

are being met inside and outside the organisation by being part of such
an exercise

- Work with the political realities and agendas of those who have the
  power to compare and evaluate
- If you are a body that has responsibility for enforcing and promoting
  the best practice model, don't pretend to be a partner or friend of the
  institution you're assessing
- Focus on finding the points of connection and difference between the
  espoused right way and lived reality

1. **Start by critically engaging with any form of comparative analysis
   between your organisation and any other – pay attention to what
   needs are being met inside and outside the organisation by being
   part of such an exercise.** Within the organisation benchmarking and
   performance evaluation against an external norm can give a sense of
   comfort and order, however stressful the effort of being part of such
   an appraisal. As identified back in the 1950s, the emotional load that
   workers are exposed to in our current model of health and social care
   is beyond the limits of what can be expected from human beings
   (Menzies, 1960). Our capacity to cope with the trauma of others is not
   limitless.

Activities such as comparative benchmarking and evaluation against a
framework of best practice can create a sense of comforting distance from
the realities of life. Better to fight against the injustice of a Red, Amber, or
Green rating than face into the storm of discontent of junior staff and angry
relatives. A CQC well-led inspection gives NHS organisations a time out, a
breather, from the trauma of the day to day. At the same time such inspec-
tions give external bodies a sense of control over a world that is inherently
uncontrollable, a sense of hope for a better tomorrow.

2. **Work with the political realities and agendas of those who have the
   power to compare and evaluate.** Behind the aspiration of the 'objective' lies a messy and complicated political reality. Organisational life is
   political, as John has explored in his recent work with Megan Reitz, and
   pretending it's not creates a world of reflecting mirrors where politics is

both there and not there and people have to play the political game of no-politics (Reitz & Higgins, 2019b). The political purpose of advocating a right way in health and social care in the UK is to address the big P political realities of there being a 'post code lottery' when it comes to the delivery of services, a pejorative headline used by all forms of the press for all sorts of ideological reasons. If the ambition of the NHS is to be universal, then part of that universality is standardisation – the provision of the same care, independent of geography.

In order to deal with the reality of a world of diverse services being delivered in diverse ways, the promotion of a standard operating model and the evaluation of the service against that template is an essential part of demonstrating that the NHS is a common service. There may be some possibility of sharing best organisational practice, although this works with a Type 1 mechanistic, technocratic view of organisational life and learning that has already been critiqued in this chapter. The most that human beings caught up in the business of organising can realistically share is their experience, of trying to get things right and the sense making in which they are practically involved as they reflexively recognise their presence and impact in the systems around them (Weick, 1995).

3.   **If you are a body that has responsibility for enforcing and promoting the best practice model, don't pretend to be a partner or friend of the institution you're assessing.** At a recent conference John attended for GPs and their evolving delivery model, he listened to a speaker from CQC responsible for grading the people in the room speak about his desire for there to be a greater sense of transparency and collegiality. Meanwhile the Chair, who operates at the most senior levels within the NHS, spoke of how his stomach lurches every time he hears that he is to be inspected. Being the guardians of the one true way means that you are always holding the high ground in a conversation, you own the template against which others will be judged.

You can be a friendly or a cantankerous judge, but you will always be a judge – and it also means that people are likely to be afraid of you in some way shape or form because you are setting the terms of reference for the conversation and are the arbiter as to whether or not they are free to practice as they currently are. People are unlikely to feel psychologically safe in such a setting while at the same time they are being held accountable, a recipe for anxiety according to psychologists like Amy Edmondson (2019).

4. **Focus on finding the points of connection and difference between the espoused right way and lived reality.** This framing focuses not on correcting reality but better understanding it and so engaging with it more richly. The right way template when used like this is a lens for inquiry into what is, a way into being curious about how things really are at the moment – rather than an evaluative framework. The non-prescriptive approach does not seek to impose a universal model regardless of the context, when it does it becomes an ideological conceit that actively distorts reality. Certainly, it is argued that the 'targets-and-terror' measurement regime introduced into the NHS by the New Labour administrations from 1997 onwards – a Soviet-style system of measurement introduced into a liberal democracy just as the USSR was sensibly abandoning it – hugely distorted the reality of health care delivery, not least through the gaming of that measurement system (Bevan & Hood, 2006). Those authors helpfully cite Goodheart's Law, which simply suggests that '...any observed statistical regularity will tend to collapse once pressure is placed upon it for control purposes' (Goodheart, 1984, p. 96). Done generatively the point of comparison becomes illumination rather than correction, a focus on inquiring more deeply into what is rather than advocating what should be.

3.15 A concluding commentary on what can be done with the 'There is a right way of doing things' myth

Stepping out of the deep shadow cast by the myth of 'the right way' creates a tension to be held. Traditionally 'right way' thinking sought to get rid of debate and tension, by announcing the answer and dictating the method to be used in developing both answer and the actions derived from it, part of the Isabel Menzies Lyth defence against anxiety (Menzies, 1960). 'Right way' thinking is good old-fashioned prescription followed by close supervision (or policing) of the patient in following the prescribed course of action and taking their medicine. For the world of health and social care a familiar and comforting way of acting.

This translates into managerial practice as the directive leadership style, which still enjoys such prevalence. The 'right way' is 'my way', as far the leader is concerned (often in those instances where they have apparently behaved in an enlightened way and 'invited' others in a meeting to express their opinions). Once 'the way' is defined and actively embraced, it is converted to a set of metrics, which the leader then sets themselves the task of scrutinising.

A more generative, but probably irritating, approach to engaging with something that is mooted to be best practice sees it as a stimulus for debate. The best practice of the 'right way' provides a pole to an argument, the voice of disagreement and opposition to an organisation's advocacy of its current order – which fits with more meaningful models of dialogue (Isaacs, 1999). Without opposition the advocacy of the status quo loses its edge and fails to see itself clearly and value both its strength and weaknesses. There is, then, an impulse to explore the tensions that exist in organisational discourses, whether they exist between how things are and how someone wants them to be, in terms of comparison with others – or whether it is merely in relation to the wishful daydreaming that goes under the business rubric of developing the corporate boilerplate of vision, mission, objectives, and values.

'Best practice' is probably in this reframe of 'the right way' myth better understood as an alternative approach, a Devil's Advocate, that seeks to hold the current order to account, rather than replace it. It may be that we let go of the idea of 'best practice' altogether, especially given how contextually specific it always is, and instead seek to offer organisations examples of 'Alternative Practice' to stimulate inquiry and insight, so stepping out of the inevitable patterns of defensiveness and rejection that arise from being told that you're wrong and I'm right. This requires the firm to start by homing in on a careful consideration of all that they do at a specific given time – and to scan the horizon to make critical judgements of what they see elsewhere. After all, even 'best practice' cannot be sensibly argued to be exclusively good; some things will be seen as positive – but that cannot be seen to preclude the fact that some elements within it will possibly be negative.

3.16 The implications of the fourth myth that 'Metrics reflect an objective reality'... and what we can do about it

The 'Metrics reflect an objective reality' myth can be summarised as: there is a reality that exists independent of human ideology, where that reality's most important aspects can be usefully described in numeric form. In short, if it can't be counted it doesn't count, a perspective that underpins the mantra of 'what gets measured, gets managed'. Its validity as a statement rests on the pre-existence of an objective world where all that is important can be tallied and where the act of tallying is a neutral act – a point of view that we find highly questionable and once again more of a theological perspective than anything else.

In the spirit of not throwing the baby out with the bathwater, how might we look to reframe the world where 'Metrics reflect an objective reality' so that measurement becomes a useful tool rather than the lousy master it has turned into? We'll do this under the following headings:

- It's a subjective world out there, baby!
- Measurement and metrics tell us more about ourselves than the 'real' world
- Rebalance valuing the territory over the map
- Make measurement matter in terms that matter to people
- Value emotional heft

1. **It's a subjective world out there, baby!** As Austin Powers would have put it if he'd become an organisational academic rather than an international man of mystery. Limits need to be set around what counts as useful measurement and a greater focus needs to be made around how to describe and share unique and particular experiences. The habits of measurement have privileged comparability over uniqueness, so what gets described in staff surveys is an experience that no one has, it is the smoothed average using an imposed scale and language – the surveys are an example of one group determining what is and isn't a legitimate way of describing experience, so the powerful hear about the experience of the less powerful in ways they are willing to tolerate.

A good rule of thumb is to assume that when it comes to understanding organisational change and how people are experiencing it, that nearly everything falls within Heifetz's school of 'Adaptive' rather than 'Technical' change i.e. it is a social experience and does not fit within the easy to evaluate, bounded mechanistic world of a technocratic understanding of the non-technocratic world. This will be a challenge to those wedded to the world of 6-Sigma management (as popularised by Jack Welch and GE), one of the more egregious examples of the misapplication of material science to the social world. To give space for the subjective world to breathe will be difficult in a world which bandies around the concept of objectivity with little rigour but a lot of institutional support.

When the Masters in Organizational Change that John studied in and has written extensively about (Critchley, et al., 2007) was being accredited by the various great and the good of the academic world, the founders were asked how they would ensure objectivity in their marking of the assignments. The response was words to the effect of: 'I don't think we recognise the notion of objectivity in this programme'. The programme was instead underpinned by a much more rigorous and sophisticated social philosophy, one of critical subjectivity – where the quality of all work was dependent on the quality of the self and relational awareness that was brought to bear.

It is essential that we pull quantitative measurement from its pedestal – but avoid seeking to grind it into the dust, as if it were a thing without value. There are instances where it may offer us insight through which we might engage with others to seek to make sense of our working lives. But we urgently need to nudge that sort of evaluation away from its ideological underpinning, which declares its precision and objectivity. Importantly, in respect to how leaders engage in this, it seems that the whole process of measurability in organisational contexts needs to be democratised, so that everyone gets to discuss what might be measured and how. Otherwise, the techniques of measurement merely constitute a surveillant apparatus, designed to direct, closely manage, and constrain everyone in the organisation.

2. **Measurement and metrics tell us more about ourselves than about the 'real' world.** It tells us what has weight, whose views matter, and what are the currencies of power when it comes to talking about what is going on in the world. Metrics are more auto-ethnographic than ethnographic when it comes to describing the world experience – they are

a keyhole into an individual and groups way of knowing the world. If an organisation relies on surveys with multiple choice answers sent out from a source approved of by senior management i.e. the HR department, that points to a number of world views in action. It assumes that the creators of the survey either see themselves as the keepers of the 'objective' truth of the workplace, they are the 'gods' who know what matters, or else they are explicitly part of the process through which senior management creates a sense of control for itself (and denies that people might be gaming this system) which has been helpfully labelled the 'leadership illusion' (Ibbotson, 2008).

WW Deming observed that the way into understanding why people behaved the way they did at work, and why it made sense, was to look at the pay and rewards system that people actually lived by. Our suggestion is that to understand how you and those around you really think about the world, your philosophy in action, simply look at what gets measured, who determined this measurement regime, and how measurement gets carried out. In one of Mark's former lives he was responsible for driving up the percentage of people who answered the staff survey, which was done by all sorts of pestering mechanisms and sleights of hand and gave senior management a comforting sense that people were now more engaged. Nothing of course had changed except that the HR department had hit its targets – engagement had turned into a function of getting HR off your back and probably fuelled a slightly more persecutory feeling about the Trust in question (which in turn sustained the sense of fear that earlier in this chapter the senior person knew he could reason out of people).

3. **Rebalance valuing the territory over the map.** The territory refers to the world of lived experience and metrics to the map that describes that territory. As a former Geography student John is very aware that cartography, the art of map making, is an activity filled with ideology and judgements – there is no true way of representing something that exists in three dimensions on a two-dimensional surface. The traditional Mercator projection, which is great for tracking direction between points, somewhat distorts areas – making many Northern states for instance look much larger and more materially significant. Then there is the small matter of what happens to the state of Israel

when you fly with some airlines over the middle east – the country is disappeared on the in-flight map. Within the workplace all sorts of sleight of hand are in action as departments offload costs onto others and claim credit for activities carried out in other parts of the system.

Cartographically we have to contend with metaphorical and literal 'phantom islands', which '...are islands that were officially charted and recorded on maps, fully believed to be real, but that turned out to be non-existent' (Nah & Perono Cacciafoco, 2018, p. 32). One such phantom island – which appeared on maps in 1876 and was finally removed due to its lack of physical existence in the world in 2012 – prompted a scientific review of its forced disappearance to observe that 'Sandy Island's life and death served as an invitation for people to question where information comes from, leading to greater insight into how the world is depicted' (Seton, et al., 2013, p. 143).

Organisational maps are famous for focusing on the structures of the organisation, profit centres, and cost centres, while maps and measures of relationships get disappeared. The organising forces of work life, rather than the ossified bones of the organisation, rarely get reported on – and at their worst deliver the disconnect between measures and practice that meant the Ford Motor Company Red/Amber/Green reports were all green while the company haemorrhaged billions (Hoffman, 2012).

4. **Make measurement matter in terms that matter to people.** Measurement is not a neutral activity; it is always for someone and in the service of a particular interest or set of interests – it always shines a light and casts a shadow i.e. to highlight one thing means putting something else on the back burner. Don't deny the purpose of measurement. In the early 1990s John was working as an IT Strategist – one project involved looking at how the Bank's headquarters in Switzerland could have some oversight of its financial position around the world, which included its activities in New York. The new system was up and running and the senior man in Switzerland pointed John at a screen in his office and proudly claimed that it was accurate to the minute for the whole global position of the Bank. On a visit to New York, John walked around the trading floor and came across a pile of paper records (this was before the days of easy automation) – on further inquiry it turned

out these held important information about the New York financial position and would be entered into the new system the senior man in Switzerland was so pleased with when they had time. For the New York operation recording the data was of no immediate importance (and possibly threatened a reduction in local autonomy), it was something head office had imposed for reasons best known to itself.

In Reitz & Higgins' work (2019b), the authors explore how the ubiquity of data and measurement could take us down two possible roots – one in which we enter into an age of self-directed learning and development enabled by access to data as we've never had it before. Have access to the information to know the world in our own self-curated fashion, see the world in a more complex and varied fashion, and find what we need to have at our fingertips. The other is an age of mass-curation and echo-chambers, where we are either corralled by powerful others or by the need to belong to a like-minded group – the intense corporate world of David Eggers' grim fictional work The Circle (Eggers, 2013) and the hyper-surveillant Chinese Sesame Credit (Kobie, 2019), which seems to have a lot in common with the language of 'bringing your whole self to work' and the seeming cult of the deliberately developmental (Kegan & Lahey, 2016).

5. **Value emotional heft.** Once something is turned into a number on a spreadsheet it loses its emotional power, which is maybe how senior corporate leaders can sound so out of touch. The initial Boeing executive response to the loss of life from the two Boeing 737 Max crashes sounded tin-eared and had more in common with a speak-your-weight machine than people who understood the magnitude of what had just happened. Subsequently, two things fought their way into the public domain: the first was that commercial pressure within the global commercial airplane duopoly had led Boeing to design, build, and deliver a fundamentally flawed product in terms of engine size and positioning (which, in turn, required a computerised fix to address, a fact that was not clearly communicated to airlines and their pilots) (Silveira Cruz & de Oliveira Dias, 2020, p. 2620). Meanwhile, the second was that the company seemed to give little opportunity for their workforce to speak up openly in respect to their concerns about the new model, although their private opinions were scathing: "'This airplane is designed by

clowns, who in turn are supervised by monkeys," said one company pilot in messages to a colleague in 2016' (Johnsson & Beane, 2020).

In his Doctoral work Steve Marshall explores how to work with the art of creating expressive photos to bring to people's attention the lived experience of people in their workplace (Marshall, 2014). His work is part of the tradition that builds on a radically different perspective on epistemology, one that seeks to value emotional expression and the wider world of experience which underpins the increasingly impoverished world of propositions and actions, based as they are on a narrow sense of what matters in the world (Heron, 1996).

3.17 A concluding commentary on the 'Metrics reflect an objective reality' myth

At the start of his Masters into Organizational Change, John recalls being advised by its Head, Bill Critchley, to: 'feel intelligently and think feeling-fully'. Measurement that is informed by this observation has the possibility to return to being a useful servant rather than the lousy master it has become. Measurement is currently out of control and largely useless, a recent maternity trust scandal that blew up in the North East of the UK reported that the Trust (Telford) was receiving large amounts of prize money (just under £1m) for the quality of its maternity care, in terms of hitting targets as adjudged by NHS Resolution, shortly before receiving a dire CQC rating of 'Inadequate' for the self-same services (O'Brien, 2020).

The late Professor Hopwood, of Oxford's Said Business School, wrote to the national papers in 2009 reporting on the complete disconnect between the management consultancy approved framework of KPIs and the tribal loyalties, blood and guts that made up the lived reality of various professional groups vying for power and authority, and the licence to operate as they saw most fit (Hopwood, 2009). This resonates with research undertaken between academics at Bristol and York, who seem to have found an inverse relationship between public sector organisations who invest heavily in traditional consultancy of this sort and improvements in productivity (Kirkpatrick, et al., 2019). Their work continues — and a newspaper report on their new findings included a case study showcasing how staff within the NHS were having their voices around ideas for improvement drowned out by the leadership's reliance on external consultancy (Kennedy, 2020).

Measurement has become the drunk who keeps popping up in this chapter, searching for their keys under the streetlight while knowing they have dropped them elsewhere. What is needed is a reframing of measurement into a broad-spectrum approach to inquiry, which people create for themselves in a way that is fit for a useful purpose. This will feel like a loss of control for the current cohorts of measurers, until they are willing to acknowledge how toxic the current practice of measurement is.

3.18 The implications of the fifth myth that 'Values bind the organisation'... and what we can do

Modern management practice and theory has sought to disappear much that shapes how people come together in much the same way that God is disappeared in the Babel Fish story we recounted earlier from the work of Douglas Adams (a tribute to the power of human logic to create any reality it wants right up until the time when a person gets run over on a zebra crossing, having successful argued that black is white). By denying the presence of difference and the need for conflict as a potentially creative way of holding the tension of difference, what has emerged are the platitudes and generalities with which we are sorely familiar (Reynolds, et al., 2020). A generative approach to creating a sense of collective belonging is achieved by adopting practices that:

- Privilege 'power with' instead of 'power over'
- Invite and expect strongly felt differences to be expressed
- Allow for individuals and groups to have diverse loyalties and group identities

1. **Privilege 'power with' instead of 'power over'.** Most workplaces are deeply controlling and punitive, the focus on compliance and standardisation are clear statements of directive power – however much they are sugar-coated by the appeal to over-arching values or some sort of common good. They tend to work from a functionalist notion of workplace power, which sees it as a zero-sum resource that is allocated

to individuals, on the basis of their positional capacity, by offering rewards to some or constraints on others in respect to getting things done (French & Raven, 1959). This echoes earlier work that sought to justify power in the workplace through an appeal to the idea of status (Goldhamer & Shils, 1939).

A more social view of this argues that: '...the three-dimensional view of power involves a thoroughgoing critique of the behavioural focus... as too individualistic and allows for consideration of the many ways in which potential issues are kept out of politics, whether through the operation of social forces and institutional practices or through individuals' decisions' (Lukes, 2005/1974, p. 28). Elsewhere Michel Foucault offers a more nuanced view of power as a dispersed, productive, and intrinsic aspect of human connection (Foucault, 1980), which – in turn – allows us to embrace the language where 'power with' is power predicated on a relationally generative notion of power, where power is in the service of growth-in-connection, a world away from competitive individualism and the imposition of will of one group over another (Fletcher, 1999).

Collective values that are discussed and debated as part of an inclusive and ongoing inquiry would be part of such a 'power with' orientation – where they are a permanent work-in-progress and don't get turned into the manicured statements that lose their relevance as soon as they are laminated. 'Power with' values will be expressed in the words that mean something to the people who wrestle with them, not the PR department or communications specialists. They might be a bit rough and ready but that is what makes them real – and they help people hold tensions between the competing priorities as specific individuals and groups experience them. Mark had the pleasure of working with an organisation in this sort of way just recently – and was impressed at the way in which the process produced values that seemed to at least resonate with the people in the organisation.

2. **Invite and expect strongly felt differences to be expressed.** Compliance to an over-arching ideology is at the heart of most so-called deliberately developmental organisations, they are underpinned by a series of unquestionable world views (often connected to a founding individual or cabal). Health and social care are much too complex to be collapsed into a single unifying ideology, predicated on a universal

assumption about what constitutes the good life and death. A healthy organisation involved in the care and lives of others should be in a permanent debate about what constitutes the right and wrong course of action, given ever shifting external contexts and personal circumstance. Argument should be the order of the day, not dull compliance, sullen subversion, or rage against an unquestioning machine-system.

The debate about the pros and cons of private provision of services in the NHS can be seen as attempt to avoid this argument and instead reduce it to a debate about cost-effectiveness of provision of an undebated philosophy of care and attitude to human mortality.

3. **Allow for individuals and groups to have diverse loyalties and group identities**. Organisations are always at risk of becoming self-regarding and self-serving and so disconnected from the world at large. The challenge is how to work with the reality of institutional flux and permeability. Very few organisational units or companies last for very long (Collins & Porras, 2005), always facing the possibility of being reconfigured and repackaged into other forms. When people become over-invested in their existing working unit as the defining part of their ethical identity, then that identity is built on sand given the mutability of organisational forms. It is therefore healthy for people to have their values connected to those more enduring parts of their lives, be that families, community groups, sports teams, political parties, trade bodies, and/or professional networks. Indeed, we suggest that an organisation would do well to seek to connect the values that are shared in common by those who have been drawn to come and work for it, rather than resort to inscribe those people into an alien and entirely artificial value set, imposed from above.

3.19 A concluding commentary on the 'Values bind the organisation' myth

Organisations rarely last. Thinking historically, one is confronted by the apparent omnipotence and seemingly timeless presence of the deeply menacing East India Company (Dalrymple, 2019). But all of that was, of course, illusory – as might be the seemingly unending quality of companies such as Amazon and Apple in contemporary times, where so many of us lodge our most treasured photos, maintain our libraries, or store our music collections – all of which will melt into the air when the winds of change finally sweep away these increasingly unedifying monoliths.

Enduring values more often come from outside an institution and provide that institution with an ethical heft that something cobbled together based on latest business school thinking is unlikely to have. Engaging with a pluralistic value culture, one where people are invited to explore and work with their different understandings of right and wrong, is a very different discipline to evaluating people's compliance with a set of decontextualised statements of what the great and good, of a here today gone tomorrow institution, think matters – and want others to think matters.

3.20 The implications of the sixth myth that 'We're all in this together'... and what we can do about it

The range of ways in which comparative advantage (Fuchs, et al., 2018) is 'disappeared' in our society and inside our organisations is part of the intellectual misdirection that asserts that the world of work is flat i.e. is a social order without stratification which at the same time often advocates itself to be a 'meritocracy' (which in turn begs the question, merit in whose eyes). This problematic flatness also co-exists with the economic-theology of the Great Chain of Being, which is underpinned by the notion that by meeting the needs of one group (in the private sector, shareholders) so the needs of all are met... or some Benthamite model of inter-connected wholeness in which assertions of shared purpose, and need, bury conflicting priorities and value sets, so hiding power and its exercise in the shadows of organisational life. In the movie *Other People's Money*, a company founder makes a hymn of praise to his business being more than its stock price. The external investor sitting in on this then says 'Amen', because to him what he's listening to is a prayer, with no connection to the nuts and bolts of commercial success.

Once these axioms are challenged, we are left with a workplace made up of a multiplicity of hierarchies made up of experiences of economic class, social identity, positional authority, group role, and personal qualities – as we see this in others and others see it in us. In this topographical world of valleys and mountains individuals and groups are not aligned and are not seeing the world from the same perspective. The view from those on the mountain top does not represent the single true view, except for those who inhabit such lofty heights – the view for those in the valley is as they see it.

The difficulty is that the mountain top is widely seen as the key vantage point, where it is presupposed that everything can be seen, like the ominous and overbearing castle at the centre of the novel of that name by Franz Kafka (Kafka, 2009). So, people aspire to that position – or acquiesce to the idea that those who 'manage' necessarily need to occupy that height, organisationally and culturally – and that this position offers special perspective. Our thinking about the contemporary context builds on this notion: whereas the castle – populated by myriad managers, drones in the hive – is built on top of the mountain and yet is part of it, the development of leadership, as a practice distinguished by its distance from the practical concerns of the organisation, floats free of the terrain and merely traverses it, casting shadow as it goes.

To return to the bureaucracy captured so supremely by Kafka, the castle at the top of the village is actually constituted not by geography but by the way in which those who work within its ramparts construct its meaning – and the way in which those in the village below comply with the expectations of the bureaucracy that inhabits that castle. The only way in which everyone implicated in this socially constructed performance are in it together is through their complicity with this alien overlay.

One NHS Trust CEO told the story of being accosted by one of the cleaning staff as she left the hospital late one night, the new finance system meant that people's pay would be two days late for the first month of its operation. For this cleaner, who lived on a financial knife edge, this delay would genuinely put her and her family at risk. Often it takes the dull compulsion of the economic to jolt us into a painful recognition that we are not in the same boat, we've simply shared the same bath. The COVID-19 pandemic was seen to have a disproportionate impact on BAME people, not necessarily because of some natural predisposition to the disease but because this group was heavily represented across the workforce in what we came to call key worker roles, where the safety of working at home was not possible. A flattener would argue that we faced the disease as humanity in common, which is the case...but that should not veil the simple difference in practical experience between a nurse, a

bus driver, and a delivery driver and those not working in such front facing roles. (In the ultimate reinforcement of this for Mark, a middle-aged
black man arrived precisely as he was editing this section in June 2020 to
make a supermarket delivery. That man and Mark were patently not 'in it
together' in any real sense.)

Instead of the catechism of alignment what we are left with is a world
which is in a permanent state of sustaining and reconstituting established
patterns of relating, as described by structuration theory (Giddens, 1984),
an idea that we tend to see as having been anticipated by the comprehensive social theories of the French sociologist and anthropologist Pierre
Bourdieu. In some parts of the society of health and social care there will
be competition for status and resources, in others there will be collaboration – at times, there will be conflict and, at others, there will be moments
of resolution. Much of the OD world seeks to amplify those patterns of
collaboration and resolution, assuming that conflict and competition are
'bad' or inferior patterns of addressing problems, rather than seeing all
these patterns and qualities having a role to play given the shifting patterns
of how organisations live out their tensions and paradoxes.

The notion that 'we're all in it together' is a vital element of the dispositif
to use a Foucauldian term that discursively gives shape and direction to the
way in which we experience power as a productive force that acts through
the formation and deployment of knowledge (Cole, 2020). In brute terms,
many of us reside in what are described as 'liberal democracies', where we
relish the notion that we enjoy a freedom guaranteed by that polity and
enjoy the opportunity to have a say in how that is shaped. However, power
remains fundamentally unchanged regardless of this supposed progress in
terms of regime – yet it has found different (and more subtle) ways in
which to operate on and through us. One of its ways has been to facilitate
the flow of the idea that hierarchy has flattened over time and through
the encouragement of an entirely non-existent egalitarianism. Whenever a
mouth falls open to pronounce that we're all in the same boat, it reminds
us that many are stuck in steerage while a precious few are dining at the
captain's table. Quite simply, it's a grotesque falsehood.

If we see the world of work through this lens of diverse perspectives
reflecting differences in hierarchal position, relational connection, and felt
capacity to speak up and engage, the priorities of leadership become very
different from those when leaders are seen as being the point at which an

organisation achieves alignment around a common purpose. We suggest that leaders in such a world need to focus on:

- Legitimising the expression of different points of view
- Acknowledging and working with established political processes
- Legitimising the decision-making authority of sub-groups
- Seeing 'empowerment' as an expression of current power relations, not an escape from them

1. **Legitimising the expression of different priorities.** These differences are of course already present, but are banned from meaningful public expression and so help sustain incoherent organisational cultures, with contradictory realities playing out in a divide between what is said and done, espoused and practised. For many senior people attached to the single narrative view of organisational life this will require a major shift in approach and a deepening of their reflexive abilities, so that they can see their defensive and habitual responses in action. Such a shift will also require persistence given the deep-seated habit of only saying some things in public and people's natural suspicion of how 'deviant' views will be received. Recognising the multitude of views – expressed through a genuine diversity of voice – and, at the same time, surrendering the positional pre-eminence of one view, namely the one announced from the mountain top, requires considerable personal insight, but is an essential leadership adjustment. Even the 'flattening' notion of *primus inter pares*, the first among equals that is so often mentioned in reference to the position of the Prime Minister in the UK government, is implicitly faulty and unhelpful.

2. **Acknowledging and working with established political processes.** All organisations will have developed ways of negotiating between the various interests and power groupings. The challenge will be to work with the actual political processes rather than the espoused ones (usually presented in a deeply rational way, devoid of human subjectivity). This is about making visible the taken-for-granted exercise of power and getting deep into its very warp and weft, finding how it is presently constituted and how it can evolve – which in turn might be very threatening to the status quo, if part of its power comes from

being undiscussable, as is so often the case in organisational settings (Tuckermann, 2018).

3. **Legitimising the decision-making authority of sub-groups.** In Robert Fuller's seminal work on rank in the workplace (Fuller, 2004), he speaks to how organisations ossify, and positional rank and decision-making authority becomes corrupted, with people who are unqualified to make decisions taking them on behalf of others. When an organisation is understood only through one lens, then there is only one type of expertise that takes people to the 'top'. In a world understood as having multiple forms of expertise, which may well not be known about ahead of time, the first question to be asked is: 'Who will give this decision legitimacy?' Closely followed by the second question: 'What decision-making process will give this decision legitimacy'?

4. **Seeing 'empowerment' as an expression of current power relations not an escape from them.** Empowerment is often advocated as a way of avoiding all of the earlier mentioned, but empowerment is simply a repackaging of the status quo, wrapped up in the tacit and explicit relational practices of the workplace. At its worst it can turn into a game in which the 'empowered' group has to second guess what the 'empowering' group really means or wants from the relationship – and then internalises these self-governing rules, so disappearing power once again. The very term implies that the powerful packages up their power as a micro-resource and bountifully allocates that to others in their organisational context. Hence, it represents incorporation – implicating us all in the vulgar to and fro of the management in a firm – whilst offering the illusion of freedom. Empowerment presupposes that power is donated to others…and, as with all the worst gift-givers, that means it can be reclaimed at any point. Empowerment is, in itself, an implicit power act.

3.21 A concluding commentary on the 'We're all in this together' myth

Currently the established organisational discourse has not paid attention to what sustains the legitimacy of a ruling class or privileged elite within an organisation – organisations are assumed to be expressions of some axiomatic 'meritocracy' and don't pay attention to how forms of power create particular truths around what constitutes merit and the common good. Positionally senior people persist in conflating that which serves them well as serving all well – in one recent interview with a senior editor at a trade magazine, the editor described how the firm's founder came back from winning a major new deal and, as was part of a pattern of the last year, expected everyone to be overjoyed at the extra work... even though the additional revenue accrued solely to the main shareholder which was himself.

We advocate an understanding of organisational life in which common cause between groups and across different parts of the system are temporary conditions, rather than an enduring and constant feature. We are in a permanent state of alliance building and reconfiguration, interests briefly coincide, but no shared agenda is for ever. For organisations to be successful requires success to be defined in many ways, and not just one, and for these different definitions of success to be continually negotiated and renegotiated.

3.22 In conclusion... reframing the six myths

The six myths point towards the habits of mind which are creating stuck and ineffective approaches to organising. Given the sectoral focus of much of our work, we are acutely aware of this in the context of health and social care in the UK. In this conclusion we offer suggestions as to how these myths can be critically interrogated collectively and actively dispelled with the aim of releasing different ways of thinking and so different (better) actions.

1. Reframing the myth that **'All is fixable'**... letting go of this myth requires people be rid of the language of 'solutions' which in the organisational context is hopelessly enmeshed with the machine metaphor and simplistic models of cause and effect. Our suggested reframe is that **'All is in flux'**... where any form of action, anything framed as an improvement to the current situation, should be understood to be both temporary and unknowable in terms of its impact, both now and in the future – which suggests that any analysis of the consequences of suggested improvement plans (often titled 'Impact Assessments') should be approached in a spirit of modesty and doubt – rather than a celebration of causal, mechanistic certainty.

2. Reframing the myth that **'Perfection is the only state worth pursu-
    ing'**... is at heart a letting go of the theology of intelligent design,
    which assumes that a divine external hand (a *deus ex machina*) can provide
    a revelatory truth about what an ideal, ahistorical, de-contextualised
    approach to health and social care should look like. Our suggested
    reframe is that **'There is no perfection, only the crooked timber of
    the here and now'** when it comes to human organising, by refocusing
    our attention on the current reality with an appreciation of human
    fallibility, needs and lived experience, any suggested improvements are
    then built out of what is in the world rather than free-floating castles
    in the air. Within the managerial discourse the visionary became delu-
    sional some time ago.

3. Reframing the myth that **'There is just one way of doing things'**...
    this requires people to step out of assuming that their reality is the
    totality of organisational experience and that there is one single per-
    spective on organisational reality that speaks to an objective truth. It
    requires an embrace of a critically subjective philosophy, which invites
    people to engage with a world of multiple truths in a rigorous fashion –
    multiplicity and subjectivity does not simply mean anything goes. The
    reframe offered is that given that health care is a dynamic social envi-
    ronment then **'Many approaches will have different and relevant
    forms of legitimacy and currency'** – from a managerial approach this
    creates a responsibility for drawing on a continuously evolving and
    multi-faceted set of approaches, removing the comforting certainty
    of working with an approved and singular methodology. Judgement,
    curiosity, and creativity become the personal qualities expected of
    those who would lead – very different from a focus on policing com-
    pliance with established and approved methods and models.

4. Reframing the myth that **'Metrics reflect an objective reality'**... meas-
    urement has become a lousy master, an end in itself... the health and
    social care system has become an impossible game, with a monstrous
    over-burden of appraisal floating free of the complex and multi-faceted
    world it keeps trying to pin down. Metrics have become 'bonkers',
    reflecting an anxious world trying to deliver the impossible and hoping
    that bold targets can be a substitute for substantive inquiry and debate.
    The reframe offered is that what is needed are **'Rich descriptions of
    diverse, felt and seen experiences reflecting a world of multiple**

realities' – the intention is to create conditions where inquiry is supported and where acts of rich description lead to new action in the moment (in tune with a philosophy of participative inquiry, where to inquire is to change).

5. Reframing the myth that **'Values bind the organisation'**... organisational units are temporary forms for configuring activities, usually without any informing moral purpose connected to this particular institutional bundling (where the language of the efficient use of assets dominates). The values that inform people's ethical choices will come from their wider and more enduring lives, the moral purposes that they have grown up with, the choices they've had to make, the tensions they hold and the extent to which a sense of belonging and identity is wrapped up in the moral universe they inhabit. The reframe offered is that **'Organisational values should not be allowed to blind people from the moral choices being made in a company – and should instead actively embrace the values that people hold in respect to work'**. Values are not abstract things that are 'brought to work', they are the orientations that people take on a moment-by-moment basis as they work collectively. By the same token, they are not abstract virtue signals to be transmitted up, down and across an organisation: instead, they manifest in the work that takes place in the organisation and the ways in which it gets done.

6. Reframing the myth that **'We're all in this together'**... this myth is a piece of magical thinking that disappears any acknowledgement of the conflicts, paradoxes, and tensions that have to be held and lived with in any multi-facetted social system. This myth cuts us off from the energising forces that give social systems their liveliness and leaves us with nothing but a dull stodge of pretend togetherness. The reframe offered is that **'We're all in a different relationship with the work of the organisation'** and by seeing the world like this we can begin to surface the differences that exist and so allow for a more robust conversation to take place around what does and doesn't count as a legitimate action.

3.23 Postscript

Our current management myths infantilise us; they serve to act as a crutch against reality, they fuel any amount of senseless activity. Our reframe is a sober reminder that we are mortal and that this knowledge must under-pin how we organise, particularly in respect to providing services, such as health and social care. It is in the ancient poets of the Judeo-Christian tradition that we can find an invitation for us to step into a more mature way of thinking about how we approach leading and managing, in a context that forces us to face into the raw existential challenge of being human, conscious of our earthly mortality. In the world of Ecclesiastes we are reminded that there is a time for everything, from birth to death, sowing and harvesting, lamentation and laughter – there's even a time for love and for hate. Leading and managing needs to draw on a much broader emotional palette than it currently allows for.

Notes

1   This observation derives from a private conversation in which John was involved with a senior leader in health and social care not so long ago.
2   Purists may cavil at what seems to be a conceptual conflation of terms used in Marxist and Foucauldian thinking, viz ideology and discourse. To an extent, though, this contentment on our part regarding using these two important terms alongside each other in support of the argument being developed here reflects fresh thinking about the linkages between these two corpuses of knowledge but also a long standing acknowledge-ment of the relationship in thought between Althusser and Foucault (Bidet, 2016).

References

Anonymous, 2019. *The cloud of unknowing.* s.l.: Digireads.com Publishing.

Bain & Company, 2020. *Complexity management.* [Online] Available at: www. bain.com/consulting-services/performance-improvement/complexity-management/ [Accessed 21 May 2020].

Baron-Cohen, S., 2011. *Zero degrees of empathy: A new theory of human cruelty.* London: Penguin.

Beard, M., 2018. *Women and power.* London: Profile Books/London Review of Books.

Beart, S., 2014. Taking my body to work: Working with relational embodiment in coaching and consulting practice. In: K. King & J. Higgins, eds. *The change doctors: Reimagining organisational practice.* Faringdon, Oxon: Libri, pp. 61–82.

Becker, E., 1997. *The denial of death.* New York: Free Press Paperbacks.

Bevan, G. & Hood, C., 2006. What's measured is what matters: Targets and gaming in the English public health care system. *Public Administration,* 84(3), pp. 517–538.

Bidet, J., 2016. *Foucault with Marx.* London: Zed Books.

Binney, G., Glanfield, P. & Wilke, G., 2017. *Breaking free of bonkers: How to lead in today's crazy world of organizations.* London: Nicholas Brealey Publishing.

Birkinshaw, J. & Heywood, S., 2010. *Putting organizational complexity in its place.* [Online] Available at: www.mckinsey.com/business-functions/ organization/our-insights/putting-organizational-complexity-in-its-place [Accessed 21 May 2020].

Boethius, 1999. *The consolation of philosophy.* London: Penguin.

Bohm, D., 1996. *On dialogue.* Abingdon: Routledge.

Boshyk, Y. & Dilworth, R. L., 2010. *Action learning: History and evolution.* Basingstoke: Palgrave Macmillan.

Branson, R., 2011. *Losing my virginity.* London: Ebury Publishing.

Brooks, J., 2000. *Thank you, comrade Stalin! Soviet public culture from revolution to Cold War.* Princeton, NJ: Princeton University Press.

Burr, V., 2003. *Social Constructionism.* Hove: Routledge.

Capra, F., 1997. *The web of life: A new synthesis of mind and matter.* London: Flamingo.

Carson, R., 1962/2000. *Silent Spring.* London: Penguin.

Child, J., 2019. *Hierarchy: A key idea for business and society.* Abingdon: Routledge.

Christensen, C. M., 2000. *The innovator's dilemma: When new technologies cause great firms to fail.* Boston, Mass.: Harvard Business Review Press.

Churchman, C. W., 1968. *Challenge to reason.* New York: Sage.

Clegg, S., Pina e Cunha, M. & Rego, A., 2012. The theory and practice of Utopia in a total institution: The pineapple panopticon. *Organization Studies,* 33(12), pp. 1735–1757.

Cole, M., 2020. *Radical organisation development.* Abingdon: Routledge.

Collins, J. & Porras, J. I., 2005. *Built to last: Successful habits of visionary companies.* London: Random House Business Books.

Coogan, S., 1995. *Gareth Cheeseman self-motivation speech.* s.l.: s.n.

Cooperrider, D. & Whitney D., 2005. *Appreciative inquiry: A positive revolution in change*. San Francisco: Berrett-Koehler Publishers Inc.

Critchley, B., King, K. & Higgins, J., 2007. *Organisational consulting: A relational perspective*. London: Middlesex University Press.

Dalal, F., 1998. *Taking the group seriously: Towards a post-Foulkesian group analytic theory*. London: Jessica Kingsley Publishers.

Dalrymple, W., 2019. *The Anarchy: The relentless rise of the East India Company*. London: Bloomsbury Publishing.

Davidson, R. & Büchel, B., 2011. The art of piloting new initiatives. *MIT Sloan Management Review*, 11 September.

Dickinson, B., 1987. *Uncle Monty – the end of an age*. [Online] Available at: youtu.be/pDl4ye22U-E [Accessed 17 June 2021].

During, E., 2006. Is there an exit from "virtual reality?" Grid and network – from Tron to The Matrix. In: M. Diocaretz & S. Herbrechter, eds. *The Matrix in theory*. Amsterdam: Rodopi, pp. 131–150.

Dweck, C. S., 2017. *Mindset: Changing the way you think to fulfil your potential*. London: Robinson.

Edmondson, A. C., 2011. *Strategies for learning from failure*. [Online] https://hbr.org/2011/04/strategies-for-learning-from-failure [Accessed 17 June 2021].

Edmondson, A. C., 2019. *The fearless organization: Creating psychological safety in the workplace for learning, innovation, and growth*. Hoboken: Wiley.

Eggers, D., 2013. *The Circle*. London: Hamish Hamilton/Penguin.

Elias, N., 2000. *The civilizing process: Sociogenetic and psychogenetic investigations*. Oxford: Blackwell.

Eliot, T. S., 2001. *Four Quartets*. London: Faber & Faber.

Fleming, P., 2014. *Resisting work: The corporatization of life and its discontents*. Philadelphia: Temple University Press.

Fletcher, J. K., 1999. *Disappearing acts: Gender, power and relational practice at work*. Cambridge, Mass: MIT Press.

Foucault, M., 1980. *Power/Knowledge: Selected interviews and other writings, 1972–1977*. New York: Pantheon Books.

Foucault, M., 1991. *Discipline and punish: The birth of the prison*. London: Penguin.

Frazer, J. G., 1998. *The golden bough: A study in magic and religion*. Oxford: Oxford University Press.

Freire, P., 2005. *Pedagogy of the oppressed*. New York: Continuum Books.

French, J. R. P. & Raven, B., 1959. The bases of social power. In: D. Cartwright, ed. *Studies in social power*. Ann Arbor, Michigan: Institute for Social Research, pp. 259–269.

Fuchs, B., Reitz, M. & Higgins, J., 2018. *Do you have "advantage blindness"?* [Online] Available at: https://hbr.org/2018/04/do-you-have-advantage-blindness [Accessed 17 November 2020].

Fukuyama, F., 2020. *The end of history and the last man*. London: Penguin.

Fuller, R. W., 2004. *Somebodies and nobodies: Overcoming the abuse of rank*. Gabriola Island: New Society Publishers.

Ghiselli, E. E. & Siegel, J. P., 1972. Leadership and managerial success in tall and flat organization structures. *Personnel Psychology*, 25, pp. 617–624.

Giddens, A., 1984. *The constitution of society: Outline of the theory of structuration*. Berkeley: University of California Press.

Gilligan, C., 1993. *In a different voice: Psychological theory and women's development*. Cambridge, Mass: Harvard University Press.

Glassdoor, 2020. *Next jump*. [Online] Available at: www.glassdoor.co.uk/Reviews/Next-Jump-Reviews-E156468.htm [Accessed 12 May 2020].

Goldhamer, H. & Shils, E. A., 1939. Types of power and status. *The American Journal of Sociology*, XLV(2), pp. 171–182.

Goodheart, C. A. E., 1984. *Monetary theory and practice: The UK experience*. London ed. London: Macmillan.

Gray, J., 2012. *The immortilization commission: The strange quest to cheat death*. London: Penguin.

Heider, J., 2015. *The Tao of leadership: Lao Tzu's Tao Te Ching adapted for a new age*. Palm Beach, Fl: Green Dragon Books.

Heifetz, R. A., 1994. *Leadership without easy answers*. Cambridge, Mass.: Harvard University Press.

Heron, J., 1996. *Co-operative inquiry: Research into the human condition*. London: Sage.

Higgins, J., 2019. *Exploring the experience of Bands 2 to 4: Who gets heard and what gets missed*. s.l.: Unpublished.

Higgins, J. & Reitz, M., 2019. If whistleblowing is the answer, ask a better question. *Journal of the Royal Society of Medicine*, 112(11), pp. 453–455.

Higgins, J., Reitz, M. & Williams, C., 2017. The hero is dead... long live the new hero. In: K. Fleming & R. Delves, eds. *Inspiring leadership: Becoming a dynamic and engaging leader*. London: Bloomsbury.

Hoffman, B. G., 2012. *American icon: Alan Mulally and the fight to save Ford Motor Company*. New York: Crown Business.

Hopwood, A. G., 2009. *Management consultants cost the NHS dear*. [Online] Available at: www.theguardian.com/society/2009/sep/07/nhs-mckinsey-health-staff-cuts [Accessed 23 November 2020].

Iacobucci, G., 2019. Life expectancy gap between rich and poor in England widens. *BMJ*, 364(l1492) doi:10.1136/bmj.l1492.

Ibbotson, P., 2008. *The illusion of leadership: Directing creativity in business and the arts*. Basingstoke: Palgrave Macmillan.

Ingerslev, K., 2014. *Healthcare innovation under the microscope: Framing boundaries of wicked problems*, Frederiksberg: Copenhagen Business School.

Isaacs, W., 1999. *Dialogue and the art of thinking together*. New York: Currency/Doubleday.

Janke, K., Propper, C. & Sadun, R., 2018. *The impact of CEOs in the public sector: Evidence from the English NHS – Working Paper 18-075*, Boston, Mass.: Harvard Business School.

Johnsson, J. & Beane, R., 2020. *'Designed by clowns... supervised by monkeys': Internal Boeing messages slam 737 Max*. [Online] Available at: www.fortune.com/2020/01/10/designed-clowns-supervised-monkeys-internal-boeing-messages-slam-737-max/ [Accessed 28 May 2020].

Kafka, F., 2009. *The Castle*. Oxford: OUP.

Kegan, R. & Lahey, L. L., 2016. *An everyone culture: Becoming a deliberately developmental organization*. Boston, Mass.: Harvard Business Review Press.

Kennedy, D., 2020. *NHS management gurus waste millions*. [Online] Available at: www.thetimes.co.uk/article/nhs-management-gurus-waste-millions-d9jlo56on [Accessed 16 November 2020].

Kierkegaard, S., 1843. *Journals IV.A.164*. [See www.homepage.divms.uiowa.edu/~jorgen/kierkegaardquotesource.html].

King, K. & Higgins, J., 2014. *The change doctors: Re-imagining organisational practice*. Faringdon, Oxon: Libri.

King, K., Higgins, J. & Schroder, H., 2018. Resilience is a team sport. *Dialogue*, Issue Q2, pp. 66–67.

Kirkpatrick, I. et al., 2019. The impact of management consultants on public service efficiency. *Policy & Politics*, 47(1), pp. 77–95.

Kobie, N., 2019. *The complicated truth about China's social credit system*. [Online] Available at: www.wired.co.uk/article/china-social-credit-system-explained [Accessed 23 November 2020].

Kohn, A., 1993. *Punished by rewards: The trouble with gold stars, incentive plans, A's, praise, and other bribes.* New York: Houghton, Mifflin and Company.

Lubitsh, G. & Higgins, J., 2001. Thinking from the heart. *Directions: The Ashridge Journal*, Summer, pp. 32–35.

Lukes, S., 2005/1974. *Power: A radical view.* 2nd ed. Basingstoke: Palgrave Macmillan.

Lyotard, J.-F., 1984. *The postmodern condition: A report on knowledge.* Manchester: Manchester University Press.

Marshall, S., 2014. Photo-dialogue: Creating the word-image that makes the difference. In: K. King & J. Higgins, eds. *The change Doctors: Re-imagining organisational practice.* Faringdon, Oxon: Libri, pp. 85–110.

Martin, T., 2020. *When Adam dolve: Pandemics and social revolution.* [Online] Available at: www.anarchiststudies.org/when-adam-dolve-pandemics-and-social-revolution-by-tom-martin/ [Accessed 13 October 2020].

McLean, A., 2013. *Leadership & cultural webs in organisations: Weavers' tales.* Bingley: Emerald Publishing.

Meadows, D., Meadows, D. L., Randers, J. & Behrens, W. W., 1972. *The limits to growth: A report for the Club of Rome's project on the predicament of mankind.* New York: Universe Books.

Menzies, I. E. P., 1960. A case-study in the functioning of social systems as a defence against anxiety: A report on a study of the nursing service of a general hospital. *Human Relations*, 13(2), pp. 95–121.

Morgan, G., 2006. *Images of organization.* Thousand Oaks, CA: Sage.

Mulgan, G., 2013. Joined-up innovation: What is systemic innovation and how can it be done effectively? In: G. Mulgan & C. Leadbetter, eds. *Systems innovation: Discussion paper.* London: NESTA, pp. 5–24.

Nah, V. E. M. Y. & Perono Cacciafoco, F., 2018. Ex-isles: Islands that disappeared. *Review of Historical Geography and Toponomastics*, 25–26(XIII), pp. 31–58.

Next Jump, 2020. *A culture of deliberate development.* [Online] Available at: www.nextjump.com/culture/ [Accessed 12 May 2020].

O'Brien, L., 2020. *Shropshire hospital trust to repay almost £1 million received for 'good maternity care' after 'incorrect submission'.* [Online] Available at: www.shropshirestar.com/news/health/2020/03/06/shropshire-trust-to-repay-almost-1-million-received-for-good-maternity-care-after-incorrect-submission/ [Accessed 23 November 2020].

O'Mahoney, J. & Sturdy, A., 2015. Power and the diffusion of management ideas: The case of McKinsey & Co. *Management Learning.* 47(3), pp. 247–265.

Oshry, B., 2007. *Seeing systems: Unlocking the mysteries of organizational life.* San Francisco: Berrett-Koehler Publishers, Inc.

Poulantzas, N., 1978. *Political power and social classes.* London: Verso.

Reitz, M. & Higgins, J., 2019a. *Managers, you're more intimidating than you think.* [Online] Available at: www.hbr.org/2019/07/managers-youre-more-intimidating-than-you-think [Accessed 17 November 2020].

Reitz, M. & Higgins, J., 2019b. *Speak up: Say what needs to be said and hear what needs to be heard.* Harlow: FT/Pearson.

Reitz, M., Nilsson, V. O., Day, E. H. J. & Higgins, J., 2019. *Speaking truth to power at work: How we silence ourselves and others – Interim survey results,* Berkhamstead, Herts.: Hult International Business School.

Reynolds, A., Houlder, D., Goddard, J. & Lewis, D., 2020. *What philosophy can teach you about being a better leader.* London: Kogan Page.

Sargent, L. T., 1994. The three faces of Utopianism revisited. *Utopian Studies,* 5(1), pp. 1–37.

Seton, M., Williams, S., Zahirovic, S. & Micklethwaite, S., 2013. Obituary: Sandy Island (1876–2012). *Eos,* 94(15), pp. 141–143.

Silveira Cruz, B. & de Oliveira Dias, M., 2020. Crashed Boeing 737-MAX: Fatalities or malpractice? *GSJ,* 8(1), pp. 2615–2624.

Slater, R., 1999. *Jack Welch and the GE way: Management insights and leadership secrets of the legendary CEO.* New York: McGraw-Hill.

Stacey, R. D., Griffin, D. & Shaw, P., 2000. *Complexity and management: Fad or radical challenge to systems thinking?* London: Routledge.

Standing, C. et al., 2016. Enhancing individual innovation in organisations: A review of the literature. *International Journal of Innovation and Learning,* 19(1), pp. 44–62.

The Bayswater Institute, 2017. *The double task.* [Online] Available at: www.bayswaterinst.org/2017/09/13/the-double-task/ [Accessed 19 May 2020].

Trompemaars, F. & Hampden-Turner, C., 2000. *Riding the waves of culture: Understanding diversity in global business.* London: Nicholas Brealey Publishing.

Tsutsui, W. M., 1996. W Edwards Deming and the origins of quality control in Japan. *Journal of Japanese Studies,* 22(2), pp. 295–325.

Tuckermann, H., 2018. Visibilizing and invisibilizing paradox: A process study of interactions in a hospital executive board. *Organization Studies*, 40(12), pp. 1851–1872.

Uhl-Bien, M., Marion, R. & McKelvey, B., 2007. Complexity leadership theory: shifting leadership from the industrial age to the knowledge era. *The Leadership Quarterly*, 18(4), pp. 298–318.

Vollmer, L., 2016. *Zurück an die arbeit: Wie aus Business-Theatern wieder echte Unternehmen werden*. Wien: Linde.

Watzlawick, P., Weakland, J. H. & Fisch, R., 1974/2011. *Change: Principles of problem formation and problem resolution*. New York: W W Norton & Company.

Weick, K. E., 1995. *Sensemaking in organisations*. Thousand Oaks, CA: Sage.

Wierman, B., Granter, E. & McCann, L., 2020. Anarchy in management today. In: M. Parker, K. Stoborod & T. Swann, eds. *Anarchism, organization and management: Critical perspectives for students*. Abingdon: Routledge, pp. 26–38.

Winnicott, D. W., 2005. *Playing and reality*. Abingdon: Routledge.

4

CONCLUSION... ENRICHESSEZ-VOUS!

In John's research with Megan Reitz into speaking truth to power (a concept we make more complicated later on in this chapter), one of the recurrent patterns is how much people see others as being the problem, while they themselves sit outside the social patterns on which they pass judgement (Reitz & Higgins, 2019). Our argument is that this is simply untrue, nobody can exist outside of the world, we are all active – if unequal – participants in sustaining what passes as common sense. In our jargon, you cannot not participate in the society of others. We are therefore all implicated in sustaining the world as it is, there is no them and us, simply us – we are all in this together, even if the rewards, benefits, and costs serve some better than others. We are both us and individuals who exist within the context of us – there is no individual who exists sovereign and apart from the society of people.

DOI: 10.4324/9781003035015-4

In this closing chapter we explore and reflect on:

- The taken-for-granted belief in magic realism and the illusions of/in leadership
- The illusion of leadership we actually live, and take part, in sustaining
- The non-dichotomy of management and leadership – the emergence of 'leaderised' management
    - Underpinning one: individualism versus individuality
    - Underpinning two: fetishisation of measurement
    - Underpinning three: displaced relationality
    - Underpinning four: headwaters and downstream thinking
- The sound of silence
- (How) time's tide will swallow you (or not)
- What we are left with to work with in the morning

Once again we have colluded with the unquestioned assumption that all arguments can be boiled down to a few quick and easy conclusions, bon mots, and aide memoires – and while providing this potentially high-risk digested summary for each section, we also want to mark it as a dangerous narcotic if seen as a substitute for rigorous, critical inquiry and reflexion.

4.1 The taken-for-granted belief in magic realism and the illusions of/in leadership

As the UK came out of its initial coronavirus lockdown in 2020, the government executed a volte-face that recast the crisis from a medical to an economic one. The message seemed to slide almost seamlessly from save lives to restart your life, as the UK government began an advertising splurge around the theme of 'Enjoy Summer Safely'. According to the advertising industry's trade magazine at the time of the launch, 'The UK government has partnered a slew of major brands in a campaign encouraging the public to resume the activities of normal life, while taking care to minimise the risk of coronavirus transmission' (Campaign, 2020).

In a report for the BBC, a number of people who had taken the government at face value and booked Spanish holidays were asked for their reactions to the introduction of a 14-day quarantine for those returning from the country. The article included the following:

> Lois Stothard, from South Yorkshire, said she had booked a holiday to Seville as a surprise for her boyfriend's 30th birthday – due to fly out on Sunday morning – but now feels that she cannot travel. "I'm a key worker – I'm a teacher – and my boyfriend has work commitments so we cannot quarantine for 14 days when we return," she said. "We can't get any money back and to change the company want double what I've already paid in fees. I'm very disappointed and upset as we're packed and ready to go".
>
> (BBC News, 2020)

There is no sense that this observation is made in order to denigrate Lois and her boyfriend. After all, who amongst us have not been hankering for things to resolve themselves so that we can begin to do the things that we used to in the ways that we have always enjoyed? Yet – for us – the story underscores the way in which the myths that we have explored frame all of our thinking. Elements of the crisis may have yielded to a certain degree of manageability – but it was a long way from being fixable through the application of a singular process that aimed to deliver a result that was perfect. To move from lockdown in the face of a deadly disease to booking surprise holidays at such a pace suggests that the government's blandishments at that time reinforced the unspoken notion that things were fixed, and we could go back to normal.

Elsewhere, an interviewee took a perspective that largely denied the nature of the world and our place in it: 'Dan says the news is stress he could have done without. "I'm particularly upset as I work for a travel company – March, April and May were hell – was never furloughed, and really needed this break," he said' (BBC News, 2020). One feels Dan's pain, for sure. Equally, one wonders at the way in which our mental attitude towards life these days has been reduced to a position of philosophical voluntarism, wherein our individual needs and personal circumstances can be mobilised to deny the reality of the impact of a pandemic.

The metaphor that springs to mind is that we all want to be Dorothy in the Wizard of Oz, who will find herself back in the warm and familiar embrace of home if she clicks her heels together three times and makes the correct wish… that there's no place like home. The bad news for Dorothy is that, however hard she tries, she's not going to wake up magically in Kansas any time soon. Instead, she has to accept the flow of time, allowing things to resolve themselves, and the simple fact that life itself is, by definition, messy and cannot simply be wished into shape.

In the course of the crisis, a companion of Mark's recounted the story of a business and budget planning meeting, wherein people were struggling to make sense of what they might be able to do in circumstances that were desperately changed and deeply unknowable. The convenor of the meeting eventually expressed their intense frustration at the failure of the participants to respond to his needs which were expressed thus: 'I just need something to put in these cells!'. Hence, his organisational reality was patently distanced from the practical character of the world, reduced merely to the void spaces that existed in the Excel spreadsheet. (In passing, it seems ripe with meaning that a cell is something in which we can become imprisoned. It is also noteworthy that business babble has moved us on from working in groups or teams – and many people now find themselves toiling away in 'work cells'. Again, one is thrown back to the cold grey rooms that one finds in gaols.)

As a story, this seems to underscore the way in which leadership resides in a never-never land, wherein the complexity of many aspects of the practical world is actively denied by a retreat into the simulacrum of: management theory (such as it is); business school research and case studies; the risibly poor 'thought leadership' of professional services companies; endless and groundless models, methods, techniques, and checklists that churn around in the business world; and the fetishised pursuit of data through a range of sources. These notionally rational elements are undergirded by the sorts of 'accepted fallacies' that express themselves in the corporate context as the sort of paradoxes and myths that we have sought to highlight. Here, it is worth flagging the way in which fallacy is properly understood in philosophical discussion, namely that, 'a fallacious argument…is one that seems to be valid but is not so' (Hamblin, 1970, p. 12).

Through all of this, two intimately related things derive: first, the superficial rationalism of much of this – with so much leadership technique being premised on the scientism that prevails in society – and its intimate connectedness to the ideas of fixability, perfection, and the ideal solution representing the illusions of leadership. Hence, those practising leadership cleave to the faulty notions that this sort of work does indeed serve a meaningful purpose in complex organisational settings. These are the illusions of leadership.

Second, the way in which these illusions of leadership circulate – both amongst those who cast themselves as leaders and those who might see themselves as 'the led' (or, to default to the decidedly ovine notion with which leadership thinking traditionally presents itself, 'followers'), generating amongst all of us an illusion of leadership. Both those who occupy positions ascribed as leader roles – or those who assume the mantle of leadership, notwithstanding their formal role – and the rest of us collectively are caught in a 'bystander effect', where none of us feel able to make a move to call out the illusion for what it is.

This psychological notion suggests that, 'When only one bystander is present in an emergency, if help is to come, it must come from him. Although he may choose to ignore it (out of concern for his personal safety, or desires "not to get involved"), any pressure to intervene focuses uniquely on him. When there are several observers present, however, the pressures to intervene do not focus on any one of the observers; instead the responsibility for intervention is shared among all the onlookers and is not unique to anyone. As a result, no one helps' (Darley & Latane, 1968, pp. 377–378).

Some punctuating summary points on 'The taken for granted belief in magic realism and the illusions of/in leadership'

- The world should bend to the established wishes of what people high and low feel they deserve, where wants exist apart from a wider social context/reality
- Within the world of work, the representation of organisational reality takes precedence over lived reality. To slightly rephrase the old saying – the map is no longer different to the territory, it is the territory
- The leader/follower construction sustains habits of passivity in those who are classified, or self-classify, as followers (the 'led')

4.2 The illusion of leadership we actually live, and take part, in sustaining

Following on from our comments about the 'bystander effect', we are all implicated in the sustaining of the present notion of what leadership is thought to be in a corporate setting, bedazzled as we are by popular representations of it in a range of cultural settings. This ordinary reality, and its bedazzlement, can readily be identified by making steady and careful progress from 'cover to cover' of a national newspaper. Partly, this exercise derived from Mark often suggesting to groups with whom he was working that a review of the news offered far better insight into the reality of leadership than engagement with any number of policies and strategies; white papers; and titles from business schools and off the shelves of the Heathrow Academy, with its ready to swallow titbits for busy leaders as they trouble shoot their way around the planet.

Mark is not alone however, a similar approach has been used to offer a grounding to an excellent work in the developing field of critical leadership studies (Learmonth & Morrell, 2019, p. 14). As a technique it helps to step out of the swamp of vested interests that sustain, complicate, and make all but undiscussable the ever-burgeoning literature being produced by those most invested in the status quo (and its complex mystification). There is a well-entrenched corpus who are nicely enriching themselves by staying uncritically within the leadership orthodoxy and are the inspiration for the title of this closing chapter – the business school tutors and researchers into leadership and their friends in the consulting industry are onto a nice little earner, rocking the boat will be bad for their pockets. Why rock the boat when you are doing so nicely out of an uncritical engagement with the established world view.

So, on July 31, 2020, Mark opened the app for The Times of London and evaluated each tab along the line in respect to the image it reflected in respect to leadership. In the section marked 'News' – what would perhaps be the front page in a hard-copy – there were two especially significant stories. The first of these reported about the UK Prime Minister apparently single-handedly managing the ongoing coronavirus crisis, under the headline: 'Johnson delays easing lockdown as infections rise'. Here, we have the image of the heroic and decisive individual, unilaterally making crucial decisions with speed and precision. It does not give insight into the collegial context in which conversations might have taken place that nudged the supposed figurehead to take action. The other focused in on the proto-fascism immanent in the Donald Trump presidency, with the heading: 'Trump uses poll delay tweet to distract from job crisis'. This implies that a single – and grotesque – personality can manage a population's understanding of the world with 140 stabs of his tiny orange thumbs. We see little reason to exercise what is laughably called balance in the face of monstrosity.

Moving along, the 'Comment' tab included one destructive piece that sought to ensure that leadership was properly located from a hierarchical perspective, with an opinion item under the heading: 'Greta's message of doom is religion not reality'. Similarly, another item challenged the assertion of Scottish politics to be taken seriously, with a column called: 'Sturgeon would rather talk about leaving the UK than saving jobs'. We note in passing – and drawing no conclusions directly from such a limited datum, although it fits within a persistent habit of misogyny – that both the alternative poles of leadership castigated herein were occupied by women. Yet, in the 'News' section, another leadership perspective with an anti-establishment bent, driven forward by some men of a right-wing persuasion, appeared under the anodyne title: 'Anti lockdown campaign raises £230,000'. Everyday sexism is too taken for granted to be even discussable; to draw attention to it is to label yourself as someone not worth listening to. After all it'll only be another 200 odd years until women get the equal pay as already legally required.

With something approaching a Shakespearean tenor, the first paragraph of this soberly reported 'Anti lockdown campaign' declared: 'A businessman leading the fight against lockdown measures has said that his movement gives its supporters something to live for. Simon Dolan, an aviation and accountancy tycoon who is said to be worth £200 million, has launched an appeal after being denied permission to seek a judicial review over the regulations imposed in March'. All the boorish leadership elements are briskly ticked off in those 54 words of journalese: Dolan puts himself at the head of a fight, on the basis of a vision that he is eager to articulate (in the face of scientific opinion and what seems to us in this case genuine common sense); in so doing, he constellates around him a group of followers – and hence assumes a messianic taint, by alleging that his self-aggrandising politicking might actually give people a motivation to continue living. And he occupies this position primarily through his access to resources, in this case a personal fortune, rather than due to a set of skills, talents, and understandings drawn out of relevant experiences.

The stories that Mark focused upon which appeared under the 'Business' tab had one thing in common: within two to four paragraphs, they were busy quoting a senior member of the board for the companies on which they reported. The item highlighting Amazon's 40% revenue increase over lockdown requires Jeff Bezos to sidle in from the wings, like some cat-stroking Bond villain, whose personal fortune is spoken off as an object of wonder (and those who even breathe a word of doubt about its virtue are howled down as consumed by envy and naïve in their understanding of the great worth of all forms of entrepreneurialism). News from the world of international beer brewing – where all the corporations are named as if they were companies in the film *Blade Runner* – speedily calls up the comments of the President of Budweiser Brewing Company who speaks in the normal corporate boilerplate expected of him. And pieces about Rentokil and their hand sanitiser and the plans for the transformation of John Lewis department stores quickly resort to remarks from the respective CEO and 'chairman' (the latter parenthesised not merely because it is an unhelpfully gendered appellation but because the post holder was, in fact, at that time, a woman).

Lastly, we went to look at 'Sport'. It was dominated by football – which, these days, of course, is increasingly inhabited by business rather than any love for the sport itself, revealing how prescient Viz magazine was in the 1980s which saw the fictional team Fulchester Rovers stop being a football team but keep its fans despite now being a property company. The fans would gather to cheer on the share price instead of goals. In this post-satire 'Sport' section we were schooled in how his background in the Basque country had shaped Mikel Arteta's (the manager of Arsenal) management style; we were invited to watch how Newcastle United was being torn apart largely by men who desperately wanted to capitalise on it as a brand; and Mark was compelled to skip over an exceptionally boring looking story, which seemed to lack any kind of hook in its headline, which was, 'Liverpool CEO Peter Moore to leave club and be replaced by Billy Hogan'. This seemed to Mark to be the newspaper equivalent of telling one's spouse on their return home that, in the course of the day, you had moved the sofa from one place to another in the sitting room. Surely neither Peter nor Billy could find the energy to read that story, despite the message it carried about the significance of leaders in large organisations? That message was not subtle: if their comings and goings are subject to this kind of scrutiny, then what they do must be significant – and the fans would need to cheer them on.

All of which underscores for us the distance that persists between what people say when they talk about leadership and what people do when they think they are leading. For us this is the superstructural conceit that sits on top of all of the other discursive elements, such as the management myths and the paradoxes, which we have described as a hard granite core of lived experience surrounded by a soft and largely illusory ideological wrapping around it. Quite simply, the very notion of leadership is the final illusion.

Some punctuating summary points on 'Looking at the leadership we actually live, and take part, in sustaining'

- The actuality of taken-for-granted assumptions about leadership are hiding in plain sight in what we see and read around us every day
- In all fields of life, the views of those who occupy the commanding heights of economic wealth are foregrounded and made significant
- The disconnect between the formally espoused and actual practice of leadership creates a discursive disconnect, making it very hard to focus on the reality of what is (compared to the endless firework display of what could, should, or might be)

4.3 The non-dichotomy of management and leadership – the emergence of 'leaderized' management (overview)

In medieval Christian theology there was the debate about how many Angels could sit on the head of a pin. This is often presented as an argument about nothing, between people who have become obsessed with their own fine distinctions. The substantive issue is about the extent to which Angels do or do not have a corporeal presence, which given the Christian tradition is based around a God made flesh in the form of Jesus Christ, actually speaks to the heart of the faith and is therefore a matter of foundational philosophy.

Within the business world there is a noisy debate about the relative nature of management and leadership, a seemingly unimportant distinction which only really matters to obsessives, but which actually points towards the heart of something of great importance. Henry Mintzberg recently underscored the tension that exists between these two terms:

> A half century ago Peter Drucker (1954) put management on the map. Leadership has since pushed it off the map. We are now inundated with stories about the grand successes and even grander failures of the great leaders. But we have yet to come to grips with the simple realities of being a regular manager.
>
> (Mintzberg, 2009, p. 1)

Now, this perspective seems to intimate a binary opposition between two practices, with one recently usurping the other. However, elsewhere Mintzberg makes an important observation suggesting that those things that are traditionally ascribed to leadership are actually merely practices that are being encouraged to inhabit traditional management:

> What we have been getting over the past 10 years is more and more of what I would call "the heroic view of management" where the chief is responsible for everything. I call it "management by deeming" because senior managers believe they can sit there and "deem" performance levels and then expect everybody to run around and reach them or else get fired. I think this has been extremely disruptive in organizations. We have more and more disconnect between senior management and the rest of the organization.
>
> (de Holan & Mintzberg, 2004, p. 208)

To our mind, this is a sanitised description of how management has 'leaderised' itself over time: we prefer the notion of 'management by shouting', where management is characterised by bombast and assertion around which is wrapped the ideological shell of vision, direction, decisiveness, wisdom, and the presence of largely bystander followers. If we accept this to be true, then it is apparent that the distinction between management and leadership is a false dichotomy, one worthy of closer attention and where we feel drawn to not only look at the linguistic currency given by the titles of leader and follower, but also the framing logic of the context within which 'leaderised' management and following happens, namely the privileging of efficiency and the disappearance of democracy and the personal authority it invites. This is a personal authority which speaks to the language of human rights and the Enlightenment tradition – which is a million miles from its milksop and disingenuous step-cousin, 'empowerment'.

We have developed this notion of 'leaderization' by seeking to situate it relationally with other developments that have taken place socially and corporately. One line of inquiry for us was to explore philosophically whether it was possible to suggest that the further away particular managers sit from the practical business of their organisations, the more likely they are to be called leaders. We alighted on this speculative and tentative conclusion on the basis of the following reasoning:

> One cannot be properly called a manager if one does not manage in practice some clearly defined element of the organisational process. Yet the managerial caste has, ..., expanded itself atop the actual business of what firms and agencies – in private and public settings – undertake but without any meaningful connection to the day to day work of those organisations. To justify that growth, particularly as it has occurred in the direction away from the practicalities of what gets done, a new caste within the caste has been entitled – by which is meant both given a name and offered privileges – and it is known as leadership.
>
> (Cole, 2020)

The expansion and transmogrification has occurred in light of the wider changing terrain of the capitalist mode of production, which – in keeping with the Foucauldian notion of disciplinary power – needs to release subjects in the workplace from visible constraint but must maintain control of the overall process. Hence, it is argued that,

> All the self-organized, creative beings on whom performance now depends must be guided in a direction decided only by a few, but without reverting to the 'hierarchical bosses' of yesteryear. This is where leaders and their visions come into the picture. Vision has the same virtues as the spirit of capitalism, for it guarantees the workers' commitment without recourse to compulsion, by making everyone's work meaningful.
>
> (Boltanski & Chiapello, 2007, pp. 75–76)

Or, rather, shrouds the brute actions of a system that increasingly merely produces for the sake of consumption with the illusion of meaning.

We will return to expand a little further on this argument later in this chapter. For the moment, it is worth restating that, in critically engaging with the notions that serve to peg the practice of leadership/leaderised management in position, we have described underpinning circumstances we perceive where:

1. The individual is unhelpfully subsumed within an ideology of individualism.
2. The fetishisation of measurement has clouded what should be a reliance on our own autoethnographic understanding of organisational life.
3. In light of the endless foregrounding in business of things like models, league tables, data, techniques and methods, the vital importance of the relational is lost in a blurry background. Indeed, the pursuit of what are to our mind epiphenomenal elements is, in fact, actively anti-relational, insofar as it allows organisations to reduce all who reside within them to mere objects, rather than active, thinking, and creative subjects, replete with agency.
4. Embracing our agency is made all the more difficult in contexts wherein we are all a long way downstream from the headwaters of management and leadership thinking, where all the assumptions about life in organisations are generated…and where the idea of critical engagement is shrouded behind a commitment to corporate cohesion.

4.3.1 The emergence of 'leaderised' management: Underpinning one. Individualism versus individuality

We have observed the way in which the vitality of the individual has effectively been subsumed by the crude celebration of an autarkic and uniform individualism. This ideology is one of the three foundations for neoliberalism, the prevailing view of the world that currently shapes our thinking in capitalist societies, the other two being argued to be an adherence to the mechanism of the so-called 'free' market and a focus on decentralisation (McGregor, 2001). Individualism in this context is argued to manifest as follows:

> One basic assumption of neoliberalism is that human beings will always try to favour themselves. As they do this, they need have no concern for others or the environment. This absence of concern can exist because each person is assumed to act independently of others and is assumed

to be restricted only by his/her natural surroundings and NOT by any other human being. The individualistic tenet of neoliberalism leads to nominal concern for the impact of current decisions and patterns of behaviour on others elsewhere, not yet born or the ecosystem.

(McGregor, 2001, pp. 83–84)

This approach, of course, denies the notion of the individual as a being able to attend reflexively to their presence in the world – and ideologically closes off the potential for human subjects to connect meaningfully and to work collectively. Hence, the key question in this respect can be posited thus:

If a rise in individualism over the last fifteen years is indeed plausible, is it not manifestly the result, not of some evolutionary process that nothing could check, but of the deconstruction of groupings (classes, firms, unions, parties, but also, in another way, churches or schools) that formed the basis for people's ability to enrol in collective perspectives, and pursue what was recognized as the common good?

(Boltanski & Chiapello, 2007, p. 532)

Such sites were not merely places wherein people found opportunities for collaboration and the capacity to act collectively; they can also be argued to be spaces in which the individual could develop their subjectivity as something other than a producer – or, crucially, as a (constant) consumer. They could escape the practice of being seen and treated as objects, a lumpen and undifferentiated mass of humanity without any sense of a unique, interior existence.

One way of accessing this concept through consideration of its practicality is to think about what is often called 'the entrepreneurial self', which focuses in on '…responsibilised individuals [who] are called upon to apply certain management, economic, and actuarial techniques to themselves as subjects of a newly privatised welfare regime' (Peters, 2001, p. 60). Overall, this is seen to be supported by two developments: first, the unbridled colonisation of life by the dismal self-claimed 'science' of economics; and second, the redefinition of roles in the workplace, particularly the recasting of workers as human resources – and, most significantly in regard to the argument being advanced here – human capital (Read, 2010, p. 5). The latter phrase is especially significant: it promulgates the idea that the individual self is something in which one invests so as to obtain an even greater return in the workplace and beyond, while promoting the view of the self as an object and inviting commensurability between the life of the human being and the unliving social construct capital.

It is certainly the case that bureaucratisation and corporatism have taken the sting out of the tail of trade unionism and rendered it less effective in terms of actively pursuing the range of grievances experienced by the memberships. But unionism remains one of the few ways in which the individualised units of production in modern organisations can connect with one another and respond to challenges collectively. However, a key triumph of neoliberalism has been to elevate individualism over collectivism, with an adjusted focus from how work groups might connect on something close to their own terms and instead onto organisational structures sanctioned by the leadership. In parallel it has created conditions for socio-economic shifts to displace the very notion of unionism as a pursuit of a common good.

That notion of common good now is defined by what is good for each and every individual in a marketised context – and the decline in the collective instinct in the economy across the UK can be usefully discussed thus:

> Trade union membership levels reached their peak in 1979 and declined sharply through the 1980s and early 1990s before stabilising from the mid-1990s to the mid-2000s. After falling during the recession and years following, the trade union membership levels among employees again stabilised between 2011 and 2015, before falling again in 2016. There was a marginal rise in trade union memberships in the period between 2016 and 2017, a trend that has continued into 2018 with a slightly larger, yet still small rise in memberships. However, trade union membership levels among employees in 2018 remains around 579,000 lower than in 2008. The proportion of employees who were in a trade union has been on a generally downward trend since 1995.
> (Department for Business, Energy & Industrial Strategy, 2019)

This is merely an indicator of the way in which the ideology of individualism has progressed at the expense of more collective ways of seeing the world. As noted, the traditional practices of trade unionism in a capitalist society are about negotiating with the system as it is, as opposed to striving to subvert it. One perspective is that such forms of non-subversive organising serve to a considerable extent to undermine the ways in which people might autonomously begin to network together, undermining alternative ways of being that make possible an entirely new way of thinking about organisation and coming together to pursue that. In that sense, the priorities of what might be called revolutionary unions can be said to be '...to build worker solidarity and to re-organize production for the benefit of the producer class' (Kinna, 2019, p. 137). In workplaces this plays out in the language of self-organisation coming from and, in practice, meaning two quite different things. In one self-organisation is in the service of the existing power structure and seeks to support the goals and ambitions of the status quo – in the other self-organisation is a self and collectively liberating experience, which seeks to challenge the very foundations of the purpose of work and whose interests are served by a particular form of organisation. This second meaning is largely notable for its absence.

Our purpose in highlighting this here is not to promulgate a position that we feel should be taken but instead to demonstrate how individualism has asserted itself in the face of past practices. Our intention is to rescue the individual from the cloying neoliberalism of the 'entrepreneurial self' so that we might better reach out – on the basis of a personal agency in the presence of others of a similar agentic energy – to create a network that embraces collective thought and action. This stands outside of the logic of the current schema of individualism, where the various elements of the organisation have colonised the very idea of what it is to be an individual, with the ultimate model encouraging us to see ourselves as a company instead of a human being – our subjective humanity is disappeared. This creation of an internalised mental frame of self-responsible individuals delivering within the given template of an unchallenged economic model creates a particular self-punishing rationality where: 'Forcing people to become individuals also means they end up having to blame themselves for failing' (Bröckling, 2016, p. 5).

This aggressive individualism compels the person to assume the traditional combined capitalist roles of both producer and consumer, and now also to behave as a unique one-person enterprise, related to others only really via the market mechanism. A key work that explores this development expresses it thus:

> The interpellations of the entrepreneurial self are totalitarian. The economic imperatives it contains resolve themselves into a system of economic imperialism. Nothing escapes the command to continually self-improve for the sake of the market. There is no expression of life, the utility of which cannot be optimized, no desire of need that cannot be commodified. Even objection, refusal and transgression can be channelled into programmes promising competitive advantages, and every instance of failure just goes to show that our performance has left room for improvement. This makes living up the entrepreneurial self a recipe for paranoia.
>
> (Bröckling, 2016, p. 196)

The underpinning of this development can be found in the turn which took place in psychology at the turn of the millennium. This pivot was articulated in this way: 'A science of positive subjective experience, positive individual traits, and positive institutions promises to improve quality of life and prevent the pathologies that arise when life is barren and meaningless' (Seligman & Csikszentmihalyi, 2000, p. 5). One senses a human science preparing itself to clamber on the rattling band-wagon of motivational gobbledegook, bracketing off the inhibiting social context of rank, race, and inequality of resource that attend a capitalist system in order to encourage a perspective wherein the individual is forced to be a cheerleader for themselves and where all is within one's grasp, providing you are positive.

This leads us to the clamour that surrounds the, to us, simplistic concepts of fixed and growth mindsets (Dweck, 2012), a framework that has been found by some researchers to be lacking in rigour (Burgoyne, et al., 2020) but which nevertheless finds a willing audience among so many involved in development in a workplace context – not least because it seems to rationalise and justify what they do. Pretty and persuasive though the whole approach might appear – particularly when viewed through the prism of neoliberalism – its scientific integrity has been scrutinised and its efficacy in relation to practice, such as within an educational context, has lately been found to be less persuasive than many would like to imagine (Sisk, et al., 2018).

Unsurprisingly, shortly after positive psychology was conceived as a corpus of thought, detractors hove into view. The eschewing of the negative in favour of what appears to be an exclusive focus on positivity lead one author to argue that,

> Aside from uncertainties and misunderstandings about what defines positive and negative, this polarity represents two sides of the same coin of life, like structure and process, stability and change, stress and coping, and so-called positive and negative emotions...[Y]ou can't separate them and make good sense. Speaking metaphorically rather than mystically, God needs Satan, and vice versa.
>
> (Lazarus, 2003)

Or more prosaically, into every life a little rain must fall.

However, others seek to nudge their critique even deeper, offering a richly textured set of observations about the development of positive psychology and its wider discursive impacts from a Foucauldian perspective. We are very much persuaded by the argument that, '...far from liberating psychology from the negative and pathological, it has instituted a new set of governmental and disciplinary mechanisms by means of defining what is 'positive' in human existence via a prescriptive set of constructs (...), and in its attempts to silence critical reflexivity and alternative perspectives' (McDonald & O'Callaghan, 2008, pp. 128–129). In fact, these authors expressly link positive psychology with the neoliberal discourse, through an exploration of a specific mechanism, namely, '...the classifying and categorizing of character strengths and virtues provides a new regulatory tool for the use of selection, control and discrimination in the workplace, in much the same way as that measures of personality have been used in the past' (McDonald & O'Callaghan, 2008, p. 136). This reminds us of a key precept in Foucault's work, namely that power acts through defining normalcy – and, in consequence, creating Otherness, or abnormality.

In fact, it goes further than this, as all of us doubtless appreciate on the basis of our exposure to corporate life. Even within the terms of that wider discussion in contrasting positivity with psychological pathologies, there is a suggestion that the neoliberal workplace will be selective in terms of the facets of positivity that managers would value in this context, such as individualism, flexibility, and entrepreneurship (McDonald & O'Callaghan, 2008, pp. 136–137). Think of your own experience of organisational life over the past two decades and consider when the notion of 'resilience' as a personal positive attribute first appeared – and how it manifested itself. Resilience is intimately linked to individualism – and we are expected to be personally responsible for bouncing back in light of our experiences of the stresses of organisational life in the context of our current form of capitalism.

For us, the final facet in respect to the individualism that prevails at this time relates directly to leadership. This observes the tally that exists between the emergence of neoliberalism and the usage of the term 'leadership' as opposed to management – and declares an interconnectivity in this regard. Research around use of terms undertaken between the 1990s and 2015 offer the following insight: at the start of the 1990s, the key term that linked with the word leader was 'Party', demonstrating that the idea of leadership broadly resided in the political context, whilst by 2015 the term at the top of the list in terms of being associated with the word leader was found to be 'Team'. Between the two analyses, the word 'Business' in relation to leadership climbed from 22nd place in the list to 4th. This linguistic research seems to demonstrate a reworking of the very idea of leadership and its contexts of operation (Learmonth & Morrell, 2019, p. 30).

This seems to suggest the displacement of the binary opposition of 'manager' and 'worker' – with the implicit suggestion that there may be divergence in terms of interests and expectations, depending on which position one structurally occupies – in favour of the seemingly consensual relationship between 'leader' and 'follower'. This is usefully explained thus:

> "Management" has the sorts of cultural associations which, in contrast to leadership, might conjure up images of diverging interests, division, strife and the need for control in workplaces. This is one of the reasons that "manager" and "follower" do not tend to go together in normal use.
> (Learmonth & Morrell, 2019, p. 38)

Patently, there is the potential for agency in respect to thinking of oneself as a worker, possibly as a member of a collective that might unite in opposition to what 'the bosses' (namely, the managers) seek to do. But the defining characteristic of followership is unidimensional, insofar as it is simply about an individual agreeing to be pulled along in the wake of the leader. Hence, the term leadership further reinforces the precepts of individualism, as a key underpinning of neoliberalism.

Behind this lies an entirely different practice in regard to how people work in and think about enterprises in a capitalist society. As a recent piece in The Atlantic magazine, exploring then US presidential candidate Pete Buttigieg and his tenure at McKinsey and the impact of that firm's views on US workers, explained,

> When management consulting untethered executives from particular industries or firms and tied them instead to management in general, it also led them to embrace the one common thing to all corporations: making money for shareholders [a key element of neoliberalism in the private sector and its public sector corollary New Public Management – MC/JH]. Executives raised on the new, untethered model of management aim exclusively and directly at profit: their education, their career arc, and their professional role conspire to isolate them from other workers and train them single-mindedly on the bottom line.
>
> (Markovits, 2020)

This, then, sees management torn away from the business – and allowed to assume an almost superstructural position, sitting as a cadre atop and across all organisations throughout the global economy. Under the prompting of the ideologists in consulting firms like McKinsey, they orient themselves not towards the business of the business – and the people therein – but to those who hold shares in those companies. The senior executives follow the instructions of consultants to strip costs out of the business to the benefit of the shareholders – and at the expense of the workforce in general and their own middle managers in particular.

In order to justify and facilitate these operations, the use of the term leadership allows for the tensions that precede and work within these economic changes to be disappeared: the 'bosses' rebadge themselves from being managers – who might be seen to be in an antagonistic relationship with the wider workforce – to being leaders. This recasts the workforce as followers, of course, and allows greater discretion to act on the part of the bosses. In real terms, we can think of this mechanism thus:

> Maximising profits almost inevitably means extracting extra value from workers – and at least for some increased insecurity and worsened conditions. The traditional terms "manager" and "worker" tacitly

acknowledge such conflict and divergence of interests. In contrast, the language of leadership seeks to make the workplace into a kind of "Santa's workshop", where everyone below the leader is imagined (against common-sense) to be [a] happy elf.

(Learmonth & Morrell, 2019, p. 7)

All of us in organisations need to recast ourselves in terms of how we perceive ourselves as a subject – and how the warp and weft of the discourse and power that surrounds us seeks to define us in light of wider developments. A starting point might be to declare quite categorically – echoing the cri de coeur of Number 6 in the 1960s TV programme, The Prisoner – 'I am not a follower' (Cox, 2017). This opens up a relational space wherein it might be possible to ask the question, 'If I am not – regardless of what organisational experience might suggest – a "follower", what sort of subject am I in this context, in terms of how I relate to other people and the aspects of the organisational setting in which I work'?

Similarly, if one is allocated the nomenclature of leader, the initial act would be to reconnect with the simple fact that you are – in real terms – a 'boss'. Importantly, you may be caught in the conundrum of those around you actively renouncing their ascribed status of 'follower', which in turn serves to problematise your adherence to the notion that you are a leader, as opposed to a manager. And, once you embrace that revision of your status, the real question becomes something along the lines of the following: 'If I am a boss, what does that mean about my priorities in this organisational context – and how do I see myself relating with those around me, and – in particular – the workforce that I seek to manage'?

Some punctuating summary points on 'The emergence of 'leaderised' management – Underpinning one. Individuality versus individualism'

- According to current practice there is no independent common good, only what is economically good for sovereign individuals in the here and now
- Formal attempts to organise collectively focus on working with, not subverting, taken-for-granted attitudes to individualism and market exchange
- The classification of how the self shows-up at work, in terms of positive and negative features, sustains a self-punishing universe based around compliance to the rules of orthodoxy

- If people are defined, or self-define, as followers in relation to a leader, how do they find a sense of being a subjective self? And how does the 'leader' step out of the strait-jacket of defining others as followers to them?
- Reimagining individuality and the common good enables, and is enabled by, new forms of workplace organising

4.3.2 The emergence of 'leaderised' management: Underpinning two. The fetishisation of measurement

The opening salvo given subsequently appears in the introduction to a diligent piece of research that seeks to explore how the proliferation of leadership research serves to generate an ever-growing repertoire of models and techniques:

> The popularity and size of the leadership literature continues to expand rapidly in both the academic and the popular press. As a byproduct of this interest in leadership, the number of leadership constructs (i.e., leader traits, behaviors, and styles) has also grown voluminously. The lack of a parsimonious nomological network is not unique to the leadership literature. Nevertheless, the creation of new constructs seems more typical to leadership research than perhaps any other topic studied in organizational behavior. Such a proliferation of constructs draws concerns regarding the potential for redundancy in the accumulated literature.
>
> (Banks, et al., 2018, p. 236)

A cursory glance across the field offers a seemingly boundless panorama of largely untested notions of how to enhance leadership efficiency. (Even this title could be said to be contributing to this swamp of sticky ideas and conceptual complexity, although our purpose is more about getting the reader to recognise – and eschew – the draw of the swamp, rather than adding to it. Only you will be able to judge whether we have managed this, of course.)

The work of Banks et al. renders that expanse manageable in terms of inquiry by focusing in just on leadership behaviour frameworks that have arisen out of the domain. In an unusually unguarded conclusion, the authors offer the following candid observation and powerful recommendation:

> The most alarming aspect of our work is that only a few of the leader behavior constructs (i.e., transformational, authentic, servant, and ethical leadership) displayed meaningful, practical correlations with outcomes. Based on these findings, we call for a moratorium on new leader behaviors (i.e., the proliferation of new theoretical approaches to leader behaviors) until we are able to cumulatively integrate what we have so far theoretically.
>
> (Banks, et al., 2018, p. 247)

The idea of a moratorium of supposedly 'fresh' ideas in this regard – so very often not new but simply re-treads, dreamt up by a 'thought leader' eager to market a model rather than engage meaningfully with the reality of the space in which they work – seems far-fetched, given the seemingly inexhaustible supply and demand in this at best questionable market. As we tried to show in our exploration of the myths, demand persists as executives seek that single solution that will perfectly fix the issue with which they are wrestling. And, where such demand exists (and budgets are aligned with it) then providers will work to offer 'product', even when taking up such an offer is akin to consuming candy floss: an overwhelming rush of sweet pleasure is soon surpassed by the return of the pangs of hunger that it momentarily offset. Leaders however they might define themselves are beset by this terrible sweet tooth and don't recognise the nutrition they would benefit from – assuming they are willing to step out of the bubble of autarkic self-interest.

How likely is the moratorium? On 10 August 2020, Mark took less than 15 minutes to run from the top of the page and through posts that had appeared for him on LinkedIn, just to get a snapshot of what was appearing on the site in regard to think-pieces, models, and techniques. Amidst the clamour, he pulled out the following as examples of the way in which organisational practice, particularly with leadership in mind, feeds on the vaguest of notions. What he found on this particular day felt not to be out of kilter with what he would usually come across in terms of volume, content, or tone.

It began with someone offering a video on the topic of 'foresight'; someone else then drawing on the experiences of elite sportspeople offering a blog article on 'goal setting'; another person shared a blog article from an individual who described themselves as a Workforce Futurist, which offered advice on 'unleashing the decentralised workforce'; as a site browser Mark was then offered supposedly rebellious insight into 'Metcalfe's Law in Organisations', a short post with an eye-catching graphic – just in case he struggled to understand the connectivity that exists between individuals when they form a network; something then promoted itself as offering HR insights and provided a podcast on 'mentoring your team through crisis'; there was a brief post accompanied by a colourful corporate graphic that pretended to offer insight into the value of 'vulnerability'; Henley Business School was offering a conference that looked at the brain in coaching; and a project called 'U Matter' was being promoted, although Mark couldn't quite fathom what it involved – and could not find the energy to pursue it.

John undertook a similar exercise and wrote up his observations of the 'noise' that exists around the whole issue of development in an organisational context, which led him to this powerful conclusion:

> The sense of making a contribution by sharing something which on the surface seems to be new, ensuring that management are up to speed with all the latest "thinking" of the business school and consulting worlds, has some appeal. It generates, perhaps, a sense of usefulness for those in roles that sit some way back from the actual work of the corporations that they seek to advise. The other part of the attraction for being an amplifier of this world view, is that it provides a sense of the new without rocking the boat – in terms of the headwaters of managerial thinking or the power structures it justifies.
>
> (Higgins, 2020)

The simple fact of the matter is that a human being would do better to spend a quarter of an hour in careful reflexive thought than immerse themselves in this cascade of what is not much more than clumsy marketing of services that, broadly speaking, are not needed in the least. We have tricked ourselves into thinking that this torrent of ill-constructed demithought somehow meets our needs in terms of 'continuing professional development', when we would be better off focusing in on a little 'progressive self-development', in terms of our personal understanding of the world, our presence within it, and the ways in which our agency impacts it and, importantly, those around us. Ultimately, it is merely a shop window chock full of products that, in keeping with the consumption patterns that one finds across the whole of capitalism, we quite simply do not need. This window, then, does not offer rich insight into the various ways and means with which we might engage with the world; instead, it opens out onto the void at the heart of our presence in organisational life, where we have abdicated our responsibility to do the heavy lifting of critical thought in relation to every facet of our work lives (and beyond).

This abdication is painfully evident in relation to the way in which we choose to relate to the practice of measurement. As with our discussion of individualism versus individuality, we seek here to acknowledge that gaining an understanding of the world requires the sort of comparing and contrasting that might be best understood as the most essential approach to getting the measure of things. But Mark's six-year-old son offers a clear pointer in this regard: when expected to engage in arithmetic without context, its abstract nature renders the exercise a mere chore, serving an agenda (that of formal education and the teachers who work within it) into which he does not have any insight and nor can he be in any real way invested. When the work relates to the practicalities of life, for instance when helping to bake biscuits or a cake, then the application of numbers has a rich and immediate purpose.

John recently had a conversation with someone responsible for overseeing equality, diversity, and inclusion activity in an organisation. They described how a good deal of their work relates to collecting and manipulating data, oftentimes so it is palatable to those at director level in the organisation. Hence, one major conceit here is the expectation that the data collected from within the organisation should not be worked on within the context where it came from; instead, the person to whom John spoke explained that they spend a good deal of time looking outwards in order to use the numbers to generate league tables and engaging in the pursuit of 'benchmarking', a notion that might be said to be cannibalising itself as some authors set themselves the maddeningly recursive task of 'benchmarking of benchmarking' (Anand & Kodali, 2008) – something that suggests that something is seriously awry in the corporate world.

As ever, first impressions around this notion can usefully be subject to scrutiny and the application of a critical frame. Within a capitalistic discourse, the assumed neutrality and pseudo-scientism of such a practice allows most people to subscribe to the practice as a means of making improvements, particularly across state financed services now beset by the neoliberalism of New Public Management. The rich potential alternative drawn from a Foucauldian perspective suggests something different:

> It is characteristic that benchmarking seeks to facilitate self-governing through normalizing comparison. The knowledge, which is produced through the comparative analysis, contributes to generating the normal as a point of reference for discussions, reflections, resistance and, in some, but far from all, cases, organizational and procedural changes. Benchmarking is informed by a broader governmental problematic, advanced liberalism, that supports a whole range of interventions, both inside and outside the public sector.
>
> (Triantafillou, 2007, p. 843)

As further indication of the way in which 'senior leaders' play at the edges of measurement and data, John's interlocutor described a time when they presented the executive group with material in respect to how the individual directors related to one another: those individuals assumed an instantly defensive position, wilfully misrepresenting the data and offering very personalised refutations of the conclusions that could be drawn. Hence, one director declared that the material did not reflect them accurately, because this was not how they ran their directorate – and you could ask anyone they worked with to confirm this. Yet, the data did draw on responses from those with whom they worked, namely their fellow directors. But the hierarchy at play, and the power that this structure had colonised, did not allow John's interlocutor to push back on such an erroneous response.

The prevalence of simplistic management models might best be explained in respect to two elements. First, there is the way in which 'crunching the data' has become a preeminent focus of what a leader in corporate life is expected to do (or that they outsource to others to do). The ceaseless quest for just the right amount of data that will enable the leader to make their self-justificatory, superficially incisive, and notionally 'correct' decision, means that there is no such thing as enough data. Who in corporate life has not taken a comprehensive package of material that they have spent long hours compiling to an Executive or Board meeting, only to sit and endure a weakly defined and ill-informed conversation around that data – before being sent away in order to collect more (albeit largely unspecified) information?

The only time that such leaders seem transfixed by the material when it is initially offered to them is when a consultancy has sent its drones crawling over their organisation in all its various manifestations. This familiar exercise tends to be encapsulated, with varying degrees of internal logic and consistency, in a multipage PowerPoint slide deck often so full of words and numbers as to be unintelligible through its busyness and unreadability – and certainly not designed with the reader in mind, except to disable them. Importantly, this represents an intermediation, something that intercedes unhelpfully between the person in charge and the practical reality of the space and time in which they work. To allow that connection to become obscured by this layering seems somewhat absurd, except perhaps in the rarefied context of leadership practice.

But it is an activity that persuades the leader that they are fully sighted in terms of a fixed 'reality' (when, of course, the kaleidoscopic shifting of the various elements of organisational life means that this fixity is utterly illusory). It disregards what was so elegantly stated in a recent crime novel: '[T]here is always a multiplicity of nodes, intersections in a fragile system of happenstance whereby the slightest divergence at one would have altered all' (Parry, 2018, p. 309). It also owes something to the distorted amplification by practitioners of organisation development of Kurt Lewin's passing and somewhat insubstantial remark about change requiring us to unfreeze, change, and then refreeze (Lewin, 1947). An explicit refutation of this exists, one that is premised on the persuasive suggestion that the ceaseless flow of change is actually the natural state in (organisational) life – and that this flux is artificially interrupted by efforts to engender change in this context (Tsoukas & Chia, 2002). It could therefore be argued that any effort by a leader to pilot through a programme of organisational change is a sleight of hand that seems to apotheosise the corporate leader.

Following on from the idea of 'crunching the data' is the second element that explains the appetite in the field for simplistic models. The tacit presumption is that this marshalled material is perhaps too complex for the leadership cadre to be able to absorb and digest successfully. Here, we can discern the provenance of the increased fascination in the corporate world with the notion of storytelling, used when the data is either too complex for leaders to absorb in metric form and followers unable to engage with the obfuscatory language of leadership.

Leaders use storytelling to engage their followers in respect to the data – and rely themselves on simplified models so that they can engage with it; this is not a communicative chain but an ideological apparatus, in pure and simple terms. In this regard, professional services companies pull together wodges of data that then have to be condensed into a palatable confection for the client through the use of models. The story is told of the development of the first management 2 x 2 matrix inside the Boston Consulting Group (BCG), where two of their people doing a diversification study for a paper company presented the usual deluge of material to their client, the company's executive in charge of strategy, who promptly declared, 'That's terrific – dress it up'. That passing instruction lead people at BCG to develop their growth-share matrix, whence flows every other glib squeezing of the world into four arbitrary quadrants (Kiechel, 2010, pp. 57–58).

We hanker after the idea of meaningful measurement that offers better clarity in respect to our collective understanding of the world. Such an approach, of course, would expose the power that precedes and inhabits our thinking and practice of metrics. Instead the fixation and fetishisation of measurement predominates as part of a wider discourse of power and – in light of maintaining the illusion of leadership – sustains the artifice of hierarchy, obfuscating the world in favour of those who enjoy rank in these structures.

Some additional remarks in this section proceed from the complex psychological relationship between planning and human agency. There has traditionally been a presupposition that the satisfaction of having a plan and thence delivering on it enhances our sense of agency. However, more recent research – which to us, as writers on organisational philosophy, had considerable resonance – challenges this simple notion and argues that,

> In the present investigation we revealed how action planning could reduce agency...[A]lthough it may be very possible that the sense of agency benefits from a comparison between *outcomes* that are intended and predicted, we show in a number of studies that the prior planning of *actions* may actually reduce agency.
>
> (Damen, et al., 2015, p. 861)

Why does any of this matter? Well, primarily from our perspective because this inhibits what passes for leadership...and, at the same time, denies people the opportunity to think meaningfully about their rich potential for collective organising. The unbridled fascination with models, techniques, checklists, and ideas – and the brimming and overflow of that grimy reservoir of these approaches that, as we have seen, is never properly flushed out – means that those who are notionally in charge of things ignore the things around them in favour of these gewgaws and their distortions of the things around them.

So stuck are these individuals in terms of their thinking, misshapen by the sorts of myths we have discussed here and the torrential volume of supposedly common-sensical takes on organisational life from business schools and consultancies – that we suggest they experience something akin to a Forer Effect when coming face-to-face with each new addition to the corpus of leadership thinking and technique. This is the psychological effect where the individual perceives themselves in a generalised description, such as might be seen by people who take astrology at face value (Forer, 1949). Hence, our leaders take the crude generalisations of leadership thought and allow it to reinforce their own assumptions about the world. The disciplines required for sustained critical inquiry into why they see the world the way they do are squeezed out by the need to play the game as it is currently configured, without consideration as to whether or not this game serves any purpose beyond sustaining the status of its players.

The way in which leaders elevate themselves by teetering on top of this body of so-called thought and approved practice puts them at the head of the hierarchy, allowing them to overshadow the capabilities that exist in those around them to connect, work, and organise together. The multiplicity of models that these positional leaders declare to be accurate reflections of reality – when they themselves are in the midst of the reality of which these models claim to reflect – denies the voice of the lived experience of those who inhabit the world as it is rather than the world as reported. Where such voices are encouraged, they are closely mediated to ensure that they sustain the illusion – and are not allowed to shatter the distorting hall of mirrors that leadership has become over the years.

Moreover, the endless fascination amongst those leaders with visions, strategies, and plans – the bread and butter of contemporary leadership,

offering the enticement that 'followers' apparently so desperately crave —
could be seen to deny those people who they are supposedly 'leading' the
chance to experience the richness of human agency in the workplace. It
seems to make an effective connection between the obsession with planning in corporate contexts and the systematic disempowerment of all those
in organisational life who are offered an invitation to 'engage' in their
work and the organisation within which they find themselves...on strictly
constrained and tightly defined managerial terms.

Hence, a recent study of the experience of those working in health care
reported that,

> ...when employees experience job autonomy and use naturally reward-
> ing self-leadership strategies, they increase their work engagement
> and health. In the end, the patients benefit from effective self-leading
> healthcare professionals. Engaged and healthy employees do all they
> can to deliver the best possible service to their clients.
>
> (van Dorssen-Boog, et al., 2020, p. 9)

Within the terms of this research, the authors offer the following helpful
description of what this means in practice:

> A self-leader is assumed to autonomously define what to do (standards
> and objectives), why to do things (strategy), and how to do things (meth-
> odology) while being less dependent on contextual control systems (...).
> True self-leadership represents autonomous functioning as one can fully
> endorse personal activities and act on a basis of higher order reflections.
>
> (van Dorssen-Boog, et al., 2020, p. 4)

For any 'leader', scratching their head in perplexity, as they seek out the
key model or method to help them do something about staff engagement
might do well to consider these findings. A simple solution to the 'empowerment' conundrum seems self-evident: surrender the idea that you are a
leader; clamber down from your position in the hierarchy; and offer people alongside whom you work the chance to explore their innate autonomy,
agency, and discretion without your unnecessary intercessions. From this
perspective, all other staff engagement activity is merely the curtaining
behind which Wizards emptily bellow to no real effect.

Some punctuating summary points on 'The emergence of 'leaderised' management – Underpinning Two. Fetishization of Measurement'

- The fetishisation of measurement is part of a wider habit of abdicating thought around the purposes and consequences of what is currently taken for granted about leadership practice
- The illusion of leadership sits within a reflecting Hall of Mirrors, decorated with reports and models that eradicate news that doesn't fit with the lived experience of those outside of the Hall
- The purpose of the current version of measurement orthodoxy is to sustain and justify the rank and hierarchy of illusory leadership, in part by creating a sense of fixity that sits outside of the flux of organisational life
- Because of the detachment from, and irrelevance to, most day-to-day organisational life, measurement activity inhibits the rich potential for collective organizing which would arise if the demand for measurement of illusory leadership were removed

4.3.3 The emergence of 'leaderised' management: Underpinning three. Displacement of the relational

Just recently, a colleague of John's started a new job as an IT change project manager with a relatively small multinational company. On the second day of her tenure, she found herself on a call with the person she described as her 'boss's boss' (BB) and at least one other C-Suite functionary. Within seconds of the start of the call, BB was shouting and swearing at many of the junior participants, instructing everyone on the call not to do anything around the project to which many had been directly recruited. At one point on the video call, by all accounts, he dropped his bright red face into his hands in despair, shook his head, and made growling noises. Throughout their time at the company, BB persisted with this behaviour – until such time as he pulled the lever on the ultimate management and sacked John's colleague.

Mark heard a similar story from someone with whom he worked earlier in his career in respect to them being recruited into a new appointment at a tiny company, only to discover that their manager (a member of something risibly referred to as the Senior Leadership Team) had failed to advise them that they were expected to take three weeks mandated leave at set times – one at Christmas and the others in Summer – when their pro-rata appointment would not actually cover those 15 days. They were also advised that whilst the new appointee would be allowed to fetch a water or coffee for themselves during the working day, it would be frowned upon if they offered to fetch drinks for others as that would be seen as encouraging an excess of unproductive fraternisation and conversation as such activity led to people simply passing the time of day. The final straw was discovering that the terms and conditions, unseen prior to their unpaid onboarding, indicated that the first two days of any period of sickness were unpaid.

In the latter example, then, we are confronted with three aspects of organisational life that modern business ideology likes to pretend have been surpassed by enlightened thinking. First, flexible working in this instance is not about a range of enlightened initiatives to attract and retain the talent that is needed by the enterprise but instead means that the employee needs to be flexible about taking their precious three weeks of annual leave only when the company allows them to…and that potentially some of that will have to be taken as unpaid leave. Flexibility is a one-way street.

Second, the very characteristic of organising that supports connectivity and a collective capacity to work together better – namely, the passing conversation – was expressly denied through a decidedly unsubtle admonition not to dawdle when rushing into the kitchen to make yourself a much-needed drink. And, lastly, we are faced with an HR policy position that seems guaranteed to create the sort of 'presenteeism' that has always been a contentious issue in corporate life – and which, in the time of coronavirus, seems absurdly short sighted and unthinkingly bureaucratic.

Meanwhile, back in the world of BB, those on the call received an email the following day that had about it the air of an apology – but instead swiftly swerved away from that and instead blithely sought to blame BB's bad behaviour on the fact that the meeting had been called 'at short notice' and this senior leader had not had adequate time to prepare for it. That notwithstanding, the managerial imperative persisted – and was reinforced in private conversation with John's colleague, who was instructed to do nothing, even if it looked easy and simple in terms of its execution. They were left wondering what on earth they were actually being paid to do, other than to keep a seat warm.

A final observation from John's recent experience: a new senior leader joined a large corporation to oversee a significant piece of strategic work and sought briskly to make a mark for himself – although there was little sense from a wider organisational context as to what that contribution might actually be and why it was important, in general (within the company) and particularly at that specific time. That deficit notwithstanding, a cult of personality began to crystallise around this individual – and it became noticeable that, in corporate communications, some in the divisional workforce began to refer this person as 'The Leader' and, indeed, 'Our Leader', which conjured – for some amongst the staff – visions of the Central Committee of the Workers' Party of Korea. To be fair, the leader did not court this adoration – but equally it was noticeable that he did nothing to discourage this increasingly striking tone of obeisance.

We offer these anecdotes to remind us all that – notwithstanding the corporate boilerplate that circulates about work being more people-focused and able to flex around the individual – things remain largely unchanged for huge numbers of people in the workplace. Largely, this is because leaders refuse to cease being the sorts of leaders that we have always had to endure and choose instead to lock themselves into their deformed world of measurement and models and the outsize rewards that being in this world insists is their right. It is a world into which – by the terms of the defining qualities of the term 'leadership' – we are expected to follow them. In that sense, 'followership' means silence in the face of a system of organisational management that is obsolete – if, indeed, it ever had any real currency in the real world, where real means delivering a useful product or service... or in healthcare, treating patients well.

As we have shown elsewhere, this issue of 'followership' is critical to the deceit that leadership promulgates. Primarily, this is because the choice to follow is inherent to the idea that this is an aspect of individualism; the individual, of course, is entirely effaced in this arrangement, their engagement in the ideologised dyad of leader-follower merely defined by proximity and position rather than human agency. By the declaration of my leadership, I unavoidably implicate and thence incorporate those who sit around me in the hierarchy that we share. My personal subjectification which derives through my occupation of a specific position serves also to subjectify those around me.

Hence, we find that the vital relational aspect of organising – in that no organisation can be said to exist without the interrelatedness and connectivity of those involved in that endeavour – is constantly effaced by the subjectivity of those who define themselves (or find themselves defined) as 'leaders'. What seems particularly figural in this taken-for-granted and impactful framing of the leader-follower relationship is how much it is anchored into a world view which starts with the analysis of people as holding individual, isolated positions, which then play out in a pre-scripted, one dimensional dance. The leader leads, the follower follows – there is little sophistication in the understanding of how people come together to co-create their collective reality in relationship with each other.

For those of us drawn to seeing the world through an inter-dependent, social constructed, relational lens i.e. one where the lived experience of reality is made by people in social engagement with each other, the unit of analysis in any relationship is the relationship itself, within which each person has agency but no unilateral autonomy. Much as we have used the word autonomy elsewhere, there is an important distinction to be drawn out between agency and autonomy (and following recent conversations, and given that words have no fixed meaning, John is acutely aware that for many 'autonomy' and 'agency' mean the same thing in practice... and there may well be some who operate with an understanding of agentic autonomy!).

The features that we wish to highlight here are that for us 'Agency', in a relational context, indicates that someone always has a presence when they are in the company of others and that presence plays out in the context of how others are present. In the case of the shouty boss on the Zoom call, there was an unsubtle showing up with aggression by someone with considerable positional power, which inevitably led to people showing up in whatever way worked for them to keep them out of the direct firing line. Pure 'Autonomy' speaks to the potential for people to act completely independently of how others are, to say and do what they like without regard to its impact on the ongoing relationship they are acting into. Professionally John is an independent researcher of by now independent means – he rarely has to pander to others, be liked, or avoid pointing out what people don't want to hear. Mark meanwhile is part of the NHS Behemoth and father of a young son. He feels he has to be mindful of the sensitivities of how he shows up in his workplace relationships, what will happen if he oversteps the mark from 'Agency' (having influence) to 'Autonomy' (engaging with others on a transactional, no-consequence basis).

One of the unhelpful habits of mind in common use is to reify relationships, treat them as things that can be manipulated and managed as any other object. This creates a stuck, fixed pattern and gets in the way of the living dynamic of relationships, which are a permanent work in progress, a flux not a fixity. The framing of the leader-follower relationship is a very fixing framing, that amplifies the power-distance while simultaneously hiding the underpinning (and enlivening) potential for difference and conflict. This creates a difficult to unpick dynamic, which tends to be highly restrictive in terms of how both leader and led are able to show up, which results in an unenlivening encounter between people who are stuck with their respective labels.

This formalised, externally imposed, power-distance defined relationship is something that fits with the mechanistic thinking which underpins nearly all approved organisational practice. For people who don't really get people, step forward most management consultants and business school cognoscenti, it is preferable to replace messy human-to-human connection with one that is a role-to-role one. How these roles are defined is another sleight of hand, with what is an ideological statement presented as an act of pure reason, which allows sources of organisational discord to be disappeared.

With the leader-follower relationship so defined, as an undiscussable transactional contract with defined boundaries and rules of engagement, so any human vitality is drained from it. This is a dehumanised, scripted connection playing out within the context of a market economy where the follower is made to feel deeply subordinate because of their relative insecurity and vulnerability. In order to develop some sense of security, followers can find themselves compelled to make themselves attractive in the eyes of their boss, sell their worth to them – and promote the value of their distinctive contribution within the rules of the leader-follower configuration.

From the perspective of those who value the capacity of an organisational unit to be formally reconfigured at the drop of a hat this form of leader-follower relationship serves a useful purpose. With its dehumanised, marketised, pre-scripted form of connection organisational units and groupings can be readily redrawn. To those willing to be impressed by such things, the illusion of 'agility' can be created, with reporting lines and structures changing at the click and drag of a PowerPoint picture. This 'agility' rests on the thinnest of human connection existing between people and their bosses (and even their endlessly redeployed colleagues). And people know how to exist and operate in these conditions, they know how to play the leader-follower relationship game whoever the actual individuals involved are – so people can slot in and out of positions, while the never-ending merry-go-round of meeting attendees, which seems part of the NHS world, can go smoothly ahead never mind who is there, as – again never mind the content – people know how to fit in with the pre-defined world of scripted relationships.

There is a downside of course, so long as you think that creativity, human connection, and a sense of individual agency are worthy of valuing. All this is lost – and with it any sense of meaningful energy, which might explain the ever-expanding world of NHS and corporate meetings where much is discussed but nothing much happens (outside of the metricised Hall of Mirrors). Strip out the agentic self, which the leader-follower framing does in practice, then you are left with a world of ritual relationships where the ritual is the end in itself.

This emasculating of relational energy inherent within the leader-follower practice, results in those wearing the leader label desperately looking for energising influences they cannot find within their workplaces. Gimmicks and technology are deployed to create the simulacrum of an enlivening encounter across the hierarchy. Meetings start with personal check-ins where people are invited to bring their whole selves into the room, share what's on their mind – while all the time carefully calculating what is the right level of disclosure based on what the Boss shares (or doesn't).

Meanwhile technologists emphasise how much data can exist outside of relational contexts, trumpeting how easy it is through the application of ever more mind-bending algorithms to make everybody's data available to everybody. All implicit data is simply explicit data waiting to happen – so the pacified follower really doesn't matter anymore, the technology will take care of keeping the Boss in touch with what is going on. A series of assumptions and claims we would assert most strongly is a nonsense from beginning to end, but which still have a real-world effect by making followers feel even more contingent and fragile in terms of their importance to the leader.

The experience of power-distance grows between leader and follower and the followers walk into a world of great silence, fearful of how they will be heard if they should step away from the party line.

Some punctuating summary points on 'The emergence of 'leaderised' management – Underpinning Three. Displacement of the Relational'

- A disconnect is experienced between espoused valuing of human connection and ingenuity and lived practice of reification and pre-scripted (role based) encounters
- Followership as the experience of being individually silenced by the leader-follower construct
- The undermining of any enlivening sense of relational energy as a consequence of their reified, power distance amplified construction
- The experience of pseudo-responsiveness and adaptability enabled by role based, dehumanised, workplace relationships
- Gimmicks and technology being deployed to create the simulacrum of an enlivening encounter

4.3.4 The emergence of 'leaderised' management: Underpinning four. Headwaters and downstream thinking

'Leaderised' management is stuck in a swamp of its own making. What is necessary to make it possible to step off the hamster wheel of instant answers and fast assessment is an all but unchallengeable pair of linked assumptions, namely that there isn't time to take longer to think about things and anyway whatever comes up must be practical – which means that it must fit within what is currently viewed as possible and useful. We would argue that this book, for instance, is deeply practical because of its invitation to re-examine the way we think about the world and what alternative ways of thinking and being become possible as a result. But we know that this is an argument that cuts little mustard in a world which glories in its need to operate at pace – even if much that is done is a complete waste of time. God save us from the doers when what is needed is that they simply sit still for a moment or two.

This trivialisation of serious thinking could be seen by John when he was running a week-long residential course at Ashridge Business School in and around the year 2000. In itself it speaks to a trivialisation of serious thinking, believing in a week that people could be 'transformed' in their capacity to engage with their own and their organisation's ability to 'lead strategy and change'. Stepping beyond the specific hubris of the programme what is of particular note is what happened next. John and his programme co-leader were approached to run a tailored version of it for a global oil company. The Learning and Development (L&D) professional requested that the five-day programme be reduced to three – after much heeing and hawing John and his colleague agreed that this might be possible, although it stripped out much of the reflective time which was the core of the design. The oil company L&D professional came back to them. He'd been told that three days was an impossibility. Over time the request collapsed into a three-hour afternoon to deliver a one-week programme. John and his colleague declined to play the game.

Within the wider Business School world, the retreat into a world of standardised tests and rote learning predominates. There is a curriculum to be learnt and tested against and much of the application of technology, such as Gamification, would seem to be in the service of rote learning and right answer thinking. There are case studies which are treated as holy writ, where the capacity to critique the ahistorical and asocial nature of what counts as a case study never happens (never mind who decided what counted as being part of the case study reality and what got edited out as unimportant). As we quoted right at the start of this book, the purpose of a Business School is to be pleasing FOR managers and leaders, it is not about educating them ABOUT how to lead and manage in organisations. When learning is treated solely as a market commodity, difficult learning is too provocative for institutions to offer (except in semi-secret offshoots, where they can be disposed of or denied should they rock the boat too much).

In many ways Business Schools should be one of the most brilliant arenas for learning, study, and research. To understand how to be a generative presence in organisational and institutional settings requires people to draw on so many schools of thought and academic disciplines. For instance, a critical appreciation of anthropology would be useful to nearly everyone, with its attention on how people create and experience culture – and the critique of the history of anthropology is also salutary, with the idea that the study of anthropology tells us more about anthropologists than about the groups they study. Such perspectives would then invite those who aspire to work in organisations to become acutely curious about how to inquire into reality of the workplace, to become critical of taken-for-granted techniques such as broadcast surveys (maybe the most useful information in a survey is what it tells us about the assumptions held by those who complied them?).

History would be an excellent guide – what a rich resource it is in terms of what can be learnt from the rise and fall of different groups, nations, and states. Combined with a sociological perspective there is nowhere better to go to learn about power and the human capacity to use and abuse power – and how the use and abuse of power in turn shapes what is valued in day-to-day practice. Psychology, Philosophy, and a certain literacy on the Physical Sciences would be no bad thing when it comes to firms appreciating their relationship with the environment. And a working familiarity with basic financial terminology would go a long way to demystifying much of what goes in organisations – John's research into 'speaking truth to power' came across at least two examples where people at all levels of an organisation were encouraged to become financially literate and did so.

We have scratched the surface here but the point is not made lightly – to understand the world of work could be the most fascinating locus of cross-disciplinary study and if people were educated to know the world in all its complexity, maybe they would be able to engage with it in a more enlightened fashion and we would be spared the casual beatification of the venal, the monomaniac, the financial engineers, and the unprincipled.

Instead we have the modern MBA with its invitation to know the world superficially. One example of this comes in the form of the Harvard MBA programme and its work around what the future business might be. It starts off with a statement of pure neoliberal orthodoxy, claiming and eulogising all that for-profit business has achieved in delivering much of the world out of poverty (as they define it) and attributing this success to the taken-for-granted practices of financially successful firms. It presents this as axiomatic and beyond question – the discussion about the future of business is already positioned within an unquestioned ideological straitjacket that fits with the beliefs of those of highest standing within the US socio-economic-political matrix.

Now there may well be an excellent case to be made about the pros and cons of the profit motive and the situations where it is most applicable, about what is meant by the word 'free' when applied to individuals and markets, but this all needs to be debated in the context of a range of philosophical perspectives, such as those which do not start from the advocacy of some normalised and ideal state – maybe including those worked on in this book – rather than presented as a fait accompli. To be blunt, most MBA programmes are remarkably silly to those of us who have taken the time to engage with the complexity of the social and material world – and how human beings can and do come together to shape and be shaped by it. Martin Parker is well ahead of us on this one with his recommendation to 'close down the business school' (Parker, 2018).

Of course this desire to widen the business school curriculum (rather than tear it down) is dismissed in an instant for the reasons we gave at the start of this section – we don't have the time to engage with such a breadth of perspective and anyway what would come out of it would be impractical. This lack of time is an interesting one given what has been happening over the last 50 years (although dipping in some parts of the US and UK now), namely the increase in life expectancy. Corporate and Institutional life still seems to be approached with the attitude of a sprinter, with everything needing to be done in a hurry – and yet most people will have more, not less, time on their hands in the years to come.

The opportunity to learn, to take time out to deepen understanding and broaden experience, is available – but it would take a shift in attitude for this to be embraced as a useful fact of life. Instead speed is all and people step into senior positions without any personal hinterland from which to draw on. Within the UK political system the 1970s saw a Prime Minister, Edward Heath, and a Chancellor of the Exchequer, Denis Healey, who had both been present at the D-Day landings in 1944. The hinterland of most senior leaders these days is piffling by comparison. What these shallowly lived highflyers may hope is that all the easy to digest models and techniques we've been questioning thus far, may be a suitable substitute for life experience acquired across multiple contexts.

This belief in easy learning and borrowed experience creates a context actively antithetical to the headwaters thinking we believe is essential if we are to step out of the habits of trivial busyness – but this is not going to be an easy sell. Whatever the argument made, what most frequently plays back to those of us attached to a more challenging inquiry into organisational practice is: 'Make it practical'. It is worth unpacking what lies behind that phrase and how it keeps people stuck in the swamp of trivial understanding and the soft words of the pedlars of what has been sold to them before.

To be practical in an organisational context is not the same as being practical in fixing a wheel on a car, although that is an attitude that has common currency. With the car, you can see whether it now works or not (although you don't know for how long). In organisational settings there is no readily observable link between cause and effect, all is judgement. People try to get round that, we've already torn what's left of our hair at the idiocy of the Fitzpatrick model for linking training interventions to systemic outcomes – but within the consulting industry there's still a band of them out there who will guarantee that a firm that employs them will get a 20-fold or so return from the money spent with them. John worked for just such an outfit in the mid-1990s. To deliver on this is very easy – you sack people or close plants or sell off assets. This may deliver in the short term, but the longer-term consequences are never considered or paid attention to. It's in nobody's interest to question the validity of what is being done here.

To be practical means to fit within the current way of seeing the world, to not rock the boat of those who are the power brokers. Practicality is an expression of a Foucauldian truth-power regime, where what fits within that regime's definition of practicality is deemed true. Headwater thinking would involve paying attention to the fitness for purpose of that truth-power regime, so it not only requires a greater breadth of knowledge about how organisations create truth than currently allowed for, it also involves an engagement with the living politics of the organisation, both licit and illicit, conscious and unconscious. No wonder people prefer to buy the next seven step programme to transformational agility, so much easier to be busy throwing mud in the swamp than doing the alternative which requires real breadth of perspective, political nous, and time to really work things through in the company of others.

Some punctuating summary points on 'The emergence of 'leader-ised' management – Underpinning Four. Headwaters and downstream thinking'

- Perceived lack of time and a definition of practicality based on existing mindsets locks out the opportunity for inquiry into unacknowledged assumptions and ideologies

- What counts as 'thought leadership' is currently determined by what is palatable and pleasing to those who occupy, or wish to occupy, the senior positions sustained by not challenging the existing status quo
- Organisational studies could be, and would benefit from being, the locus of significant inter-disciplinary study

4.4 The sound of silence

Let an institution be created which shall have for its object to keep correct doctrines before the attention of the people, to reiterate them perpetually, and to teach them to the young; having at the same time power to prevent contrary doctrines from being taught, advocated, or expressed. Let all possible causes of a change of mind be removed from men's apprehensions. Let them be kept ignorant, lest they should learn of some reason to think otherwise than they do. Let their passions be enlisted, so that they may regard private and unusual opinions with hatred and horror. Then, let all men who reject the established belief be terrified into silence. Let the people turn out and tar-and-feather such men, or let inquisitions be made into the manner of thinking of suspected persons, and when they are found guilty of forbidden beliefs, let them be subjected to some signal punishment. When complete agreement could not otherwise be reached, a general massacre of all who have not thought in a certain way has proved a very effective means of settling opinion in a country. If the power to do this be wanting, let a list of opinions be drawn up, to which no man of the least independence of thought can assent, and let the faithful be required to accept all these propositions, in order to segregate them as radically as possible from the influence of the rest of the world.

(Peirce, 1877)

Many of us spend inordinate amounts of precious time in the tinny echo chamber of the Twittersphere (although John has chosen to turn his back on all of the social media platforms that simply cause him vexations), transfixing Mark with its capacity to show the actual ideology of the age in action. In that netherworld, those of us who remain are familiar with the internet memes that draw attention to the fact that something like Twitter is more about contestation than communication – and it does little or nothing to draw people together (other than helping the like-minded to coalesce around one another in opposition to everyone else).

A typical encounter will see something like the following unfold:

> Mark: *I like a soft fig in the morning*
> Anonymous: *So you hate a cooked breakfast? What do you want to do? Starve farmers who go out in all hours? And what about your carbon footprint? Figs are not indigenous! Open your eyes and get educated!*

These channels are unmediated other than through the communities that develop around particular sets of ideas, which – in turn – encourages further use of that conduit for similar (and hence reinforcing) opinion. Indeed, it is argued that there are three defining elements of social media, all of which give us pause for concern:

> First, social media allow users to not only consume but to also produce information, whereas the supply of information in traditional media markets is typically concentrated in the hands of a small number of outlets. Second, the information to which users are exposed depends upon self-chosen links among users. That is, users may be exposed to significantly different information depending on the set of individuals with whom they are connected and the content created by this set of individuals. Third, information on social media travels more rapidly and broadly than in other forms of social interactions. For example, a tweet from a user on Twitter is simultaneously transmitted to all of that user's followers, and each time one of these followers retweets this tweet, another set of followers is exposed to the information.
>
> (Halberstam & Knight, 2014, p. 3)

This reflects to us two things: the closure of the critical mind and the associated intensification of intolerance. Hence, whilst it derives from a classical liberal perspective (and hence contains within it all manner of shortcomings in respect to the slippery notion of 'free speech'), we opted to open this section with an extended quote from the back end of the 19th Century, not least because – as an incisive set of observations – it still has powerful contemporary currency. Just to underscore this general philosophical observation, it is worth reminding ourselves of the grim horror of how these two elements of lack of criticality and intolerance intersected in the early phase of the COVID crisis, when a research paper found the following:

> Only half the population showed little evidence of conspiracy thinking...[A]lmost half of participants endorsed to some degree the idea that "Coronavirus is a bioweapon developed by China to destroy the West" and around one-fifth endorsed to some degree that "Jews have created the virus to collapse the economy for financial gain". The conspiracy beliefs were connected to a number of markers of excessive mistrust: paranoia, endorsement of other conspiracy beliefs, mistrust in institutions and experts, and a conspiracy mentality.
>
> (Freeman, et al., 2020, p. 12)

Read that again, we urge you. One fifth. Twenty per cent. One in five. All content to give voice to the oldest of old prejudices. Here we can see in outline the myths that we deconstructed earlier: if everything is fixable, if perfection is the only acceptable position, and if there's only one way in which to achieve that, then anything that seems to confound these deeply but erroneously held beliefs – such as a zoonosis – must be someone's fault, whether it's a nation, a racial group, or a provider of 5G services. Significantly, it is apparent within this belief system that, whilst science is deemed to underpin this view of the world (medicine just needs to mobilise to save us), the failure of science's presumed mythical promise breaks that covenant. In such a model, it serves a dual purpose: to offer mythical foundations and then betraying the myth when it is deemed to be unable to address the unexpected.

Back in 1877, Peirce stated that,

> We generally know when we wish to ask a question and when we wish to pronounce a judgment, for there is a dissimilarity between the sensation of doubting and that of believing...The feeling of believing is a more or less sure indication of there being established in our nature some habit which will determine our actions. Doubt never has such an effect. Nor must we overlook a third point of difference. Doubt is an uneasy and dissatisfied state from which we struggle to free ourselves

and pass into the state of belief; while the latter is a calm and satisfactory state which we do not wish to avoid, or to change to a belief in anything else. On the contrary, we cling tenaciously, not merely to believing, but to believing just what we do believe. The irritation of doubt causes a struggle to attain a state of belief. I shall term this struggle inquiry, though it must be admitted that this is sometimes not a very apt designation.

(Peirce, 1877)

This triangulation of doubt, inquiry, and belief seems vital to where we would hope that leadership might take itself. And the important observation that our innate desire to bridge as speedily as possible the gap between doubt and belief means that inquiry can never be as pure a practice as we might wish to imagine it to be. Moreover, our capacity to get stuck in the reassuring treacle of belief – particularly where that belief is sustained by homophily, possibly engineered by personal technologies – means that we oftentimes close off the idea that belief contains within itself tiny but potentially catastrophically disruptive seeds of doubt. Hence, unless we acknowledge that within belief itself resides doubt – and hence this fluid and dynamic model requires us to apply inquiry to both doubt…and the doubt that can sometimes be subtly disguised within the belief with which we reassure ourselves.

In so many organisational spaces these days, the beliefs that prevail are seen to be monolithic, utterly solid, and uninhabited by anything that might resemble doubt. Indeed, the intolerance that prevails – so ably facilitated by the crazed frenzy on social media – denies anyone but the most committed parrhesiastes (a term mobilised by Foucault in order to explore the associated practices of self-care and speaking truth to power) the opportunity to break the silence (Foucault, 2011). And, while to do so is unlikely to result in the ultimate sanction, it remains potentially profoundly impactful, professionally and personally, to give voice to doubt. Within some discourses, it can appear as if the very notion of doubt has attained an ideological complexion, which doubles down on this tension and actively creates regimes of silence: the belief carries with it the notion of perfection and hence immutability, so doubt becomes a crime against the faith-like belief that has asserted itself through its enmeshment in the complex relational matrix of power in which we all find ourselves.

As public discourse – particularly in respect to its transmission through the polarising lens of social media – has been driven to its extremes, it is important not to assume that one side of that debate seeks to conserve things whilst the other aims to support progress. Largely, these terms are redundant, in light of the human thought and practice that underpins both perspectives. As people retreat into the comfort of their own echo chambers – and, from that comfortable position, discharge their volumes of aggressive bile at those who are sitting outside of those ramparts – the very idea of 'speaking truth to power' as something that exclusively goes up a hierarchy to those who sit at its apex is thrown into sharp relief.

A nuanced understanding of power, such as that offered by Foucault, reminds us that its 'normalising' effect acts across all relations – and not merely from top to bottom. In its simplest expression, one can perceive of the intimate relationship between discourse, knowledge, and power thus: 'When one says "this is true" he (sic) also means "and therefore you must yield"' (Harter, 2017, p. 8). In light of this adjusted philosophical underpinning, it is possible to observe that,

> In the attempt to institute power structures that do not openly coerce, we have created systems to do two things: (a) persuade most people to conform on their own and (b) quarantine the rest in institutions where everybody else is unwelcome. Control requires the impression of widespread conformity. The nonconforming have to be removed from the scene. Foucault was to call these "dividing practices".
>
> (Harter, 2017, p. 8)

Such dividing practices can now be clearly scene as the exclusive preserve of one political perspective...which means that speaking up takes a considerably more nuanced position to what might be traditionally thought about this practice.

All of which is offered in order to revise our understanding of what a leader might be expected to do in order to acknowledge this considerably more complex picture of power and speech in the workplace than might be familiar to us at first sight. The linear scientism of traditional leadership tends to take a processual view of the interrelatedness of '"doubt ⇨ inquiry ⇨ belief'. Oftentimes, it is couched in different words, specifically: first, there seems to be a 'problem' (which invariably the leader is expected to see from their elevated position – and to articulate, so that resources can then be deployed in response to it); second, the leader compels people across the organisation to gather data, invariably with a focus on volume rather than quality, and to bring it to them in order that they might use the material to make sense of the problem and design a response; and, third, there is a sanctioned reaction, which appears in order to solve the problem that was identified.

In contrast to this clumsy formalism, itself determined by the myth of fixability, we argue for a fluid engagement with the challenge of voice, power, and belief, which should be reflected in all discourse, including that which takes place in an organisational context. We should all strive to embody doubt as a constant state, applying it equally to that which is not known at any time – and that which is presumed to be known, in terms of prevailing certainty. And that means that inquiry needs to be rethought from its very foundation: it should provide a space wherein critical thinking can be applied in respect to an understanding of circumstances that is not merely derived from the fetishised pursuit of all of the data around a particular topic. Such criticality subjects everything to scrutiny, not simply the metrics that seem to speak to the reality at hand; it also encompasses the freshest thinking and practical experiences of everyone.

Some punctuating summary points on 'The sound of silence'

- Swimming in a sea of toxic contestation, sustained by people belonging to communities of like-minded ideologues and uncritical believers, those who wish to inquire, be critical, or hold to their doubts are silenced
- A diminishing of the discipline of critical thinking and an intensification of intolerance towards those who are other to us in how they know the world, reinforced by the speed and scope with which the like-minded can be rallied to the cause, silences those who are outside the pale
- Inquiry into leadership, and staying with our doubts about what we believe about leadership, is an uncomfortable place to stay in as we are invited to move swiftly away from doubt and embrace uncritical belief
- Giving voice to doubt at work is rarely encouraged – people do not want to give it room to breathe for fear it will be a distraction from the practice of staying with the status quo

- Silencing is a pan-dimensional phenomena, not just something that exists within a hierarchical context. It is systemic and pervasive
- Control requires the impression of widespread conformity. The non-conforming have to be removed from the scene

4.5 (How) time's tide will swallow you (or not)

Mark is inordinately fond of the phrase 'Time's tide will swallow you', given his abiding affection for The Smiths – notwithstanding Morrissey's best efforts on an almost daily basis to befoul his own legacy. It comes from an exquisite song on the *Meat is Murder* album, musically soaring and lyrically entrancing (Smiths, 1985). However, despite the role it plays in underscoring the melancholy that haunts the track, it is broadly inaccurate. Time does not, after all, ebb and flow like a tide. Instead, we sit in what is often referred to as a specious present. Where The Smiths elsewhere posed the question of *How soon is now?*, philosophy – in its phenomenological guise – restructures this inquiry to read, 'How long is now'?...and in so doing accords the present a sense of duration rather than a single point on a linear flow of time itself (Roselli, 2018).

This specious present, then, is where life occurs and where we sense our agency. But, as we have suggested elsewhere, our corporate focus is exclusively on the future, not least because that is where perfection can be built (as it patently does not reside in the present). The managerial imperatives endlessly throw us forward, where we find ourselves immersed in visions, strategies, plans and project outlines, budget and sales projections, and so on. Our corporate lives are spent in an endless and ultimately fruitless search for that perfection, which is adumbrated in the data representation that exists in all of this future-focused material. There is a cartoon that shows someone presenting a graph to a small group of people in an office. The graph is a grid, with a line slightly zigzagging up and down but moving upwards overall. The presenter, by way of explanation, observes to their audience: 'And this shows a range of mountains viewed through a tennis racquet'.

Even within the terms of this visual gag, we are reminded of the way in which graphic representations – even at their most schematic – are charged with semiotic meaning. We know – having been entrained throughout our organisational experience – that this is a control chart, which overall directs us to think about ways in which to keep the line climbing (notwithstanding the minor tremors along its trajectory) so as to achieve some peerless state, one that, of course, will be eternally deferred but sought forever. Hence, even the simplified models about which we spoke earlier in this chapter – in the section on measurement – serve to reinforce this constant future-focus. Indeed, the corporate engagement with storytelling in relation to looking to the narrative arc throws up what one author sees as a fascinating contrast:

> The aim of corporate storytelling as a medium for internal communi-cation has less to do with anchoring the organization in the past (as in marketing, in which the business is linked to its history and thus valorized) and more to do with orienting it toward an uncertain future in a way that is flexible and promotes learning.
>
> (Schoenthaler, 2018, p. 14)

In this formulation, then, the past is not solely as we have argued a place where failure resides, a repository of efforts that failed to deliver and which are thence seen as negative experiences that are really only fit to be forgotten as we cast our ambitions into the future. The past also offers a parallel source of cultural artefacts that serve – to our mind – not merely to give historical grounding in terms of the company (encapsulated in England by the term 'since' followed by date to confer a sense of longevity and permanence – and mirrored by exactly the same capitalist usage of 'desde' in Spain and 'dal' in Italy) but also to reinforce the pre-eminence and per-manence of a brand, which is such an ephemeral notion in our disruption addicted world of commerce these days.

A leadership practice liberated from the constraints that we have sought to outline in this book needs to reorient itself to time with a significant dif-ference in terms of its focus. It requires an active encouragement of people (including one's self) to attend to the present as the place where inquiry and agency is situated. It needs a leader to draw the focus back from the hazy uncertainties of the future – and away from the future being the destination to which we are meant to be heading on an endless trek for perfection, to a world where things are finally fixed. And time's velocity needs to be addressed, particularly where traditional leadership is seen to impel this end-lessly, demanding greater and greater filling of time with activity. This 'busy-ness' signals nothing but a desire to make the puppets dance around you, so is a thoroughly depraved pursuit more about aggrandisement than achievement, given that this busyness is largely disconnected from the present time and so is detached from engaging with the world of the here and now.

4.6 What is left that we can do in the morning

This book is not a hymn of hopelessness but it is an invitation to engage quite differently with how the social experience of organisational life is created and re-created. Let us start with four headline prescriptions and then explore the seriousness behind them:

- To change how power is exercised change the bodies that exercise power
- Banish all external consultants and shred all business books
- Free people to talk together about how they want to engage with shaping what the organisation does, how people are paid, and how they will organise to deliver what the organisation needs to do (including engaging with external bodies)
- Do it

To change how power is exercised change the bodies that exercise power

As part of one of his research projects John has been exploring how an organisation called The Orchid Project is going about bringing about the end of Female Genital Cutting. Its founder was greatly influenced by another organisation called Tostan who have adopted an approach to social development a million miles away from the Global North saviour trope. Their approach is about meeting people eye to eye as equals, where communities explore what Tostan has to offer, and then choose to participate or not. The only entry requirement if they want to participate is that the community sets up its own decision-making committee, comprised of 17 people, who represent all of the major interest groups and are chosen by the community itself. What is distinctive is that there must always be nine women on the committee. In communities where women have traditionally lived in the shadows, or had decisions made on their behalf, this is the first step towards them having a voice and experiencing having some agency in their lives.

This is very different from the skin-deep veneer of diversity which can often play out. One colleague of John's was tasked with facilitating a global conference of NGOs in Bangladesh a few years back. She was overwhelmed by the presenting difference in the room, how she found herself to be the only European woman there. How exciting to see global diversity in action! Until the next day by when she had realised they had all been to the same elite graduate schools in the US and Europe (but mainly the US...)

Some questions to consider

- Which bodies within your organisation currently make decisions and how would they need to be reconstituted if a broader range of perspectives and organisational options were to be considered?
- Who would make the case, and how would it be made, for such a reconfiguration of existing decision-making bodies?

Banish all external consultants and shred all business books

Maybe even this one... once it has been used to help make the case mentioned earlier.

Business books have become the crack cocaine of organisational thinking; they rot the brain. Read Adam Smith not those who claim to speak from his canon. Hayek may not be our cup of tea but there is seriousness in his thinking about what it takes to escape a slave mentality. Want to learn about change? Read Gibbon's 'Decline and fall of the Roman Empire', that'll teach you much more about institutional longevity than anything by Collins & Porras. If that's not to your taste, John's favourite historical writer is Marc Ferro who wrote about the use and abuse of history, revealing how different ideologies construct history – an important prompt for all of us to pay attention to the way we've been taught to see the past and the present. Want to be understand realpolitik? Study the life of Bismark or simply take Machiavelli's The Prince seriously, not as a curio to one side of the more anodyne studies of Branson and Welch.

Create a book group where people can share the writers that they most draw on, some may find that fiction packs a greater punch than the McKinsey business book of the year – which will of course be on the banned list! 1984 has more to say about the consequences of a pacified leader-follower construct than any number of MBA approved texts. As we talked about earlier, the great management thinker (one of very few worthy of the title) Charles Handy handed out Greek Tragedy alongside the accounting text books when teaching at the LBS.

And get those quack consultants off your premises and out of your head. The only people who can make sense of what the reality of your organisational life is are those who are currently participating in it. If these consultants represented some Platonic ideal then maybe they could be tolerated, but even then they'd get in the way of you making sense of things for yourself and rip you out of time present and plant you into the disembodied fantasy of the future. And they are all purveyors of dodgy ideologies dressed up as 'the truth' rather than 'a truth' created by them – and which serves their own self-interest. Find your own path in your own way – stop hoping that others can answer impossible questions which only you and yours have even an inkling of an answer to.

Some questions to ask

- What does the use of external consultancies allow you and yours not to pay attention to for yourselves?
- What are the best non-business books you know of that speak to what a healthy organisational life looks like?

Free people to talk together about how they want to engage with shaping what the organisation does, how people are paid, and how they will organise to deliver what the organisation needs to do (including engaging with external bodies)

A friend of John's was employed to work alongside the Kingdom of Uganda to help them work on their strategy. The defining quality of the process was for everyone to talk, for every group to be heard, for no short cuts to be taken. People talked and talked until there was no more to say, no more to hear that had not been said and heard by those who needed to say it and hear it. The promoters of this process knew to their bones that this is not just talk, this is the process through which collective understanding is created, through which true transparency and participation are engendered. Luckily for John's friend this approach worked with a centuries old tradition, which did not need to be imported. People just knew that participating in such a collective experience is the only way for a community to make a decision that will live.

Now this presents a challenge for the Global North, where habits of collective inquiry have been lost in the mist of time, driven out by the drumbeat of the clock and the need to rush to actions imposed on those who didn't even know they were being taken. Of course there are still vibrant communities out there who live and breathe the reality of engaging dialogue, and get frustrated and angry with it as well. Attempts to bastardise these processes, import them into contexts where the basic leader-follower construct rules the roost, ensures that their use is deeply manipulative and ill-intentioned. People can smell bullshit, however much perfume is poured over it.

Some questions to ask

- What would a first stab at a genuine inclusive inquiry process look like and what would give it at least a gram of credibility?
- How do you acknowledge and work with ingrained attitudes which may find sustained conversations difficult?
- How do you work with the reality that people have different life commitments which means they have to work with other constraints beyond that of the workplace?

Do it.

And do it in the now. Enough said.

*   *   *   *   *   *   *   *   *   *   *   *   *

We believe that the current way of organisational life is unhealthy and anti-life, for leader, led, and all those in-between. You may agree or disagree with some or even most of our advocacy and framing, but if it speaks to you even in part we urge you to do what you can because the status quo really is not good for anyone.

References

Anand, G. & Kodali, R., 2008. Benchmarking the benchmarking models. *Benchmarking: An international journal*, 15(3), pp. 257–291.

Banks, G. C. et al., 2018. Construct redundancy in leader behaviors: A review and agenda for the future. *The Leadership Quarterly*, Volume 29, pp. 236–251.

BBC News, 2020. *Coronavirus: Travellers react to Spain quarantine rules*. [Online] Available at: www-bbc-com.cdn.ampproject.org/c/s/www.bbc.com/news/amp/uk-53541503 [Accessed 30 July 2020].

Boltanski, L. & Chiapello, E., 2007. *The new spirit of capitalism*. London: Verso.

Bröckling, U., 2016. *The entrepreneurial self: Fabricating a new type of subject*. London: Sage.

Burgoyne, A. P., Hambrick, D. Z. & Macnamara, B. N., 2020. How firm are the foundations of mind-set theory? The claims appear stronger than the evidence. *Psychological Science*, 31(3), pp. 258–267.

Campaign, 2020. *UK Government "Enjoy summer safely" by MullenLowe.* [Online] Available at: www.campaignlive.co.uk/article/uk-government-enjoy-summer-safely-mullenlowe/1688665 [Accessed 30 July 2020].

Cole, M., 2020. *On the "leadership (r)evolution".* [Online] Available at: radicalod.org/2020/10/28/on-the-leadership-revolution/ [Accessed 24 November 2020].

Cox, A., 2017. *I am (not) a number: Decoding the prisoner.* Harpenden: Kamera.

Damen, T. G. E., van Baaren, R. B., Brass, M. & Henk, A., 2015. Put your plan into action: The influence of action plans on agency and responsibility. *Journal of Personality and Social Psychology*, 108(6), pp. 850–866.

Darley, J. M. & Latane, B., 1968. Bystander interventions in emergencies: Diffusion of responsibility. *Journal of Personality and Social Psychology*, 8(4), pp. 377–383.

de Holan, P. M. & Mintzberg, H., 2004. Management as life's essence: 30 years of The Nature of Managerial Work. *Strategic Organization*, 2(2), pp. 205–212.

Department for Business, Energy & Industrial Strategy, 2019. *Trade union membership: Statistical bulletin*, s.l.: s.n.

Dweck, C. S., 2012. *Mindset: How you can fulfil your potential.* London: Constable & Robinson.

Forer, B. R., 1949. The fallacy of personal validation: A classroom demonstration of gullibility. *The Journal of Abnormal and Social Psychology*, 44(1), pp. 118–123.

Foucault, M., 2011. 1 February 1984: First hour. In: F. Gros, ed. *The courage of truth: The government of self and others II (Lectures at the College de France 1983–1984.* s.l.: Palgrave Macmillan, pp. 1–19.

Freeman, D. et al., 2020. Coronavirus conspiracy beliefs, mistrust, and compliance with government guidelines in England. *Psychological Medicine.* doi:10.1017/S0033291720001890

Halberstam, Y. & Knight. B., 2014. *Homophily, group size, and the diffusion of political information in social networks: Evidence from Twitter (Working Paper 20681)*, Cambridge, Mass.: National Bureau of Economic Research.

Hamblin, C. L., 1970. *Fallacies.* London: Methuen.

Harter, N. W., 2017. *Foucault on leadership: The leader as subject*. Abingdon: Routledge.

Higgins, J., 2020. *Happy, shiny thinking!* [Online] Available at: www.radicalod. org/2020/11/12/happy-shiny-thinking/ [Accessed 24 November 2020].

Kiechel, W., 2010. *The lords of strategy: The secret intellectual history of the new corporate world*. Boston, Mass.: Harvard Business Press.

Kinna, R., 2019. *The government of no one: The theory and practice of Anarchism*. London: Pelican.

Lazarus, R. S., 2003. Does the positive psychology movement have legs? *Psychological Inquiry*, 14(2), pp. 93–109.

Learmonth, M. & Morrell, K., 2019. *Critical perspectives on leadership: The language of corporate power*. Abingdon: Routledge.

Lewin, K., 1947. Frontiers in group dynamics: Concept, method and reality in social science; social equilibria and social change. *Human Relations*, 1(5), pp. 5–41.

Markovits, D., 2020. *How McKinsey destroyed the middle class*. [Online] Available at: www.theatlantic.com/ideas/archive/2020/02/how-mckinsey-destroyed-middle-class/605878/ [Accessed 17 July 2020].

McDonald, M. & O'Callaghan, J., 2008. Positive psychology: A Foucauldian critique. *The Humanistic Psychologist*, 36(2), pp. 127–142.

McGregor, S., 2001. Neoliberalism and health care. *International Journal of Consumer Studies*, 25(2), pp. 82–89.

Mintzberg, H., 2009. *Managing*. San Francisco: Berrett-Koehler Publishers, Inc.

Parker, M., 2018. *Shut down the business school: What's wrong with management education?* London: Pluto Press.

Parry, A., 2018. *The way of all flesh*. Edinburgh: Canongate.

Peirce, C. S., 1877. *The fixation of belief*. [Online] Available at: www.peirce.org/writings/p107.html [Accessed 12 August 2020].

Peters, M., 2001. Education, enterprise culture and the entrepreneurial self: A Foucauldian perspective. *Journal of Educational Enquiry*, 2(2), pp. 58–71.

Read, J., 2010. A genealogy of homo-economicus: Neoliberalism and the production of subjectivity. In: S. Binkley & J. Capetillo, eds. *A Foucault for the 21st Century: Governmentality, biopolitics and discipline in the new millenium*. Newcastle upon Tyne: Cambridge Scholars Publishing, pp. 2–15.

Reitz, M. & Higgins, J., 2019. *Speak up: Say what needs to be said and hear what needs to be heard*. Harlow: FT/Pearson.

Roselli, A., 2018. How long is now? A new perspective on the specious present. *Disputatio*, X(49), pp. 119–140.

Schoenthaler, P., 2018. *Portrait of the manager as a young author: On storytelling, business, and literature*. Cambridge, Mass.: MIT Press.

Seligman, M. E. P. & Csikszentmihalyi, M., 2000. Positive psychology: An introduction. *American Psychologist*, 55(1), pp. 5–14.

Sisk, V. F. et al., 2018. To what extent and under which circumstances are growth mind-sets important to academic achievement? Two meta-analyses. *Psychological Science*, 29(4), pp. 549–571.

Smiths, T., 1985. *That joke isn't funny anymore*. [Sound recording] (Rough Trade Records).

Triantafillou, P., 2007. Benchmarking in the public sector: A critical conceptual framework. *Public Administration*, 85(3), pp. 829–846.

Tsoukas, H. & Chia, R., 2002. On organizational becoming: Rethinking organizational change. *Organization Science*, 13(5), pp. 567–582.

van Dorssen-Boog, P., de Jong, J., Veld, M. & Van Vuuren, T., 2020. Self-leadership among healthcare workers: A mediator for the effects of job autonomy on work engagement and health. *Frontiers on Psychology*, 11(1420). doi:10.3389/fpsyg.2020.01420

INDEX

Note: Page numbers followed by n indicate notes.